The Missouri Persecutions

by

B. H. Roberts

The Missouri Persecutions
by B. H. Roberts

ISBN: 978-93-59326-69-6

Published by

DOUBLE 9 BOOKS
2/13-B, Ansari Road
Daryaganj, New Delhi – 110002
info@double9books.com
www.double9books.com
Tel. 011-40042856

This book is under public domain

ABOUT THE AUTHOR

Brigham Henry Roberts (March 13, 1857 – September 27, 1933) was a Church of Jesus Christ of Latter-day Saints (LDS Church) historian, politician, and leader. He independently wrote the six-volume Comprehensive History of the Church of Jesus Christ of Latter-day Saints and edited the seven-volume History of the Church of Jesus Christ of Latter-day Saints. Roberts also wrote Studies of the Book of Mormon, which was released posthumously and explored the Book of Mormon's authenticity as an ancient record. Because of his polygamy, Roberts was denied a seat in the United States Congress. Roberts was born in Warrington, Lancashire, England, the son of alcoholic blacksmith and ship plater Benjamin Roberts and seamstress Ann Everington. Both of his parents converted to the LDS Church the year he was born. Then Benjamin Roberts abandoned his family. "My childhood was a nightmare; my boyhood was a tragedy," Roberts later wrote. B. H. Roberts and a sister departed England in April 1866, aided by the Perpetual Emigrating Fund. They boarded a wagon train in Nebraska and walked—barefoot for much of the way—to Salt Lake City, where they were met by their mother, who had preceded them.

CONTENTS

PREFACE

My chief purpose in publishing this book, and the one which will immediately follow — "The Rise and Fall of Nauvoo" — is to place in the hands of the youth of the Latter-day Saints a full statement of the persecutions endured by the early members of The Church in this last dispensation, in the States of Missouri and Illinois, that they may be made acquainted with the sacrifices which their fathers have made for the word of God and the testimony of Jesus Christ. And I indulge the hope that by becoming acquainted with the story of the suffering of the early saints, the faith of the Gospel will become all the more dear to the hearts of their immediate posterity and all the youth of Zion for many generations to come.

I think without depreciating at all any other narrative of these events in our Church literature, I may claim that the story of the Missouri Persecutions in these pages is told more thoroughly than in any other of our present publications. This arises from the fact that this book deals with but a brief period in the history of The Church—from 1830 to 1838—and therefore admits of such a consideration of details as could not possibly be given to that period in any general history of The Church. This detailed treatment of the subject, in the opinion of the author, is justified because of the very important events which the treatise covers, and also for the reason that it is a period of our history which has been very much misrepresented, upon which misrepresentations false accusations are made against The Church and its leaders to this day. Those who have thought themselves called upon to oppose, if not to persecute, The Church in later years, frequently attempt to justify their present opposition by insinuating that The Church was driven from Missouri and Illinois for other reasons than adherence to an unpopular religion. The impression is sought to be created that it was for some overt acts against the State or National government, or for some offense against the spirit of American institutions, or because The Church leaders "were determined to be a law unto themselves," in disregard of the rights of others.

It is, in part, to correct these false statements, and guard our youth against the influence of such calumnious insinuations, that I tell this story of the Missouri Persecutions; not that the history in these pages is written for the purpose of glozing over the defects in the character of the early members of The Church, or to claim for them absolute freedom from errors in judgment, or actual sinfulness in conduct. I have not written what may be called "argumentative history," only so far as a statement of the truth may be considered an argument. After these pages are read I feel sure that no one will be able to accuse me of failing to point out the errors of the early members of The Church; indeed, I have been careful to call attention to the complaints which the Lord made against their conduct; the reproofs of his inspired servants; and the repeated warnings sent to them by the Prophet Joseph Smith concerning the results of their conduct if there was not a speedy repentance.

In Appendices will be found accounts of these same persecutions as told by writers of Missouri history. I quote these extracts from the *"History of Jackson County,"* published by the Union Historical Company of Kansas City, Missouri, 1881; the *"History of Clay County,"* published by the National Historical Company, 1885; the *"History of Daviess County,"* by D. L. Kort; the *"History of Caldwell County,"* by Crosby Johnson; and the *"History of Missouri,"* published by the Union Historical Company.

While these alleged histories of the "Mormon War," "Mormons in Jackson County," "Mormon Exodus," etc., etc., are contemptible for their distortion of facts and misrepresentations, the reader by having them at hand will at least have both sides of the story presented to him, and will be able by the means of comparison thus afforded, to judge where the truth of the matter lies; and it will contribute to the making of this book a valuable work of reference to the student of Church history.

One other thing I ought to say in justice to myself, both in reference to this book and "The Rise and Fall of Nauvoo." Very much of the matter contained in the two volumes, indeed most of it, was published in a series of twenty-four articles some fifteen years ago, in *The Contributor*, under the respective titles now used. Since that time very extensive quotations have been made from those articles, sometimes with, but often without, acknowledgement of the authorship; and to such extent has this been the case, that I feel it necessary to make mention of it, that I myself may not be charged with using the matter prepared by others, when in reality I am but using my own. Having called attention to this subject, I feel that it will not be out of place to say something further upon it. The fault, not to say literary crime, of plagiarism is by far too common. Some men who would never think of stealing a man's property, or even of using it without his permission, sometimes do not hesitate in public speech or in written articles or books to take all sorts of liberties with another's writings, quoting without acknowledgement not only sentences and paragraphs, but whole pages, and often page after page. And thus they bedeck themselves, not with "old, odd ends stolen out of Holy Writ," but in borrowed phrases and sentences—the fruits of another's research and thought and genius, if the writer from whom they steal possesses any. It is true that plagiarism is not a crime under the law. A man, if he so elects, may steal both the ideas and the literary construction of another, without fear of fine or imprisonment, but no writer or speaker worthy of respect would be found pilfering the thoughts or expressions of another, any more than a self-respecting, honest man would be found with stolen goods upon his back. Gradually there is being built up in The Church a very considerable and stately literature, historical, doctrinal and poetical; and for one I hope to see it, first of all, of a character that will be in harmony with the great Dispensation of the Gospel which it celebrates, that is, that it be honest.

THE AUTHOR.

CHAPTER I
THE FACTS IN WHICH THE CHURCH OF JESUS CHRIST OF LATTER-DAY SAINTS HAD ITS ORIGIN

The story of the persecutions endured by the Latter-day Saints in Missouri, one of the sovereign States of the United States of America, properly begins with the advent of a mission to the Lamanites,[A] at Independence, Missouri, in the winter of 1830. But in order that those not acquainted with the history of The Church may understand how there came to be a mission to the Lamanites in 1830, and how there came to be a Church of Jesus Christ of Latter-day Saints to be persecuted, I think it proper to state briefly those facts in which The Church had its origin.

[Footnote A: American Indians]

I know the story has often been told—so often indeed that all novelty in relation to it has long since passed away. But in history there are certain foundation facts that are as essential to the right understanding of some particular phase of history as the employment of the first principles of the science of mathematics is to the solution of some particular problem in algebra; and the historical writer is as much bound to state those foundation facts as the mathematician is to use the first principles of his science in the solution of his problem.

In the present instance, however, though I deem it necessary to tell again such a well known story as the rise of The Church, I shall attempt no embellishment of it; nor shall I deal with the religious condition of the world at the time of the origin of The Church with any view to establish the probability of the story; nor stop to call attention to the reasonableness and strength of it; nor the evidences of its truth, or necessity, although the temptation to do this is always strong whenever the facts of that story are passed before me in review. I shall content myself on this occasion with a mere statement of the facts, such as an annalist might make, without any further consideration of them whatsoever; and this because such a statement will serve my present purpose.

Joseph Smith, the man who, under the direction of God, was the founder of The Church, was born at the little village of Sharon, Windsor County, in the State of Vermont, on the 23rd of December, in the year of our Lord 1805.

When he was ten years of age the Smith family moved from Vermont to the State of New York, settling in Palmyra, Wayne County. Four years later the family moved a few miles south to the town of Manchester, Ontario County.

Here, in the spring of 1820, a great religious revival agitated the community, and Joseph Smith was much affected by it.

In the course of this religious excitement he was much perplexed over the discussion and strifes of the different Christian sects, and often wondered how it was that the Church of Christ could be so divided into contending factions. "I found," he said some years later when writing his recollections of those early days of his religious experience—"I found that there was a great clash in religious sentiment; if I went to one society they referred me to one plan, and another to another—each one pointing to his own particular creed as the *summum bonum* of perfection. Considering that all could not be right, and that God could not be the author of so much confusion, I determined to investigate the subject more fully, believing that if God had a Church it would not be split up into factions, and that if he taught one society to worship one way and administer in one set of ordinances, he would not teach another principles which were diametrically opposed." [B]

[Footnote B: From a letter to Mr. John Wentworth, written in 1842. Mr. Wentworth at the time was the editor of the *Chicago Democrat*.]

In the midst of these perplexities Joseph's attention was called to the first chapter of the epistle of James, where it is written: "If any of you lack wisdom, let him ask of God, that giveth to all men liberally, and unbraideth not; and it shall be given him."

This instruction the youth determined to follow, and accordingly repaired to a secret place in the woods near his father's house, where he called upon God for wisdom.

While so engaged he was seized upon by some power of darkness which threw him violently to the ground, and it seemed for a time that he was doomed to sudden destruction. It was no imaginary power, but some actual being from the unseen world who thus seized him. His tongue for a time was bound that he could not speak; darkness gathered about him; but, exerting all his powers, he called upon God to deliver him out of the hands of his enemy, and at the very moment he was ready to give up in despair and abandon himself to destruction, he beheld a pillar of light immediately over his head descending towards him. Its brightness was above that of the sun at noonday, and no sooner did it envelop him than he was freed from the enemy who had held him in his power.

When the light rested upon him he beheld within it two personages standing above him in the air, whose brightness and glory defied all description. They exactly resembled each other in form and features. One of them, pointing to the other, said:

"JOSEPH, THIS IS MY BELOVED SON, HEAR HIM."

As soon as the youth gained his self-possession, he asked the personage to whom he was thus introduced, which of all the religious sects was right, that he might join it.

He was answered that none of the sects were right; that their creeds were an abomination to God; that their professors were corrupt; that they drew near to God with their lips but their hearts were far removed from him; that they taught for doctrine the commandments of men; that they had a form of godliness but denied the power thereof; and he was strictly commanded to join none of them: but was informed that at some future time the fullness of the Gospel would be made known to him.[C]

[Footnote C: Letter to Mr. John Wentworth, 1842.

I cannot refrain at this point from calling attention, at least in a foot note, to the importance of this great vision which lies at the very foundation of what the world calls "Mormonism."

At a glance it gives the reason for the existence of the Church of Jesus Christ of Latter-day Saints; and also the reason for the proclamation of the new dispensation of the Gospel it presents to the world.

It makes known the awful fact that the Gospel was not on the earth at that time; that none of the churches were acknowledged of God as his; that divine authority to preach and administer the ordinances of salvation was not among men. Therefore if men were to have the Gospel of Jesus Christ it must be restored from heaven; the Church of Christ must be again established; divine authority must be renewed.

Moreover, this splendid vision dispelled the vagaries that men had conjured up in respect to the person of Deity. Instead of being a personage without body, parts or passions, it revealed the fact that he had both body and parts, that he was in the form of man, or, rather, that man had been made in his image.

The vision clearly proves that the Father and Son are distinct persons, and not one person as the Christian world believes. The oneness of the Godhead, so frequently spoken of in scripture, must therefore relate to oneness of sentiment and agreement in purpose—to likeness.

The great revelation swept away the rubbish of human dogma, tradition and speculation that had accumulated in all the ages since Messiah's personal ministry on earth, by announcing that God did not acknowledge any of the sects of Christendom as his Church, nor their creeds as his gospel. Indeed, the Lord himself declared that they taught for doctrine the commandments of men. Thus the ground was cleared for the planting of the truth.

The vision showed how mistaken the Christian world was in claiming that all revelation had ceased—that God would no more reveal himself to man.

The vision created a witness for God on the earth: a man lived who could say to some purpose that God lived and that Jesus was the Christ, for he had seen and talked with them. Thus was laid anew the foundation for faith in God.—*Roberts*.]

This heavenly visitation Joseph Smith related to many of his acquaintances, including some sectarian ministers, who generally disbelieved his story and ridiculed him for telling it; all said inspired dreams and revelations from God were no more to be expected.

After an interval of three years Joseph Smith again received a heavenly visitant. On the 21st of September, 1823, after having retired to his chamber, he betook himself to prayer, seeking to know his standing before the Lord. While so engaged his room began to be filled with beautiful light, in the midst of which he beheld a personage who announced himself to be Moroni, one of the ancient prophets of the western hemisphere, now raised from the dead, and made an angel of God. He said he was sent from the Divine Presence to reveal the existence of an ancient record engraven upon plates of gold, giving an account of the origin of the American Indians; of God's hand-dealings with their forefathers; of the rise and fall of their civilization; of the ministry of the Lord Jesus Christ among them after his resurrection from the dead and of the establishment of the Christian religion and the Church of God in their midst.

Joseph Smith was also informed that this record was concealed in a hill not far distant; and that with it would be found a Urim and Thummim,[D] consisting of two stones fastened in silver bows attached to a breast-plate, by means of which the record could be translated through the power of God. The Prophet then beheld in a vision the hill where the plates were hidden.

[Footnote D: Those who would be informed concerning the Urim and Thummim and its use among the ancients, should consult the following scriptures: Ex. 28:30; Lev. 8:8; Deut. 33:8; Ezra 2:63; Neh. 7:65; Num. 17:21; I Sam. 28:6.]

When this vision was passed the angel quoted a number of ancient prophecies relating to the gathering of Israel in the last days, and the judgments of God upon the wicked, all of which he declared would soon be fulfilled.[E] The angel visited him three times during that same night, repeating to him each time the message he first announced.

[Footnote E: The passages quoted are as follows: Malachi, part of chapter 3. (most likely the first part); Malachi, chapter 4; Isaiah 11; Acts 3:22, 23; Joel 2:28-32.]

The next day Moroni again appeared to him when he was crossing a field, and announced to him once more the message of the night before, and instructed the youth to make a confidant of his father, Joseph Smith, Sen., and make known to him the visitations he had received and the things revealed, which the youth promptly and gladly did, and from that hour received consolation and encouragement from his father.

The same day, namely, 22nd of September, 1823, Joseph Smith went to the place where the record was deposited—called by Moroni, Cumorah—and there in a rude stone box, the crowning cover of which he could see above the surface of the hillside, he found the record, together with the Urim and Thummim.

Moroni appeared to him again while he was viewing the sacred treasure, and forbade him taking the plates from their place of concealment, as the time had not yet come for him to take possession of them. He was required to meet the angel at that place in one year from that time, and from year to year, until the time should come for the record to be given to him for translation.

These annual visits at Cumorah continued until the 22nd of September, 1827, when the plates were committed to his keeping with instructions to translate them. He received a strict commandment to show them to no man, except such as God would appoint to see them, and bear witness of their existence and the truth of what they contained; nor was he to have any other object in view in obtaining and translating the record than the glory of God and the establishment of his Church in the earth.

With the assistance of a man of the name of Martin Harris, and another of the name of Oliver Cowdery, the latter acting as his scribe, Joseph translated the record in about two years and a half, and published it at Palmyra, New York, early in the spring of 1830.

The stone box in which the record had been preserved, and the record itself, is thus described by Joseph Smith:

> Convenient to the village of Manchester, Ontario County, New York, stands a hill of considerable size, and the most elevated of any in the neighborhood. On the west side of this hill, not far from the top, under a stone of considerable size, lay the plates, deposited in a stone box. This stone was thick and rounding in the middle on the upper side, and thinner towards the edges, so that the middle part of it was visible above the ground, but the edge all round was covered with earth. Having removed the earth, and obtained a lever, which I got fixed under the edge of the stone, and with a little exertion raised it up, I looked in, and there indeed did I behold the plates, the Urim and Thummim and the breast-plate, as stated by the messenger. The box in which they lay was formed by laying stones together in some kind of cement. In the bottom of the box were laid two stones crossways of the box, and on these stones lay the plates, and the other things with them.[F]

[Footnote F: Millennial Star, Supplement to Vol. 14, p.6.]

These records were engraven on plates which had the appearance of gold; each plate was six inches wide and eight inches long, and not quite so thick as common tin. They were filled with engravings, in Egyptian characters, and bound together in a volume as the leaves of a book, with three rings running through the whole. The volume was something near six inches in thickness, a part of which was sealed. The characters on the unsealed part were small, and beautifully engraved. The whole book exhibited many signs of antiquity in its construction and much skill in the art of engraving.[G]

[Footnote G: Letter to Mr. Wentworth.]

The following is a summary of this interesting record as given by the Prophet in his letter to Mr. Wentworth:

> In this important and interesting book the history of ancient America is unfolded, from its first settlement by a colony that came from the Tower of Babel, at the confusion of languages,

to the beginning of the fifth century of the Christian era. We are informed by these records that America in ancient times had been inhabited by two distinct races of people. The first was called Jaredites and came directly from the Tower of Babel. The second race came directly from the city of Jerusalem, about six hundred years before Christ. They were principally Israelites, of the descendants of Joseph. The Jaredites were destroyed about the time that the Israelites came from Jerusalem, who succeeded them in the inheritance of the country. The principal nation of the second race fell in battle towards the close of the fourth century (A.D.) The remnant are the Indians that now inhabit this country. This book also tells us that our Savior made his appearance upon this continent after his resurrection; that he planted the gospel here in all its fullness, and richness, and power, and blessing; that they had apostles, prophets, pastors, teachers and evangelists; the same order, the same priesthood, the same ordinances, gifts, powers and blessings, as were enjoyed on the eastern continent; that the people were cut off in consequence of their transgressions; that the last of their prophets who existed among them were commanded to write an abridgment of their prophecies, history, etc., and to hide it up in the earth, and that it should come forth and be united with the Bible for the accomplishment of the purposes of God in the last days.

The Book of Mormon was not brought forth without serious opposition. The commandment not to show the plates to anyone except those whom God should appoint to be witnesses of their existence and their truth, necessarily enjoined secrecy upon Joseph Smith, and involved more or less of mystery in his movements; and yet it became necessary for some to know of his having the records, or else how could he obtain the necessary assistance to translate them? These prohibitions upon the Prophet and the necessary secrecy they involved, gave rise to a perfect flood of misrepresentations and slanders; enemies pursued him at every turn; the vilest calumnies were circulated both with respect to himself and his family; they were charged with the grossest ignorance, superstition, idleness, and all things that go to the making of vicious and low characters; and yet it is evident from the testimony of those who personally knew them, that the Smiths, while poor, were nevertheless people of upright lives, kind neighbors, and good citizens. This is not said for the purpose of claiming for Joseph Smith exemption from many boyish follies, and the common weaknesses of humanity—the existence of these weaknesses, in fact, he himself freely admits and deplores; and as much has been made of his own admissions on that head, I think it proper that what he has said upon the subject should be given in full, and hence I republish here a letter of his to Oliver Cowdery which the Prophet wrote upon hearing that Cowdery, in 1834, was about to publish a series of letters on the subject of "Early Scenes in the Church." Following is the letter:

Oliver Cowdery:

DEAR BROTHER: Having learned from the first number of the *Messenger and Advocate,* that you were not only about to "give a history of the rise and progress of the Church of the Latter-day Saints," but that said history would necessarily embrace my life and character, I have been induced to give you the time and place of my birth; as I have learned that many of the opposers of those principles which I have held forth to the world, profess a personal acquaintance with me, though when in my presence, represent me to be another person in age, education, and stature, from what I am.

I was born (according to the record of the same, kept by my parents) in the town of Sharon, Windsor County, Vermont, on the 23rd of December, 1805.

At the age of ten my father's family removed to Palmyra, New York, where, and in the vicinity of which, I lived, or made it my place of residence, until I was twenty-one; the latter part in the town of Manchester.

During this time, as is common to most or all youths, I fell into many vices and follies; but as my accusers are and have been forward to accuse me of being guilty of gross and outrageous violations of the peace and good order of the community, I take the occasion to remark that, though as I have said above, "as is common to most, or all, youths, I fell into many vices and follies," I have not, neither can it be sustained, in truth, been guilty of wronging or injuring any man or society of men; and those imperfections to which I allude, and for which I have often had occasion to lament, were a light, and too often, vain mind, exhibiting a foolish and trifling conversation.

This being all, and the worst, that my accusers can substantiate against my moral character, I wish to add that it is not without a deep feeling of regret that I am thus called upon in answer to my own conscience, to fulfill a duty I owe to myself, as well as to the cause of truth, in making this public confession of my former uncircumspect walk, and trifling conversation and more particularly, as I often acted in violation of those holy precepts which I knew came from God. But as the "Articles and Covenants" of this Church are plain upon this particular point, I do not deem it important to proceed further. I only add, that I do not, nor never have, pretended to be any other than a man "subject to passion," and liable, without the assisting grace of the Savior, to deviate from that perfect path in which all men are commanded to walk.

By giving the above a place in your valuable paper, you will confer a lasting favor upon myself, as an individual, and, as I humbly hope, subserve the cause of righteousness.

I am, with feelings of esteem, your fellow-laborer in the Gospel of our Lord,
JOSEPH SMITH.

It is clear from this letter that Joseph Smith, while acknowledging his imperfections, does not accuse himself of any dark crimes of a nature to disqualify him for his subsequently exalted station or the great work to which he was called. He goes no further than to confess to lightness and vanity of mind, resulting in "a foolish and trifling conversation;" but even that, on account of his quick conscience and innocent life, occasioned him much remorse.

While the Book of Mormon was in process of translation, namely, in May, 1829, the question of baptism came up between Joseph Smith and Oliver Cowdery. They repaired to the woods to inquire of the Lord concerning it, when an angel from heaven appeared to them and announced himself to be John the Baptist, of the New Testament, now raised from the dead, and sent to them by the Apostles Peter, James and John, under whose direction he acted, to confer upon them the Aaronic Priesthood.[H] He placed his hands upon their heads and said:

[Footnote H: Elsewhere the writer has said concerning this event: "When the work reached that stage of development that men could be taught repentance, and receive baptism for the remission of sins, who so qualified or who with more propriety could be sent to deliver the keys of the priesthood that is especially appointed to cry repentance and administer baptism, than *the* teacher of repentance and *the* Baptist?" —*New Witness for God, p. 221.*]

Upon you, my fellow servants, in the name of Messiah, I confer the Priesthood of Aaron, which holds the keys of the ministration of angels and of the gospel of repentance, and of baptism for the remission of sins, and this shall never be taken from the earth until the sons of Levi do offer again an offering unto the Lord in righteousness.

They were then commanded to each baptize the other, which they did, and thus baptism for the remission of sins, under divine authority, was again commenced on earth. This ordination received under the hands of the angel gave them the right and power to preach the gospel, call men to repentance, and baptize them for a remission of their sins. This they began to do and in a short time quite a number had been baptized.

Soon after this first ordination, namely, some time in the month of June, 1829, Joseph Smith and Oliver Cowdery were again visited by angels. The ancient Apostles Peter, James and John came to them on the banks of the Susquehanna River, between Harmony, Susquehanna County, and Colesville, Broome County, and conferred upon them the holy Apostleship, the keys of the higher or Melchisedek Priesthood, which gave them power not only to preach the gospel and administer baptism, but to lay on hands for the Holy Ghost, together with right to all the offices in The Church. This Priesthood gave them power to organize The Church, set in order the affairs thereof in all the world, and preside over it as God's representatives.

The authority of God thus restored to earth, the way was prepared for the organization of The Church. Still the young men to whom had been entrusted these great powers waited further direction from the Lord, and did not proceed with so great an undertaking until he commanded them.

At length the commandment came, and the 6th day of April, 1830, was appointed as the day on which to effect the organization of The Church. A number of the people who had been baptized met with Joseph Smith and Oliver Cowdery, on the day appointed, at the house of Peter Whitmer, Sen., in Fayette, Seneca County, New York, to effect that organization. The meeting was opened by solemn prayer, after which, according to previous instructions from the Lord, the Prophet Joseph called upon the brethren present to know if they would accept himself and Oliver Cowdery as their teachers in religion, and if they were willing that they should proceed to organize The Church according to the commandment of the Lord. To this the converts to the faith consented by unanimous vote. Joseph then ordained Oliver an Elder of the Church of Jesus Christ; after which Oliver ordained Joseph an Elder of said Church. The sacrament was administered, and those who had been previously baptized were confirmed members of The Church, and received the Holy Ghost by the laying on of hands. Some enjoyed the gift of prophecy, and all rejoiced exceedingly.

While The Church was yet assembled a revelation was received from the Lord, directing that a record be kept, and that in it Joseph Smith be called a Seer, a Translator, a Prophet, and an Apostle of Jesus Christ, an Elder of The Church; and The Church was commanded to give heed to all his words and commandments which he should receive from the Lord, accepting his word as the word of God in all patience and faith. On condition of their doing this, the Lord promised them that the gates of hell should not prevail against The Church; but on the contrary he would disperse the powers of darkness before them, and shake the very heavens for their good.

In addition to the ordination of Joseph and Oliver to be Elders in The Church, as stated above, other brethren were called and ordained to different offices in the Priesthood as the Spirit directed. "And after a happy time," says the Prophet, "spent in witnessing and feeling for ourselves the power and blessings of the Holy Ghost, through the grace of God bestowed upon us, we dismissed with the pleasing knowledge that we were now individually, members of, and acknowledged of God, The Church of Jesus Christ, organized in accordance with commandments and revelations given by him to ourselves in the last days, as well as according to the order of The Church as recorded in the New Testament."

On Sunday, the 11th of April, the public ministry of The Church may be said to have begun. Oliver Cowdery on that day preached the first public discourse of the new dispensation then opening. Of the nature of the discourse we know little or nothing. The meeting was held by previous appointment at the house of Mr. Peter Whitmer, in Fayette, and was largely attended by people of the neighborhood, and the preaching was certainly successful, as upon the same day, and doubtless as a result of the explanations, teachings, doctrines and spirit of the discourse, a number came forward for baptism, and a few days later a number more—thirteen in all. And so the work grew and prospered.

Fayette, in Seneca County, New York, and Colesville, Broome County, in the same State, were the centers of activity for The Church in those early days. In both places meetings were occasionally held, and baptisms were frequent, in the clear, beautiful waters of Seneca Lake. What historical associations will yet gather about these localities! Fayette! Seneca Lake! I venture to predict that these places will in the ages to come be as famous as Capernaum and Lake Gennesaret. The latter were the scenes of Christ's early ministry. The former the scenes of Joseph Smiths. The latter were identified with the Dispensation of the Meridian of Time. The former with the Dispensation of the Fullness of Times. Capernaum and Gennesaret are associated with memories of the Christ, with Simon Peter, with John, with Andrew and Nathaniel, and Mary of Magdala. Fayette and Seneca with Joseph Smith, with Oliver, with David Whitmer, with Joseph Knight and Newel, his son, with Emily Coburn and others. Gennesaret was but the widening of the Jordan; Seneca but one of the river valleys once occupied and modified by the glaciers which in ancient times filled that land.[I] The site of the ancient Capernaum is now unknown; so, too, the Fayette of our Church history is no more; but of the latter as of the former, and of Seneca as of Gennesaret it may be said: If every vestige of human habitation should disappear from beside it, and the jackal and the hyena should howl about the shattered fragments where Joseph once taught, yet the fact that he chose it as the scene of his ministry will give a sense of sacredness and pathos to its lovely waters till Time shall be no more.

[Footnote I: Enc. Brit., Art. New York.]

On the first of June The Church held its first conference as an organized body. At that conference—held in Fayette—more brethren were ordained to the various offices of the Priesthood; a number who had been baptized were confirmed; the sacrament was administered, and many spiritual manifestations were enjoyed, such as beholding heavenly visions and prophesying.

Thus The Church was organized and well started upon its career, the history of which was to be so thrilling; the success of which was to be so great; and the final victory of which over every opposing power is assured by the promises of God.

CHAPTER II
THE MISSION TO THE LAMANITES

The Book of Mormon, the coming forth of which has already been detailed, contains many promises to the Lamanites—that is, to the American Indians, whom it reveals to be the remnants of mighty nations that once inhabited the Americas, and also proclaims them to be descendants of the house of Israel. Their present fallen state arises from their departure from the ways of the Lord, and the instructions and doctrines of their ancient prophets; the very blackness of their skin is the result of God's curse upon them for their unrighteousness; yet are they promised that they shall know their origin—the favored race from which they are descended; it is promised that the gospel of Jesus Christ shall be declared among them, and they shall regard it as a blessing from the hand of the Lord; "and their scales of darkness shall begin to fall from their eyes, and many generations shall not pass away among them save they shall be a white and delightsome people." [A] It is promised that Zion, the New Jerusalem, shall be built upon the land of their fathers—the Americas—which, according to the Book of Mormon, is a land especially dedicated to the seed of Joseph, of Egyptian fame, the son of Jacob, "and they are the ten thousands of Ephraim, and they are the thousands of Manasseh;" and in this great work of building up the Zion of God, the Lamanites are assigned a special part, which will be a manifestation of God's favor towards them.[B]

[Footnote A: II Nephi, chap. 30.]

[Footnote B Book of Mormon, Ether 13, and III Nephi 20.]

Very naturally, of course, those who accepted the Book of Mormon as true, possessed a lively interest in this people, that is, in the Lamanites; and anxiously looked forward to the commencement of the fulfillment of the words of their ancient prophets concerning them; and hence at the close of a conference held in the last days of September, and which also extended into the early days of October, "a great desire," says the Prophet, "was manifested by several elders respecting the remnants of the house of Joseph—the Lamanites residing in the west—knowing that the purposes of the Lord were great to that people, and hoping that the time had come when the promises of the Almighty in regard to that people were about to be accomplished, and that they would receive the gospel and enjoy its blessings. The desire was so great that it was agreed upon that we should inquire of the Lord as to the propriety of sending some of the elders among them, which we accordingly did." [C]

[Footnote C Millennial Star, (Supplement), Vol. 14, p. 44.]

The result of this inquiry was a revelation in which Oliver Cowdery, Peter Whitmer, Parley P. Pratt and Ziba Peterson were called to go on a mission to the Lamanites who then inhabited the western states and the Indian Territory. On their journey westward the Indian missionaries stopped at Kirtland, Ohio, where they converted a number of people to the gospel, and organized a branch of The Church.

It was here that Sidney Rigdon, a somewhat noted Campbellite preacher, resided and had a large following. These Campbellites, or Disciples of Christ, as they preferred to be called, were reformed Baptists: that is, in addition to believing that immersion is the only acceptable mode of baptism, they also taught that baptism, when preceded by true faith in God and sincere repentance, was "for the remission of sins;" and that forgiveness of sins really followed every proper baptism. It was on the occasion of this visit of the Indian missionaries to Kirtland, that Sidney Rigdon first heard of Joseph Smith and Mormonism; and the first time he ever saw the Book of Mormon was when young Parley P. Pratt, himself formerly a Campbellite preacher, presented a copy of it to him to read. I think it important to make this statement here, because it has been asserted that Sidney Rigdon had much to do with producing the Book of Mormon; the theory of some being that it was he who stole from a printer in Pittsburg—a Mr. Patterson—a manuscript story written by a sort of harebrained, retired minister, of the name of Solomon Spaulding; and that, after making some changes in the text, he then connived with Joseph Smith to palm it off upon the world as a new revelation from God—a theory which, in addition to being absolutely untrue, always was inadequate as an explanation of the origin of the Book of Mormon, and is now quite generally abandoned, since the manuscript of Solomon Spaulding most unexpectedly came to light in 1884, verbatim copies of which have been widely published; the original now being in Oberlin College, in the State of Ohio. It needs only a perusal of the "Manuscript Found" to satisfy anyone that it never could in the remotest manner have suggested the Book of Mormon, or any part of it; while the fact that Sidney Rigdon knew nothing of the Book of Mormon until Parley P. Pratt presented it to him at Kirtland, Ohio, on the occasion above referred to, is a complete refutation of the idle stories that he was associated with Joseph Smith in writing the Book of Mormon.

Sidney S. Rigdon was born in St. Clair Township, Allegheny County, Pennsylvania, on the 19th of February, 1793, and was the youngest son of William and Nancy Rigdon. On his father's side his forefathers were English; on his mother's, Irish. In his youth and early manhood he followed the vocation of a farmer and tanner. At the age of twenty-five he became associated with a Baptist society, and possessing a natural gift of oratory he drifted into the ministry of that society. He seems to have been much in doubt as to the Baptist church possessing the fullness of the truth, and he at last severed his connection with it and joined in the reform movement inaugurated by one Alexander Campbell, of Bethany, Virginia, founder of the church of the "Disciples," or "Christians." This new religious movement was very successful in what was called the Western Reserve, that region of country lying south of Lake Erie, and constituting the present State of Ohio. It derived its name, Western Reserve, from the fact that the State of Connecticut in ceding its claims upon western lands reserved to itself this magnificent tract for the purposes of a school fund. Among the settlers on this Western Reserve, I repeat, the doctrines of faith, repentance and baptism for the remission of sins, preached by Alexander Campbell, Sidney S. Rigdon, Parley P. Pratt and others, as the cardinal doctrines of Christianity, and the means provided in the gospel for man's salvation, had great success. Sidney Rigdon's labors in this new ministry led him to settle at Kirtland, where he had a large congregation, the members of which, in addition to accepting the primitive faith and ordinances referred to above, were also trying to carry out that order of things incidentally mentioned in the early Christian writings,[D] namely, none of them said that which he possessed was his own; but they had all things in common.

[Footnote D: Acts 4:32-37.]

Such was the state of affairs in Kirtland, and with Sidney Rigdon, when Parley P. Pratt and his associates arrived there in the fall of 1830, and presented the Book of Mormon to him, and preached the gospel of the Dispensation of the Fullness of Times.

Here it may not be amiss to speak a word with reference to the character of Sidney Rigdon. His subsequent prominence in The Church, both the good and the injury he did it, warrant my doing so, and will doubtless be a key to his conduct. That he possessed talents of an extraordinary nature goes without saying, especially in the line of public speaking. Few men in The Church, perhaps none, have possessed the gift of oratory to an equal degree; spontaneous, fervid, rapid, brilliant, captivating; abounding in flights of fancy, rich in coloring and original in its wealth of historical illustration, which his wide and various reading made possible. It can well be imagined how one so gifted would be useful in the work just beginning to come forth through the instrumentality of Joseph Smith—what a welcome the young Prophet would give to such a help-meet, and what influence he would have in The Church then struggling into existence. The Prophet could receive the word of the Lord through the Urim and Thummim, and by the visitation of angels; but at that time he was evidently lacking in ability to expound it or show that what he brought forth was in harmony with the predictions of ancient prophets, a part of a great whole, and admirably dovetailed into the general purposes and designs of God. Neither his powers of expression nor his historical information fitted him for this task. Whatever his abilities in the later years of his ministry, in the earlier days of it he was somewhat slow of speech. He was as Moses waiting for Aaron, and that Aaron, that spokesman, he found in Sidney Rigdon, and bade him welcome.

But talented as Sidney Rigdon was, moral, too, and spiritually minded and sincere as we believe him to have been in these early days of his career, he possessed traits of character which neutralized to a very great extent his great abilities. He was vain of his talents; vainglorious of his importance; too proud of what he regarded as his sacrifices for the truth. The very qualities which made him brilliant prevented him from being profound. The fervid imagination which enabled him to clothe with such splendid imagery his speech, made him a dangerous man when called to act with reference to stern and often disagreeable and prosy realities. He was constitutionally unsound. Remarkably gifted in one or two directions, he was markedly deficient in others. He was wanting in soundness of judgment, steadiness of purpose, a high sense of honor. He was moody, petty, jealous, selfish; and in a word, lacked that mysterious quality so well expressed by the phrase, "weight of character." But with all his imperfections he was useful, and for many years was faithful and devoted to the Prophet and the work of God. He was an instrument in the hands of the Almighty through whom was accomplished much good. He endured much for the truth's sake— persecution, poverty, imprisonment, mob violence, almost death. For such men, whatever may be their defects of character,—especially when such defects are constitutional, the effect of temperament—we can have but the kindest sentiments; and only make mention of such defects as they may have possessed in order to bring to pass a proper understanding of events with which they were associated.

At Kirtland, Frederick G. Williams, who subsequently occupied an important station in The Church—counselor to the Prophet Joseph in the

First Presidency—was also baptized. He volunteered to accompany the Indian missionaries on their journey westward.

The Indian missionaries arrived at Independence, Missouri, in midwinter. Independence was then a frontier town; one of the outposts of Anglo-American advancement westward. It was on the line that divided our frontier from the possessions of the red man west of the great Missouri River; and it can be very well understood that its civilization was not of the highest order. Here had drifted many outcasts from society, and there was, at the time of which we are writing, very little regard for God, religion, refinement, or for civilization. As the Indian missionaries were destitute and weary from the extended journey on foot through what, at that time, was at best but a sparsely-settled country, and very much of it wilderness— it was arranged that two of the company who had been tailors should obtain work at their trade in Independence, while the three others should cross the frontier line and enter the reservation occupied by the Shawnees and the Delaware Indians.

The chief of the Delawares, who is described by Elder Parley P. Pratt as a "venerable looking man," and the "sachem of ten nations or tribes," called together some forty chief men of his people, and to these Oliver Cowdery delivered, in substance, the following message:

> Aged Chief and Venerable Council of the Delaware nation: We are glad of this opportunity to address you as our red brethren and friends. We have traveled a long distance from towards the rising sun to bring you glad news; we have traveled the wilderness, crossed the deep and wide rivers, and waded in the deep snows, and in the face of the storms of winter, to communicate to you great knowledge which has lately come to our ears and hearts; and which will do the red man good as well as the pale face.
>
> Once the red men were many; they occupied the country from sea to sea—from the rising sun to the setting sun; the whole land was theirs; the Great Spirit gave it to them, and no pale faces dwelt among them. But now they are few in numbers; their possessions are small, and the pale faces are many.
>
> Thousands of moons ago, when the red man's forefathers dwelt in peace and possessed this whole land, the Great Spirit talked with them and revealed his law and his will,

and much knowledge to their wise men and prophets. This they wrote in a book; together with their history, and the things which should befall their children in the latter days.

This book was written on plates of gold, and handed down from father to son for many ages and generations.

It was then that the people prospered, and were strong and mighty; they cultivated the earth; built buildings and cities, and abounded in all good things, as the pale faces now do.

But they became wicked: they killed one another and shed much blood; they killed their prophets and wise men, and sought to destroy the book. The Great Spirit became angry, and would speak to them no more; they had no good and wise dreams; no more visions; no more angels sent among them by the Great Spirit; and the Lord commanded Mormon and Moroni, their last wise men and prophets, to hide the book in the earth that it might be preserved in safety, and be found and made known in the latter day to the pale faces who should possess the land; that they might again make it known to the red men; in order to restore them to the knowledge of the will of the Great Spirit and to his favor. And if the red men would then receive this book and learn the things written in it, and do according thereunto, they should be restored to all their rights and privileges; should cease to fight and kill one another; should become one people: cultivate the earth in peace, in common with the pale faces, who are willing to believe and obey the same book, and be good men and live in peace. Then should the red men become great, and have plenty to eat and good clothes to wear, and should be in favor with the Great Spirit and be his children, while he would be their Great Father, and talk with them, and raise up prophets and wise and good men amongst them again, who should teach them many things.

This book, which contained these things, was hid in the earth by Moroni, in a hill called by him Cumorah, which hill is now in the State of New York, near the village of Palmyra, in Ontario County.

In that neighborhood there lived a young man named Joseph Smith, who prayed to the Great Spirit much, in order that he might know the truth; and the Great Spirit sent an angel to him, and told him where this book was hidden by Moroni; and commanded him to get it. He accordingly went to the place, and dug in the earth, and found the book written on gold plates.

But it was written in the language of the forefathers of the red men; therefore this young man, being a pale face, could not understand it; but the angel told him and showed him, and gave him knowledge of the language and how to interpret the book. So he interpreted it into the language of the pale faces, and wrote it on paper, and caused it to be printed, and published thousands of copies of it among them; and then sent us to the red men to bring some copies of it to them, and to tell them this news. So we have now come from him, and here is a copy of the book, which we now present to our red friend, the chief of the Delawares, and which we hope he will cause to be read and known among his tribe; it will do them good.

To these remarks the Indian chief made the following reply:

We feel truly thankful to our white friends who have come so far, and been at such pains to tell us good news, and especially this news concerning the book of our forefathers; it makes us glad in here, [placing his hand on his heart]. It is now winter, we are new settlers in this place; the snow is deep, our cattle and horses are dying, our wigwams are poor; we have much to do in the spring—to build houses, and fence and make farms; but we will build a council house, and meet together, and you shall read to us and teach us more concerning the book of our fathers and the will of the Great Spirit.[E]

[Footnote E: Autobiography of Parley P. Pratt, ch. 8.]

The interest awakened among the Indians by the brethren aroused the jealousy of sectarian missionaries who were also at work among this tribe. They falsely charged the Elders with disturbing the peace, and through their influence with the Indian agents, secured the banishment of the Mormon mission from the reservation.

The Indian missionaries, after their banishment, met with their brethren at Independence, on the 14th of February, 1831, for consultation as to their future movements. It was finally agreed by the meeting that Parley P. Pratt should return to Ohio, and report their labors to the Prophet. Elder Pratt immediately set out upon this long journey, and after enduring much fatigue and sickness, he arrived early in the spring at Kirtland, where he found the Prophet Joseph Smith, to whom he reported the labors of himself and companions.

How Joseph Smith came to be in Ohio at this particular time is of some interest. After joining The Church at Kirtland under the ministrations of Oliver Cowdery, Parley P. Pratt and others, Sidney Rigdon, in company with Edward Partridge (who had not yet received baptism), determined upon a personal visit to the Prophet in New York. They arrived at Fayette, New York, early in the month of December, and soon thereafter the Prophet received revelations which must have been a source of great comfort to these brethren. Sidney Rigdon was declared to have been inspired of God and sent forth to prepare the way before the coming of the Lord and of Elijah, though he knew it not. He had baptized by water unto repentance, but those who received his ministrations did not receive the Holy Ghost; now he was called to a greater work, and was promised that the baptism of the Holy Ghost, under his hands, should follow the baptism of the water, even as was the case with the apostles of old. He was commanded to tarry with Joseph Smith and assist him in writing and in counseling with him in relation to the great work that the Lord was bringing forth.

Edward Partridge, who is described by the Prophet as a pattern of piety, one of the Lord's great men, and, like Nathaniel of old, a man in whom there was no guile, after some investigation of the truth, was baptized by the Prophet in Seneca Lake, and was also called by revelation to the ministry.

The addition of these brethren to The Church greatly strengthened the ministry; they preached almost daily, and were frequently engaged in receiving the word of the Lord by revelation and through the revision of the scriptures; for it had been made known that in consequence of imperfections in translation in some instances, and the omission of many plain and precious parts in other instances, the scriptures—the Old and New Testaments—were imperfect, and hence the necessity for the revision. Finally the brethren received a commandment that after they had strengthened The Church in these parts, they should go to Ohio. The Church in New York was also commanded to gather to Ohio, which commandment, by the way, is the first one given to The Church to gather together in this dispensation. Obedient to this commandment, Joseph Smith, in company with Elders Rigdon and Partridge, and with his family, about the latter part of January removed to Kirtland, where he received a hearty welcome, and was there when Parley

P. Pratt arrived from the west with his report of the labors of the Indian missionaries, as already stated.

What effect this Indian mission report had upon the mind of the Prophet he has left no word to indicate; but that a deep impression was made upon him, and that he attached much importance to that mission, can scarcely be doubted, because of the mighty consequences which subsequently grew out of it.

Since the departure of the Indian missionaries for the west a very great amount of knowledge had been revealed concerning the work of the Lord in the last days. Soon after the arrival of Sidney Rigdon at Fayette, in New York, as already related, work upon the translation of scripture was begun, and among the ancient scriptures that were revealed in the course of this work, was "The Prophecy of Enoch," which is alluded to in the writings of Jude,[F] in the New Testament. According to this "Prophecy of Enoch" the Lord revealed to that patriarch very much that would take place in the last days, among which is the following:

[Footnote F: Jude 14, 15 and 16.]

> And righteousness and truth will I cause to sweep the earth as with a flood, to gather out mine own elect from the four quarters of the earth, unto a place which I shall prepare, a holy city, that my people may gird up their loins, and be looking forth for the time of my coming; for there shall be my tabernacle, and it shall be called Zion, a New Jerusalem. And the Lord said unto Enoch, then shall you and all your city meet them there, and we will receive them unto our bosom, and they shall see us, and we shall fall upon their necks, and they shall fall upon our necks, and we will kiss each other, and there shall be my abode, and it shall be Zion, which shall come forth out of all the creations which I have made; and for the space of a thousand years shall the earth rest.[G]

[Footnote G: Prophecy of Enoch, Pearl of Great Price.]

This is the city also spoken of in the Book of Mormon, to which reference before has been made.[H]

[Footnote H: Page 24.]

Again, before the Prophet and his companions departed from Fayette, in the month of January, speaking of the provisions that he would make for the poor, the Lord said:

I have made the earth rich; and behold it is my footstool, wherefore, again I will stand upon it; and I hold forth, and deign to give unto you greater riches, even a land of promise, a land flowing with milk and honey, upon which there shall be no curse when the Lord cometh: and I will give it unto you for the land of your inheritance, if you seek it with all your hearts. And this shall be my covenant with you, ye shall have it for the land of your inheritance, and for the inheritance of your children forever, while the earth shall stand, and ye shall possess it again in eternity, no more to pass away.[I]

[Footnote I: Doc. & Cov. Sec. 380.]

After the Prophet's arrival in Kirtland, the branch of The Church there in the meantime having increased to about one hundred members, the elders of The Church were sent out into the surrounding country, two and two, to preach the gospel; and a promise of a future mission was given to them in which it was said:

And from this place ye shall go forth into the regions westward; and inasmuch as ye shall find them that will receive you, ye shall build up my Church in every region, until the time shall come when it shall be revealed unto you from on high, when the city of the New Jerusalem shall be prepared, that ye may be gathered in one, that ye may be my people and I will be your God.[J]

[Footnote J: Ibid Sec. 42.]

Moreover, in the same revelation, something of the law under which the holy city is to be built up unto the Lord was revealed, of which we shall say more in the course of this history.

In the latter part of February a brief revelation was given, making known that it was the will of the Lord that the elders who had been sent out to preach in the regions round about should be called together; and this led to the appointment of a somewhat notable conference of The Church that was called to meet on the sixth day of June ensuing. On the 7th of March (1831), the Lord gave a somewhat lengthy revelation setting forth the judgments that should come upon the generation in which this new dispensation of the gospel came forth, in the course of which it is said:

Wherefore I, the Lord, have said, gather ye out from the eastern lands, assemble ye yourselves together ye elders of my Church; go ye forth into the western countries, call upon the inhabitants to repent, and inasmuch as they do repent, build up churches unto me; and with one heart and with one mind, gather up your riches that ye may purchase an inheritance which shall hereafter be appointed unto you, and it shall be called the New Jerusalem, a land of peace, a city of refuge, a place of safety for the saints of the Most High God; and the glory of the Lord shall be there, insomuch that the wicked will not come unto it, and it shall be called Zion.

And it shall come to pass, among the wicked, that every man that will not take his sword against his neighbor, must needs flee unto Zion for safety. And there shall be gathered unto it out of every nation under heaven; and it shall be the only people that shall not be at war one with another. And it shall be said among the wicked, Let us not go up to battle against Zion, for the inhabitants of Zion are terrible; wherefore we cannot stand.[K]

[Footnote K: Doc. & Cov. Sec. 45.]

For a time, however, both the saints who had come from New York in obedience to the commandment from the Lord, and also the saints in Ohio, were commanded by revelation to remain in Ohio for the present, the saints in the latter State being called upon to share their lands with their eastern brethren. "It must needs be necessary," continues the revelation, "that ye save all the money that ye can, and that ye obtain all that ye can in righteousness, that in time ye may be enabled to purchase land for an inheritance, *even the city*. The place is not yet to be revealed, but after your brethren come from the east, there are to be certain men appointed, and to them it shall be given to know the place, or to them it shall be revealed. And they shall be appointed to purchase the lands, and to make a commencement to lay the foundation of the city." [L]

[Footnote L: Doc. & Cov. Sec. 48]

Thus it will be seen that considerable knowledge had been imparted to The Church concerning "Zion" during the absence of the Indian missionaries; and as all the revelations indicated that the location of Zion was in the west, very naturally the interest of The Church was intense concerning this Indian mission operating on the very western borders of American civilization.

This brings us to the before mentioned conference, appointed for the 6th of June, 1831.

CHAPTER III
IN SEARCH OF ZION

The conference of The Church appointed for the 6th of June assembled on that date, in Kirtland. It was an occasion of great importance. In what way it was done is not recorded, but the Prophet in speaking of the matter says: "The Lord displayed his power in a manner that could not be mistaken." He further recounts that the Man of Sin was revealed, and the authority of the Melchisedek Priesthood was manifested and conferred for the first time upon several of the elders. "It is clearly evident," says the Prophet, "that the Lord gives us power in proportion to the work to be done, and strength according to the race set before us, and grace and help as our needs require."

The day following (June 7th), the Lord, in a revelation given through the Prophet, appointed the next conference to convene in Missouri, "upon the land which I will consecrate unto my people, which are a remnant of Jacob, and them who are heirs according to the covenant. Wherefore, verily I say unto you, let my servants Joseph Smith, Jr., and Sidney Rigdon take their journey as soon as preparations can be made to leave their homes, and journey to the land of Missouri. And inasmuch as they are faithful unto me, it shall be made known unto them what they shall do; and it shall also, inasmuch as they are faithful, be made known unto them the land of your inheritance."

This announcement caused great joy to the conference. The place for the Zion of God—the New Jerusalem—was to be made known! It was to be the land of their inheritance! The city which Enoch, the seventh from Adam, saw in its splendor—the city of refuge for the righteous in the last days; the city of peace; the joy of the godly; the terror of the wicked—this city was to be located, and they were to be instruments in the founding of it! Small wonder if the thought of it exalted them until even the weak felt strong, and the strong yet more powerful.

Twenty-eight elders in all were called by name to go in different directions through the western states, two by two—"preaching by the way in every congregation, baptizing by water and the laying on of hands by the water's side." They were to meet in western Missouri in a conference appointed at that place, and there learn the location of Zion.

Soon after the close of the conference the elders started upon this mission, some going on foot, others going part way by stage and steamboat. The Prophet, in company with Sidney Rigdon, Martin Harris, Edward Partridge, W. W. Phelps, Joseph Coe, A. S. Gilbert and wife, left Kirtland for Missouri *via* Cincinnati and St. Louis.

At Cincinnati the Prophet Joseph had an interview with Rev. Walter Scott, the associate of Alexander Campbell in founding the sect of "The Disciples," or "Campbellites." It was with these gentlemen that Sidney Rigdon was associated in a religious reform movement, to which reference has already been made. Their design was to re-establish primitive Christianity. This object they proposed to achieve by discarding all man-made creeds and accepting the Bible alone—and especially the New Testament—as the authority and groundwork of their faith. Their cardinal doctrines were, faith in God and in Jesus Christ, repentance of sin, and baptism by immersion for the remission of sins, followed by righteousness of life. This unquestionably was a good beginning in the way of restoring the primitive Christian faith. Most of the fundamentals of the Christian faith are here; and if Sidney Rigdon, as the Lord declared, was sent forth even as John the Baptist to prepare the way before the Lord Jesus and Elijah—though he knew it not—then undoubtedly Alexander Campbell and Walter Scott, who were engaged in the same work, were also sent forth to prepare the way before the Lord. Certain it is that Alexander Campbell did a great work among the Protestant sects of the United States in getting them to turn from the creeds of men to the scriptures; and the elders of the Church of Jesus Christ of Latter-day Saints have found in the sect of "The Disciples" more who would listen to their teachings, and a greater proportion of them who would accept the fullness of the gospel, than among any other sect. And those among them who have rejected the fullness of the gospel when it was presented to them, have failed to understand aright the meaning of the Campbell-Scott-Rigdon reform movement—they have failed to recognize in that movement merely a preparation for the incoming of the fullness of the gospel.

That their teaching was not a complete return to the Christianity of the New Testament ought to have been clear to them, especially to the originators of the movement. They lacked divine authority—divine commission from God to administer the sacraments of the gospel. They baptized only with water for the remission of sins. The baptism of the Holy Ghost—apparently unknown to them—is equally a vital part of primitive Christianity, and is as plainly taught in the New Testament as an essential to salvation as water baptism. They lacked the organization of the primitive Church—apostles, prophets, bishops, elders, teachers, deacons, etc., etc.; and especially were they lacking in the enjoyment of those spiritual gifts of the gospel, so prominent a characteristic of the primitive Christian Church.

Unfortunately, and very unlike Sidney Rigdon, both Mr. Campbell and Mr. Scott violently opposed the work of God brought forth by Joseph Smith. Alexander Campbell, through his "Millennial Harbinger," bitterly assailed both the Book of Mormon and the character of Joseph Smith; and Mr. Scott in this Cincinnati interview with the Prophet, opposed the work strenuously for that it set forth that men accepting the gospel of Jesus Christ were now entitled to the same spiritual powers and gifts as were enjoyed in the primitive Church. "Before the close of our interview," says the Prophet, "he manifested one of the bitterest spirits against the doctrine of the New Testament, (that these signs shall follow them that believe, as recorded in the 16th chapter of the Gospel according to St. Mark), that I ever witnessed among men."

From St. Louis, those who continued in the company of the Prophet made the journey on foot to Independence, where they arrived about the middle of July.

In a few days the other elders of this mission through the western states began to arrive. These men had suffered all the hardships incident to a long journey performed for the most part on foot through a sparsely settled country and in the hot summer months; but the consciousness that they were seeking the place of the city of Zion; that they had been promised, on condition of their faithfulness, that its location would be revealed to them; that it should be the land of their inheritance—sustained them in every trial and made the journey pleasant to them.

The meeting between these brethren from the eastern states and the elders of the Indian mission who had remained at Independence since the departure of Elder Pratt to report their operations to the Prophet at Kirtland, was a memorable one. Those from the east could tell their brethren of the west of the expansion of The Church both in numbers and in doctrine; of the commandment of The Church to gather from New York to Ohio; of the appointment of a Bishop in The Church; of the revelation of the prophecy of Enoch, in which they had learned more about the city of Zion; of the other revelations that had been given upon that same subject—the city of Zion—the promise of God to reveal the place where eventually it is to be founded; the laws that must govern its inhabitants; of the glory which at last it shall possess; and finally of their God-commanded journey toward the place where it had been indicated its location was, and all the incidents that had happened on the way westward. All these and a thousand other things—their hopes for the advancement of the Kingdom; the peace of Zion that shall be; the safety, the glory;—all these were interesting themes for conversation.

Of their meeting the Prophet himself said:

> The meeting with our brethren who had long waited our arrival, was a glorious one, and moistened with many tears. It seemed good and pleasant for brethren to meet together in unity. But our reflections were great, coming as we had from a highly cultivated state of society in the east, and standing now upon the confines or western limits of the United States, and looking into the vast wilderness of those that sat in darkness; how natural it was to observe the degradation, leanness of intellect, ferocity and jealousy of a people that were nearly a century behind the times, and to feel for those who roamed about without the benefit of civilization, refinement or religion; yea, and to exclaim in the language of the prophets: When will the wilderness blossom as the rose? When will Zion be built up in her glory, and where will Thy templestand, unto which all nations shall come in the last days?

The brethren were not long left in doubt upon this subject, for within a day or two—the date of the revelation is not definitely known further than the fact that it was given in July—a revelation was given in which the Lord made known that Missouri was the land which the Lord had appointed and consecrated for the gathering of his people: "Wherefore this is the land of promise," said the Lord, "and the place for the city of Zion," and "behold, the place which is now called Independence, is the center place, and a spot for the temple is lying westward, upon a lot which is not far from the court house." [A]

[Footnote A: Doc. & Cov. Sec. 57.]

The Saints were commanded to purchase this land, and that lying westward to the extent of their ability, that they might "obtain it as an everlasting inheritance."

Sidney Gilbert was appointed an agent to The Church to receive money and to purchase lands, and also to engage in the business of a general merchant, the proceeds of which business were to be used in the purchase of lands.

Edward Partridge, by virtue of his office as bishop, was to divide to the Saints their inheritance as the lands were purchased.

W. W. Phelps was to be established as a printer and publisher to The Church in Zion, assisted by Oliver Cowdery.

Immediate preparations were to be made by the bishop and his agents for settling the families then on their way from the east to settle in Zion.

The first Sunday after the arrival of the elders of this western mission, a public meeting was held over the western boundary of the United States. Such a congregation was present as was only possible in an American frontier district—Indians, Negroes (then slaves), and all classes and conditions of people from the surrounding counties—Universalists, Atheists, Deists, Presbyterians, Methodists, Baptists, both priests and people—a motly crowd, truly! At the conclusion of the services two were baptized, but they were not the fruits of this meeting as they previously believed the gospel.

During the week following, the Colesville branch of The Church, which had emigrated bodily from Colesville, Broome County, State of New York, arrived and settled in the edge of an extensive prairie about twelve miles west of Independence, and in what must now be the suburbs of Kansas City. It is worth while observing as we pass, that this branch of The Church was made up wholly of northern people, and therefore constituted a different class of settlers from the old inhabitants of Independence, who came chiefly from the south. They had been commanded to come to western Missouri in a body, with a view to permanently settling in the land of Zion, when that place should be designated; and in this their mission differed from that given to the twenty-eight elders who were commanded to travel two and two, preaching the gospel through the western states en route for Missouri.

These people were unquestionably plunged into new conditions. They had been reared in a district of New York where the land was heavily timbered, and where to clear a farm for cultivation took well-nigh the lifetime of one generation. But here they found alternate woodland and prairie, great stretches of open country which only needed to be fenced to be ready for plowing, and doubtless their hearts swelled with gratitude when they contemplated the possibilities and prosperity that could come to the industrious in such a goodly land.

They soon set about their work of founding Zion, for on the 2nd day of August they began the erection of a log house. The first log was carried and placed by twelve men—of whom the Prophet was one—in honor of the twelve tribes of Israel; and Sidney Rigdon who had arrived at Independence sometime after the Prophet, from whom he separated at St. Louis, dedicated the land of Zion for the gathering of God's people. "It was a season of joy to those present," writes the Prophet, "and afforded a glimpse of the future which time will yet unveil to the satisfaction of the faithful."

Sidney Rigdon was also commanded to write a description of the land of Zion, but of that more later.

It will be remembered that a site for the temple in Zion was also revealed at the time Independence was declared to be the center place thereof, and that it was described as lying a short distance west from the court house. A scant half mile from the latter place one comes to the summit of a hill—

A gentle hill of mild declivity

—the crown of which is about an acre and a half in area, perhaps more. On the 3rd day of August, 1831, upon this spot then covered with a rich growth of timber, the Prophet and a number of the brethren, among whom were Sidney Rigdon, Edward Partridge, W. W. Phelps, Oliver Cowdery, Martin Harris and Joseph Coe—assembled to dedicate the place as the temple site in Zion. In the course of the impressive ceremonies then conducted, the 87th Psalm was read:

His foundation is the holy mountains.

The Lord loveth the gates of Zion more than all the dwellings of Jacob.

Glorious things are spoken of thee, O city of God.

I will make mention of Rahab and Babylon to them that know me; behold Philistia, and Tyre, with Ethiopia: this man was born there.

And of Zion it shall be said, This and that man was born in her; and the Highest himself shall establish her.

The Lord shall count when he writeth up the people, that this man was born there.

As well the singers as the players on instruments shall be there: all my springs [i. e. hopes] are in thee.

The Prophet Joseph then dedicated the spot where the temple is to be built—a temple, by the way, on which the glory of God shall visibly rest; yea, the Great God hath so declared it, saying: "Verily this generation shall not all pass away until an house shall be built unto the Lord, and a cloud shall rest upon it, which cloud shall be even the glory of the Lord, which shall fill the house; * * * the sons of Moses and also the sons of Aaron shall offer an acceptable offering and sacrifice in the house of the Lord, which house shall be built unto the Lord in this generation, upon the consecrated spot as I have appointed." [B]

[Footnote B: Doc. & Cov. Sec. 84:4-6, 31.]

On the 4th of August a conference was held at the house of Joshua Lewis, in Kaw Township, Jackson County, among the Colesville saints. This was the conference that was appointed to convene by the revelation received on the 7th of June, directing the elders to go westward in search of Zion.

Thus the work of building up the center place of Zion was commenced, and although the commencement was humble in the extreme, the final result shall be the erection of a city that shall be the crowning glory of the western world—a city from which shall go forth the law of the Lord unto all nations, for it is written: "The law shall go forth from Zion." [C]

[Footnote C: Isaiah 2:3.]

It shall be a city of refuge, for the Lord has said that "every man that will not take his sword against his neighbor, must needs flee unto Zion for safety." [D]

[Footnote D: Doc. & Cov. Sec. 45:68.]

The wicked will consider her inhabitants terrible, while the righteous out of every nation will come unto her with songs of everlasting joy in their hearts.[E]

[Footnote E: Doc. & Cov. Sec. 45:69-71.]

CHAPTER IV
THE LAND AND THE CITY

The land in which the city of Zion is to be built will ever be of interest to the saints, and I therefore give the following description of that section of Missouri.

The Missouri River, though flowing east in the main, takes a meandering course through the State to which it has given its name. The "river bottom" is a low strip of land on either bank of the stream, and varies in width from a few hundred yards to several miles. The character of the soil in the bottom is, of course, alluvial, and very fertile. The Missouri is said to be a "treacherous stream" by the people living on its banks. By that they mean it frequently changes its channel. Several places were pointed out to me, as I passed down it, that used to be the main channel of the stream; but which are now overgrown with trees, underbrush, and fields of waving corn; while here and there the stream is cutting its banks, and mass after mass of sandy, alluvial deposit of former times is caving in—the river is cutting for itself a new channel—or moving obstructions from an old one in which it flowed ages ago.

But however often the Missouri may change its banks, the main stream never leaves the river bottoms, for the reason that these bottoms are walled in by the "bluffs." The word bluff naturally suggests to the mind rugged cliffs rising almost perpendicularly from the bottoms to dizzy heights—but such are not the bluffs of the Missouri. While occasionally one may see a bold cliff rising from the water's edge, yet they are not numerous. The Missouri bluffs are sharp, rolling hills that run parallel with the river on either side, and are usually timbered. They vary in width, sometimes extending ten or fifteen miles, and then again narrowed down to a few hundred yards by some patch of prairie that approaches very nearly to the river bank.

Back from these bluffs are stretched out great rolling prairies, the extent of which quite bewilders one. They are divided into what appear to be immense meadows by the strips of timber land which invariably border the winding streams. Standing on an eminence that overlooks these alternate prairie and timber lands, extending as they do as far as the eye can reach—

with here and there a crowning hill ornamented with a pretentious farm house, or some more humble dwelling half hidden from your view by the thick foliage of the trees, with cattle feeding on a thousand hills—all this is very likely to make the beholder imagine himself in some enchanted realm. But to be more particular:

Jackson County, which is the center place of Zion, is in ninety-four west longitude, and thirty-nine north latitude, being nearly equally distant from the northern boundary of the United States and the Gulf of Mexico. It is also about midway between the Atlantic and the Pacific Oceans, making it the most central point within the United States, and, with reference to both North and South America, a central place in this western hemisphere, of which in the future it will be the great capital. The climate is delightful, being mild at least three-fourths of the year The soil of Missouri is, for the most part, a rich, black loam, in places intermingled with sand and clay, and is from two to ten feet in depth, with a sub-soil of a fine quality of clay. Both climate and soil are favorable to the production of all the fruits and vegetables of the warm temperate climate: not only the hardy cereals, such as oats, barley, wheat, rye, buck-wheat, corn, etc., but also tobacco, cotton, flax, sweet-potatoes and all other common vegetables, as also fruit, apples, pears, apricots, persimmons, plums of many varieties, the luscious peach, the delicious grape, and a great many kinds of berries grow in abundance. It is either Stanley or Livinstone who, in speaking of some parts of Africa, says: "The people tickle the soil with a hoe, and it laughs with plenty." It is so with the land of Zion.

Though the supply of timber useful for lumber purposes is nearly exhausted, you still find luxuriant growths of hickory, some black walnut, a variety of oaks, plenty of elm, cherry, honey-locust, mulberry, bass-wood and boxelder; huge sycamores and cottonwoods grow in the river bottoms, as also hard and soft maple.

Formerly many wild animals roamed over the prairies or lived in the woods; such as the buffalo, elk, deer, bear, wolf, beaver, and many smaller animals; wild turkeys, geese, quail, and a variety of singing birds: in short, it was once the hunter's paradise. Civilization, however, has driven away nearly all these animals, especially the larger ones; but they are replaced by the domestic species so useful to man, both for food and clothing, as well as being of valuable assistance in his labors.

The clay, of which there is unlimited quantities, makes a fine quality of brick. Stone quarries which supply a good quality of light-colored sand-stone, are abundant, so that substantial building material may be said to be plentiful. Such is the land of Zion as I found it—a land with resources well-nigh unlimited, a land yielding an abundance of all useful products though but indifferently cultivated by the husbandmen who possess it—a land of surpassing loveliness, though its beauties are often marred rather than increased by those who inhabit it; while its magnificent resources are very far from anything like complete development.

The land being thus beautiful in its products when only partially developed, the mind naturally inquires what will it be when its resources are fully developed—when the idleness and indifference of its people shall be banished—when it shall be possessed by the saints of the Most High, who will consecrate their substance for the building of Zion; and all their exertions will be to glorify God, and benefit mankind—when covetousness is subdued and virtue and righteousness shall reign in every heart—and when under the blessings of Jehovah the land shall yield in its strength! When the glory of Lebanon shall be brought to Zion, the fir tree, the pine tree and the box tree together; when for brass, will be brought gold; and for iron, silver; for wood, brass; and for stones, iron, to glorify the place of God's sanctuary! Surely when this shall come to pass, the land of Zion shall be the perfection of beauty.

Independence, designated as the center place of Zion, is in the northern part of Jackson county, about three or four miles south of the Missouri River. It is located nearly midway between two small rivers which flow northward and empty into the Missouri; the stream on the west is called "Big Blue," and the one on the east "Little Blue." The town is situated in the river bluffs already described as sharp, rolling hills, many of which at one time were covered with fine growths of timber and even now some of them are partially covered with beautiful groves. Independence in 1831, as stated in a previous chapter, was a frontier town with all the disadvantages implied by that term. It had a mixed population of white men from many sections of the Union, chiefly, however, from the south, some of whom had moved into the western wilderness to escape the consequences of unlawful deeds committed elsewhere; vagabond Indians and renegades who had mingled with them; besides a number of negro slaves. Society was as varied as the character of the population, but on the whole may be described as being without stability, regard for law, or religion. Of late years, of course, the character of Independence has been entirely changed. Western Missouri is no longer the frontier of the United States, nor is Independence a frontier town. It is now a delightful residence suburb of Kansas City, Missouri, with many attractive homes.

Having given a description of the land of Zion and the town of Independence, it may be interesting to learn something concerning the city of Zion that shall yet stand there to the glory of God. Of necessity the description will be imperfect, as the available materials for such description are very meagre. While the prophets have written much concerning Zion and her future glory, their rapturous effusions do not furnish matter for a definite description of the city. In June, 1833, however, Joseph Smith and the elders in Kirtland, Ohio, sent a plat of the city to the brethren in Missouri. We have been unable to find the plat, but an explanation of it is recorded in the history of Joseph Smith,[A] from which we learn the following:

[Footnote A: Millennial Star, Vol. 14, p. 438]

The city plat is one mile square, divided into blocks containing ten acres each—forty rods square—except the middle range of blocks running north and south; they will be forty by sixty rods, containing fifteen acres, having their greatest extent east and west. The streets will be eight rods wide, intersecting each other at right angles. The tier of blocks forty by sixty rods will be reserved for public buildings, temples, tabernacles, school houses, etc.[B]

[Footnote B: By this arrangement, it will be observed that the blocks in the city cannot be uniformly forty rods square (if the middle range of blocks running north and south are made forty by sixty), as the plat east and west would lack twenty-eight rods, and north and south eight rods, of being sufficient for such an arrangement. Either the outside tier of blocks must be less than forty rods square, or the city plat must be more than a mile square. It must be three hundred and forty-eight rods east and west, (instead of three hundred and twenty) by three hundred and twenty-eight north and south.—B. H. R.]

All the other blocks will be divided into half-acre lots, a four rod front to every lot, and extending back twenty rods. In one block the lots will run from the north and south, and in the next one from the east and west, and so on alternately throughout the city, except in the range of blocks reserved for public buildings. By this arrangement no street will be built on entirely through the street; but on one block the houses will stand on one street, and on the next one on another street. All of the houses are to be built of brick or stone; and but one house on a lot, which is to stand twenty-five feet back from the street, the space in front being for lawns, ornamental trees, shrubbery, or flowers according to the taste of the owners; the rest of the lot will be for gardens, etc.

It is supposed that such a plat when built up will contain fifteen or twenty thousand population, and that they will require twenty-four buildings to supply them with houses for public worship and schools. These buildings will be temples, none of which will be less than eighty-seven feet by sixty-one, and two stories high, each story to be fourteen feet, making the building twenty-eight feet to the square. I say none of these temples will be smaller than this, but of course there will be others much larger; the above, however, are the dimensions of the one the saints were commanded to build first.

Lands on the north and south of the city will be laid off for barns and stables for the use of the city, so there will be no barns or stables in the city among the homes of the people.

Lands for the agriculturist are also to be laid off on the north and south of the city plat, but if sufficient land cannot be laid off without going too great a distance, then farms are to be laid off on the east and west also; but the tiller of the soil as well as the merchant and mechanic will live in the city. The farmer and his family, therefore, will enjoy all the advantages of schools, public lectures and other meetings. His home will no longer be isolated, and his family denied the benefits of society, which has been, and always will be, the great educator of the human race; but they will enjoy the same privileges of society, and can surround their homes with as much refinement as will be found in the home of the merchant or banker.

"When this square is thus laid off and supplied, lay off another in the same way," said Joseph to those to whom the city plat was sent, "and so fill up the world in these last days, and let every man live in the city, *for this is the city of Zion.*"

CHAPTER V
SETTLEMENT OF THE SAINTS IN MISSOURI—
THEIR ERRORS—REPROOFS AND WARNINGS

On the 4th of August, 1831, a conference was held among the Colesville saints, at the house of Joshua Lewis, in Kaw Township; and about this time a number of revelations were given in which the Lord made known his will to his servants and gave his reasons for calling them to Missouri. Those reasons were:

1. That the Lord's servants might give to him a witness of their obedience;

2. That they might have the honor of laying the foundation of Zion;

3. That they might bear record in all their travels hereafter, where the city of Zion shall stand;

4. That the testimony of these things might go forth from "the city of the heritage of God." [A]

[Footnote A: Doc. & Cov. Sec. 58:1-13]

The Lord commanded the saints to purchase lands in Jackson County, to the extent of their ability; and for the better accomplishment of this object, Sidney Gilbert was appointed agent for The Church. Having accomplished these things, the elders, except Edward Partridge and a few others whom the Lord appointed to settle permanently in Missouri, were commanded to return to their homes, bearing record by the way of what had been revealed.

The saints and elders who remained in the land of Zion began the work of building up permanent homes. They had arrived too late to raise crops that season, but they cut hay for their cattle, and prepared some ground for cultivation. The fall and winter were occupied in building log cabins; but with all their industry they were not able to provide shelter for all. Through that long, cold winter the saints cheerfully submitted to all kinds of inconveniences, such as several families living in an open, unfinished log room, without windows, and nothing but the frozen ground for a floor. Their food consisted chiefly of beef and a little bread, made of coarse corn meal, manufactured by rubbing the ears of corn on a tin grater. The spirit of peace, union and love, however, was in their midst, and at their prayer meetings, and in their family worship, they were blessed with many seasons of refreshing from the presence of the Lord.

Thus the winter of 1831 passed away.

As soon as the churches scattered abroad learned that the Lord had revealed the place where the city of Zion was to be built, preparations to purchase inheritances absorbed the minds of the faithful; and money was sent to The Church agent from all quarters to buy lands. Edward Partridge had been appointed the bishop in Zion, and it was made his duty to divide unto the saints their inheritances.[B] As early as February, 1831, the Lord had said that those who loved him would remember the poor, and consecrate of their property to sustain them, for inasmuch as they did it to the poor, they did it unto him; and that which was consecrated to the poor, should be imparted to them with a deed and a covenant that could not be broken. Moreover every man was to be made a steward over his own property.[C]

[Footnote B: Doc. & Cov. Sec. 57:7.]

[Footnote C: Doc. & Cov. Sec. 42:29-35.]

This law of consecration and stewardship was as follows: Every man was to consecrate his property to the bishop of The Church without reserve, with a covenant that could not be broken; and then from this consecrated property receive an inheritance from the bishop—sharing equally with his brethren, according to his family and circumstances—this inheritance being deeded [D] to him by the bishop; which inheritance then became his stewardship, upon which he was to improve according to the measure of wisdom he possessed. Every man is to be independent in the management of his stewardship. By every man consecrating his property to the bishop, and then receiving back as his stewardship only sufficient for his support, there was a surplus left in the hands of the bishop to be placed in the Lord's storehouse. Then if in the management of his stewardship a man obtained more than was needful for his support, it, too, was put into the Lord's storehouse, and that, as well as the surplus first named, was to be used in giving inheritances to the poor; and in assisting the brethren in the improvement of their respective stewardships, as should be appointed by the high council of The Church, and the bishop and his counselors.[E] And thus the saints were to be made equal in temporal things as well as in things that are spiritual.[F]

[Footnote D: Doc. & Cov. Sec. 51:4.]

[Footnote E: Doc. & Cov. Sec. 42:33, 53-55.]

[Footnote F: Doc. & Cov. Sec. 78.]

The hearts of the saints in Zion were made glad in the spring of 1832 by a visit from their youthful Prophet and Sidney Rigdon, both of whom had suffered much for the truth's sake, during the winter that had just past, at the hands of a furious mob in Ohio.

At the time the mobbing referred to occurred, the Prophet was living at the house of a Brother John Johnson, Sen., (usually called "Father Johnson" by Joseph and the saints), in the little town of Hiram, Portage County, Ohio, about thirty miles from Kirtland. Before removing to that place, the Prophet's wife had taken two children (twins) to rear, their mother, the wife of a Brother John Murdock, having died when the children were a few days old. Emma Smith received them when they were nine days old, and at the time of the event to be related they were eleven months old.

Nothing of unusual importance had occurred in Hiram since the Prophet's arrival. He had occupied his time in the revision of the Bible that he had been commanded to make, and in holding public meetings in the evenings and on the Sabbath day. Here, too, he received a number of revelations, among them the one called the "Vision," [G] which describes the different degrees of glory to which men may attain in the future life.

[Footnote G: Doc. & Cov. Sec. 76.]

A number of men, however, had apostatized from the truth and left The Church; among them one Ezra Booth, formerly a Methodist minister. He had been converted on seeing a person healed of an infirmity of many years' standing, and, as is so frequent in such cases, he required a constant succession of miracles to keep him in The Church. "But when," as the Prophet remarks in stating his case, "he actually learned that faith, humility, patience, and tribulation were before blessing, and that God brought low before he exalted; that instead of the Savior's granting him power to smite men and make them believe (as he said he wanted God to do with him), he found he must become all things to all men, that he might peradventure save some; and that, too, by all diligence, by perils, by sea and land, as was the case in the days of Jesus" — when he found this was the course the servants of God must run, he was disappointed and turned away from the faith and The Church. So, too, did one Simonds Rider, and also Eli Johnson, Edward Johnson, and John Johnson, Jr.

This by way of introducing the matter, the rest is as related by the Prophet himself:

> On the 25th of March, 1832, the twins before mentioned, which had been sick of the measles for some time, caused us to be broke of our rest in taking care of them, especially

my wife. In the evening I told her she had better retire to rest with one of the children, and I would watch with the sickest child. In the night she told me I had better lie down on the trundle bed, and I did so, and was soon after awakened by her screaming *murder!* when I found myself going out of the door in the hands of about a dozen men, some of whose hands were in my hair, and some hold of my shirt, drawers and limbs. The foot of the trundle bed was towards the door, leaving only room enough for the door to swing. My wife heard a gentle tapping on the windows which she then took no notice of, (but which was unquestionably designed for ascertaining whether we were all asleep), and soon after the mob burst open the door and surrounded the bed in an instant, and as I said, the first thing I knew I was going out of the door in the hands of an infuriated mob. I made a desperate struggle as I was forced out, to extricate myself, but only cleared one leg, with which I made a pass at one man and he fell on the door steps. I was immediately confined again, and they swore by God they would kill me if I did not be still, which quieted me. As they passed around the house with me, the fellow that I kicked came to me and thrust his hand into my face, all covered with blood, (for I hit him on the nose,) and with an exulting hoarse laugh, muttered, "Gee, gee, God damn ye, I'll fix ye."

They then seized me by the throat, and held on till I lost my breath. After I came to, as they passed along with me, about thirty rods from the house, I saw Elder Rigdon stretched out on the ground whither they had dragged him by the heels. I supposed he was dead.

I began to plead with them, saying, "you will have mercy and spare my life, I hope?" To which they replied, *"God damn ye, call on yer God for help,* we'll show ye no mercy;" and the people began to show themselves in every direction; one coming from the orchard had a plank, and I expected they would kill me and carry me off on the plank. They then turned to the right and went on about thirty rods further— about sixty rods from the house and thirty from where I saw Elder Rigdon, into the meadow, where they stopped, and one said, "Simonds, Simonds," (meaning, I supposed, Simonds Rider,) "pull up his drawers, pull up his drawers, he will take cold." Another replied, "a'nt ye going to kill 'im, a'nt ye going to kill 'im?" A group of mobbers collected a little way off, and said: "Simonds, Simonds, come here;" and Simonds charged those who had hold of me to keep me from touching the ground (as they had done all the time), lest I should get a spring upon them. They went and held a council, and as I could occasionally overhear a word, I supposed it was to know whether it was best to kill me. They returned after awhile, when I learned they had concluded not to kill me, but pound and scratch me well, tear off my shirt and drawers, and leave me naked. One cried, "Simonds, Simonds, *where's the tar bucket?*" "I don't know," answered one, "*where 'tis, Eli's left it.*" They ran back and fetched the bucket of tar, when one exclaimed, "*God damn it, let's us tar up his mouth;*" and they tried to force the tar paddle into my mouth; I twisted my head around so that they could not; and they cried out, "*God damn ye, hold up yer head and let us give ye some tar.*" They then tried to force a vial into my mouth and broke it in my teeth. All my clothes were torn off me except my shirt collar; and one man fell on me and scratched my body like a mad cat, and then muttered out: "*God damn ye, that's the way the Holy Ghost falls on folks.*"

They then left me and I attempted to rise, but fell again; I pulled the tar away from my lips, so that I could breathe more freely, and after awhile I began to recover, "and raised myself up, when I saw two lights. I made my way towards one of them, and found it was Father Johnson's. When I had come to the door I was naked, and the tar made me look as though I was covered with blood, and when my wife saw me she thought I was all mashed to pieces, and fainted. During the affray abroad, the sisters of the neighborhood had collected at my room. I called for a blanket; they threw me one and shut the door: I wrapped it around me and went in.

* * * * * * * *

My friends spent the night in scraping and removing the tar, and washing and cleansing my body; so that by morning I was ready to be clothed again. This being Sabbath morning, the people assembled for meeting at the usual hour of worship, and among those came also the mobbers, viz.:

Simonds Rider, a Campbellite preacher and leader of the mob; one McClentic, son of a Campbellite minister; and Pelatiah Allen, Esq., who gave the mob a barrel of whiskey to raise their spirits; and many others. With my flesh all scarified and defaced, I preached to the congregation as usual, and in the afternoon of the same day baptized three individuals.

It was during this visit to Missouri in the spring of 1832, that Joseph was acknowledged by The Church and Priesthood in Zion, "President of the High Priesthood." It was on the occasion of this visit, too, that he sought to so "organize The Church that the brethren might, eventually, be independent of every incumbrance beneath the celestial kingdom, by bonds and covenants of mutual friendship and mutual love." [H]

[Footnote H: History of Joseph Smith. Millennial Star Vol. 14, p. 162.]

In a revelation given July, 1831, W. W. Phelps had been appointed a printer unto The Church in the land of Zion. Accordingly a press and type were purchased, and in June, 1832, the first number of a monthly paper was issued, called the *Evening and Morning Star*. This was the first periodical published by The Church. According to its prospectus it was to be a messenger of truth; a harbinger of peace and good will; to bring good tidings of great joy to all people, but more especially to the house of Israel scattered abroad, telling them that the day of their redemption was near; to proclaim the ensign to which all nations must come, in order to worship God acceptably; to declare that goodness consists in *doing* good, not merely in teaching it; and to show that all men's religion is vain without charity; and as the paper was to be devoted to the great concerns of eternal things, and the gathering of the saints, it would leave politics, broils, the gainsayings of the world, and many other matters for their proper channels.[I]

[Footnote I: Millennial Star Vol. 14:146-8.]

So rapidly did the saints gather to Zion during this summer that the *Star* for November reported eight hundred and thirty souls in the new settlements. The Lord had blessed them both with food and with raiment, and there was plenty in Zion. A feeling of insubordination, however, existed among the brethren of the priesthood. Seven high priests had been appointed to preside over the affairs of The Church in Zion, viz., Oliver Cowdery, W. W. Phelps, John Whitmer, Sidney Gilbert, Edward Partridge, Isaac Morley and John Corrill. These brethren, with the common consent of the several branches comprising The Church in Missouri, were to appoint elders to preside over the respective branches, and attend to all the affairs of The Church in that land. But a number of those high priests and elders who went up to Zion, ignored the authority of the seven who were placed there to preside, and began setting some of the branches in order without being appointed to do so; and it resulted in some confusion. Others who went there sought to obtain inheritances in some other way than according to the laws of consecration and stewardship; and these things, together with jealousies, covetousness, light-mindedness, unbelief, and general neglect to keep the commandments of God, enkindled the displeasure of the Almighty against Zion and her inhabitants.

This state of affairs coming to the knowledge of the Prophet Joseph, through his correspondence with the leading elders in Zion, he wrote a letter to the saints in Missouri, severely reproving them for their neglect to keep the commandments of God; and as the communication is full of prophecy of those calamities which eventually befell the Church, I quote it entire:

KIRTLAND, January 11, 1833.

Brother Wm. W. Phelps:

I send you the Olive Leaf which we have plucked from the tree of Paradise, the Lord's message of peace to us; for though our brethren in Zion indulge in feelings towards us which are not according to the requirements of the new covenant, yet we have the satisfaction of knowing that the Lord approves of us and has accepted us, and established his name in Kirtland for the salvation of the nations; for the Lord will have a place from which his word will go forth, in these last days, in purity, for if Zion will not purify herself, so as to be approved of in all things, in his sight, he will seek another people; for his work will go on until Israel is gathered, and they who will not hear his voice must expect to feel his wrath. Let me say unto you, seek to purify yourselves, and also the inhabitants of Zion, lest the Lord's anger be kindled to fierceness. Repent, repent, is the voice of God to Zion; and strange as it may appear, yet it is true, mankind will persist in self-justification until all their iniquity is exposed, and their character past being redeemed, and that which is treasured up in their hearts be exposed to the gaze of mankind. I say to you (and what I say to you, I say to all), hear the warning voice of God, lest Zion fall, and the Lord swear in his wrath, "The inhabitants of Zion shall not enter into my rest."

The brethren in Kirtland pray for you unceasingly, for, knowing the terrors of the Lord, they greatly fear for you. You will see that the Lord commanded us, in Kirtland, to build a house of God, and establish a school for the prophets; this is the word of the Lord to us, and we must, yea, the Lord helping us, we will obey; as on conditions of our obedience he has promised us great things; yea, even a visit from the heavens to honor us with his own presence. We greatly fear before the Lord lest we should fail of this great honor, which our Master proposes to confer upon us; we are seeking for humility and great faith lest we be ashamed in his presence. Our hearts are greatly grieved at the spirit which is breathed both in your letter and that of Brother G— —'s; the very spirit which is wasting the strength of Zion like a pestilence; and if it is not detected and driven from you, it will ripen Zion for the threatened judgments of God. Remember, God sees the secret springs of human action, and knows the hearts of all living.

Brother, suffer us to speak plainly, for God has respect for the feelings of his saints, and he will not suffer them to be tantalized with impunity. Tell Brother G— —that low insinuations God hates; but he rejoices in an honest heart, and knows better who is guilty than he does. We send him this warning voice, and let him fear greatly for himself, lest a worse thing overtake him; all we can say by way of conclusion is, if the fountain of our tears is not dried up, we will still weep for Zion. This from your brother who trembles for Zion, and for the wrath of heaven which awaits her if she repent not.

JOSEPH SMITH, JUN.

P. S.—I am not in the habit of crying peace, when there is no peace, and, knowing the threatened judgments of God, I say, Woe unto them that are at ease in Zion; fearfulness will speedily lay hold of the hypocrite. I did not expect that you had lost the commandments, but thought from your letters you had neglected to read them, otherwise you would not have written as you did.

It is in vain to try to hide a bad spirit from the eyes of those who are spiritual, for it will show itself in speaking and in writing, as well as in all our other conduct. It is also needless to make great pretensions when the heart is not right; the Lord will expose it to the view of his faithful saints. We wish you to render the *Star* as interesting as possible, by setting forth the rise, progress and faith of our Church, as well as the doctrine; for if you do not render it more interesting than at present, it will fall, and The Church suffer a great loss thereby.

J. S.

A council of high priests at Kirtland also appointed Hyrum Smith and Orson Hyde to write a letter of reproof and warning, in which they cried, "Repent! repent! or Zion must suffer, for the scourge and judgment must come upon her." The whole of this communication, however, is likewise so full of prophetic warning to the saints in Zion that I consider it too important to be omitted, and hence give it *in extenso*:

KIRTLAND MILLS, GEAUGA COUNTY, OHIO,

January 14, 1833.

From a conference of twelve High Priests, to the Bishop, his Council, and the inhabitants of Zion:

Orson Hyde and Hyrum Smith being appointed by the said conference to write this epistle in obedience to the commandment, given the 22nd and 23rd of September last which says: "But verily I say unto all those to whom the kingdom has been given, from you it must be preached unto them that shall repent of their former evil works, for they are to be upbraided for their evil hearts of unbelief; and your brethren in Zion, for their rebellion against you at the time I sent you."

Brother Joseph, and certain others, have written to you on this all-important subject, but you have never been apprized of these things by the united voice of a conference of those high priests that were present at the time this commandment was given.

We, therefore, Orson and Hyrum—the committee appointed by said conference to write this epistle—having received the prayers of said conference, that we might be enabled to write the mind and will of God upon this subject, now take up our pen to address you in the name of the conference, relying upon the arm of the great Head of The Church.

In the commandment alluded to, the children of Zion were all, yea, even every one, under condemnation, and were to remain in that state until they repented and remembered the new covenant, even the Book of Mormon, and the former commandments, which the Lord had given them, not only to say but to do them, and bring forth fruit meet for the Father's Kingdom; otherwise there remaineth a scourge and a judgment to be poured out upon the children of Zion; for "shall the children of the kingdom pollute the holy land? I say unto you, nay!"

The answers received from those letters which have been sent to you upon this subject, have failed to bring to us that satisfactory confession and acknowledgment, which the spirit of our Master requires. We, therefore, feeling a deep interest for Zion, and knowing the judgments of God that will come upon her except she repent, resort to these last and most effectual means in our power to bring her to a sense of her standing before the Most High.

At the time Joseph, Sidney and Newel left Zion, all matters of hardness and misunderstanding were settled and buried (as they supposed), and you gave them the hand of fellowship; but afterwards you brought up all these things again, in a censorious spirit, accusing Brother Joseph in rather an indirect way of seeking after monarchial power and authority. This came to us in Brother Carroll's letter of July 2nd. We are sensible that this is not the thing Brother Joseph is seeking after, but to magnify the high office and calling whereunto he has been called and appointed by the command of God, and the united voice of this Church. It might not be amiss for you to call to mind the circumstances of the Nephites, and the children of Israel rising up against their prophets, and accusing them of seeking after kingly power, etc., and see what befell them, and take warning before it is too late.

Brother Gilbert's letter of December 10th has been received and read attentively, and the low, dark, and blind insinuations which were in it were not received by us as from the fountain of light, though his claims and pretensions to holiness were great. We are not unwilling to be chastened or rebuked for our faults, but we want to receive it in language that we can understand, as Nathan said to David, "Thou art the man." We are aware that Brother G——is doing much and has a multitude of business on hand, but let him purge out all the old leaven, and do his business in the spirit of the Lord, and then the Lord will bless him, otherwise the frown of the Lord will remain upon him. There is manifestly an uneasiness in Brother Gilbert, and a fearfulness that God will not provide for his saints in these last days, and these fears lead him on to covetousness. This ought not to be, but let him do just as the Lord has commanded him, and then the Lord will open his coffers, and his wants will be liberally supplied. But if this uneasy, covetous disposition be cherished by him, the Lord will bring him to poverty, shame and disgrace.

Brother Phelps' letter of December 15th, is also received, and carefully read, and it betrays a lightness of spirit that ill becomes a man placed in the important and responsible station that he is placed in. If you have fat beef and potatoes, eat them in singleness of heart and boast not yourselves in these things. Think not, brethren, that we make a man an offender for a word; this is not the case; but we want to see a spirit in Zion, by which the Lord will build it up; that is the plain, solemn, and pure spirit in Christ. Brother Phelps requested in his last letter that Brother Joseph should come to Zion; but we say that Brother Joseph will not settle in Zion until she repent and purify herself and abide by the new covenant, and remember the commandments that have been given her, to do them as well as to say them.

You may think it strange that we manifest no cheerfulness of heart upon the reception of your letter; you may think that our minds are prejudiced so much that we can see no good that comes from you, but rest assured, brethren, that this is not the case.

We have the best of feelings, and feelings of the greatest anxiety for the welfare of Zion; we feel more like weeping over Zion than rejoicing over her, for we know that the judgments of God hang over her, and will fall upon her except she repent, and purify herself before the Lord, and put away from her every foul spirit. We now say to Zion, this once, in the name of the Lord, Repent! repent! awake, awake, put on thy beautiful garments, before you are made to feel the chastening rod of him whose anger is kindled against you. Let not Satan tempt you to think we want to make you bow to us, to domineer over you, for God knows this is not the case; our eyes are watered with tears, and our hearts are poured out to God in prayer for you, that he will spare you, and turn away his anger from you.

There are many things in the last letters of Brothers G——and P——that are good, and we esteem them much. The idea of having "certain ones appointed to regulate Zion, and traveling elders have nothing to do with this part of the matter," is something we highly approbate, and you will doubtless know before this reaches you, why William E. McLellin opposed you in this move. We fear there was something in Brother Gilbert when he returned to this place from New York last fall, in relation to his brother William, that was not right. For Brother Gilbert was asked two or three times about his brother William, but gave evasive answers, and at the same time he knew that William was in Cleveland; but the Lord has taken him. We merely mention this that all may take warning to work in the light, for God will bring every secret thing to light.

We now close our epistle by saying unto you, the Lord has commanded us to purify ourselves, to wash our hands and our feet, that he may testify to his Father and our Father, to his God and our God, that we are clean from the blood of this generation; and before we could wash our hands and our feet we were constrained to write this letter. Therefore, with the feelings of inexpressible anxiety for your welfare, we say again, Repent, repent, or Zion must suffer, for the scourge and judgment must come upon her.

Let the bishop read this to the elders that they may warn the members of the scourge that is coming, except they repent. Tell them to read the Book of Mormon and obey it; read the commandments that are printed and obey them: yea, humble yourselves under the mighty hand of God that peradventure he may turn away his anger from you. Tell them that they have not come up to Zion to sit down in idleness, neglecting the things of God, but they are to be diligent and faithful in obeying the new covenant.

There is one clause in Brother Joseph's letter which you may not understand; that is this, "If the people of Zion did not repent, the Lord would seek another place and another people." Zion is the place where the temple will be built, and the people gathered, but all people upon that holy land being under condemnation, the Lord will cut them off, if they repent not, and bring another race upon it that will serve him. The Lord will seek another place to bring forth and prepare his word to go forth to the nations, and as we said before, so we say again, Brother Joseph will not settle in Zion, except she repent and serve God, and obey the new covenant. With this explanation the conference sanctions Brother Joseph's letter.

Brethren, the conference meets again this evening to hear this letter read, and if it meets their minds, we are all agreed to kneel down before the Lord, and cry unto him with all our hearts, that this epistle, and Brother Joseph's, and the revelations also, may have their desired effect, and accomplish the thing whereunto they are sent, and that they may stimulate you to cleanse Zion, that she mourn not. Therefore, when you get this, know ye that a conference of twelve high priests have cried unto the Lord for you, and are still crying, saying, Spare thy people, O Lord, and give not thy heritage to reproach. We now feel that our garments are clean from you and all men, when we have washed our feet and hands according to the commandment.

We have written plain at this time, but we believe not harsh. Plainness is what the Lord requires, and we should not feel ourselves clear, unless we had done so: and if the things we have told you be not attended to, you will not long have occasion to say, or to think rather, that we may be wrong in what we have stated. Your unworthy brethren are determined to pray unto the Lord for Zion, as long as we can shed the sympathetic tear, or feel any spirit to supplicate a throne of grace in her behalf.

The school of the prophets will commence, if the Lord will, in two or three days. It is a general time of health with us.

The cause of God seems to be rapidly advancing in the eastern country; the gifts are beginning to break forth so as to astonish the world, and even believers marvel at the power and goodness of God. Thanks be rendered to his holy name for what he is doing. We are your unworthy brethren in the Lord, and may the Lord help us all to do his will, that we may at last be saved in his kingdom.

ORSON HYDE. HYRUM SMITH.

N. B.—We stated that Brother Gilbert knew that William was in Cleveland last fall when he was in Kirtland. We wrote this upon the strength of hearsay: but William being left at St. Louis, strengthened our supposition that such was the fact. We stated further, representing this matter, or this item, than the testimony will warrant us. With this exception the conference sanctions this letter.

These words of reproof and warning had the effect of awakening in the hearts of the saints the spirit of repentance. A solemn assembly was called at which a sincere and humble repentance was manifested. A general epistle to The Church authorities in Kirtland, bearing date of 26th of February, 1833, was adopted at a conference of the saints in Zion, expressing their repentance, and desires to keep the commandments of God in the future. This was satisfactory to the brethren in Kirtland; and the Lord said in a revelation given the 8th of March, that the brethren in Zion *"began"* to repent; and that the angels rejoiced over them. Still there were many things with which the Lord was not well pleased, and he said that he would contend with Zion, and plead with her strong ones, and chasten her until she overcame.[J]

[Footnote J: Doc. & Cov. Sec. 90:32-36.]

CHAPTER VI
STORM CLOUDS.

The spring of 1833 opened early in western Missouri. The streams, which had been so long locked up in ice, broke loose under the genial rays of the returning sun, and rushed madly on to swell the majestic current of the Missouri. The winter snows early melted before the balmy breath of spring, and grass and flowers in rich profusion and of varied hue clothed the great rolling prairies of the west in their loveliest attire. The forests along the water courses put forth their tender buds, and the birds that had migrated to the south in the autumn, to escape the severity of the winter, joyfully returned to build their nests in the same old woods, and make the wilderness glad with their sweet songs. All nature rejoiced, and the saints who had gathered to that land to build up Zion rejoiced with her. They had repented of the sins which had called forth the reproofs of the servants of God: and although there were some persons among them with whom the Lord was not well pleased, yet they had received assurances from God that the angels rejoiced over them.

Under these auspicious circumstances eighty officials and a large number of the members of The Church met for the service of God, and to be instructed in the things of eternal life, at the Ferry on Big Blue, a small forest-lined stream a few miles west of Independence. Their conversation and discourses ranged over immense periods of time; extending back to that time when the morning stars sang together, and the sons of God shouted for joy in anticipation of the blessings that would follow the creation of this earth.[A] They spoke of the cruel persecutions endured by the disciples of Jesus in former ages, little dreaming that the time was at hand when they, too, would be required to endure like trials for the truth's sake—for the word of God and the testimony of Jesus. Their minds were absorbed in contemplating the future glory of Zion; their souls were filled with joy unspeakable—filled with that spirit which ages before caused men and angels to unite in singing, "Peace on earth; good will to man." This occurred on the 6th of April, and was the first attempt of The Church to celebrate the anniversary of her birthday. Only three years before, in the house of Peter Whitmer The Church had been organized; and now the saints in Missouri were exclaiming, How The Church has grown! How much has been accomplished! The Gospel had been preached in nearly all the states of the Union: thousands had hailed the message with delight, and numerous branches of The Church had been established. The place of the city of Zion had been revealed, and nearly a thousand of the saints gathered there. A printing establishment had been founded, and the precious truths from heaven were being published to the world; and all this had been accomplished in the face of poverty and bitter opposition.

[Footnote A: Job 38:3-7.]

During the summer of 1833, a school for the elders was organized in Zion, presided over by Elder Parley P. Pratt, who labored with all the zeal of an apostle in teaching them the things of God. They held their meetings in the shady groves—in "God's first temples," and their instructor frequently walked several miles bare-footed to meet with them. How strange it seems to record the above as occurring in this age! It appears to be quite out of joint with the times, and smacks rather of that age in which John the Baptist preached the gospel in the wilderness of Judea, clothed with camel's hair, and a girdle of skin about his loins; and whose food was locusts and wild honey. Some day, however, when a parallel shall be drawn between the introduction of the gospel in this dispensation, and that in which John figured, it will appear that the men who have been chosen of the Lord in this age to perform his work, possess the same simplicity of character as those whom he chose in Judea, nineteen hundred years ago—the same guileless honesty of purpose; the same child-like confidence in God, and the same unwavering fidelity to their Master's cause; as willing to undergo privations, hunger and cold, and toil and nakedness; as willing to endure the scorn and hatred of the world; as willing to suffer bonds and even death.

The migration of the saints to Missouri in the early summer of 1833, exceeded that of the previous season; but they were settling among a people who possessed characteristics with which, from the nature of things, they were bound to be at variance. The "old settlers" of Jackson County were principally from the mountainous portions of the Southern States. They had settled along the water-courses, in the forests which lined their banks, instead of out on the broad and fertile prairies, which only required fencing to prepare them for cultivation. It was the work of years to clear a few acres of the timber lands, and prepare them for cultivation, but with these small fields the "old settlers" were content. They had no disposition to beautify their homes, or even make them convenient or comfortable. They lived in their log cabins without windows, and very frequently without floors other than the ground; and the dingy, smoked log walls were unadorned by pictures or other ornaments. They were uneducated; those who could read or write being the exception and not the rule; and they had an utter contempt for the refinements of life. It is needless to add that they were narrowminded, ferocious, and jealous of those who sought to obtain better homes, and who aspired to something better in life than had yet entered into the hearts of these people.

There was another element in western Missouri which did not tend to the improvement of its society. Western Missouri at the time of which I write, and as before remarked, was the frontier of the United States, and therefore a place of refuge for those who had outraged the laws of society elsewhere. Here they were near the boundary line of the United States, and if pursued by the officers of the law, in a few hours they could cross the line out of their reach, as the officers could not operate outside of their own nation. These outcasts helped to give a more desperate complexion to the already reckless population of western Missouri.

The Saints could not join the Missourians in their way of life—in Sabbath-breaking, profanity, horse-racing, idleness, drunkenness, and debauchery. They had been commanded to keep the Sabbath day holy, to keep themselves unspotted from the sins of the world. The fact of people having so little in common with each other was of itself calculated to beget a coldness and suspicion, which would soon ripen into dislike. The saints, too, had come, for the most part, from the Northern and New England States, and the hatred that existed at that time between the people of the slave-holding and free states, was manifested toward the saints by their "southern" neighbors. Moreover, the old settlers were dear lovers of office, and the honors and emoluments growing out of it; and they greatly feared that the rapidly increasing saints would soon outnumber them, and that the offices would be wrested from them. Political jealousy is always cruel and unscrupulous; and is not slow to find excuses for destroying the object of its hatred. To the politician as well as to the lover,

> "Trifles light as air,
> Are to the jealous confirmations strong
> As proofs of Holy Writ."

And where these "trifles" do not exist, we shall see in the progress of our narrative that sectarian meanness and political jealousy do not hesitate to manufacture them.

As early as the spring of 1832 there began to appear signs of an approaching storm. In the deadly hours of the night the houses of some of the saints were stoned, the windows broken, and the inmates disturbed. In the fall of the same year a large quantity of hay in the stack belonging to the saints was burned, houses shot into, and the people insulted with abusive language. In the month of April, 1833, the old settlers to the number of some three hundred met at Independence, to consult upon a plan for the destruction, or immediate removal, of the "Mormons" from Jackson County. They were unable, however, to unite on any plan, and the mob becoming the worse for liquor, the affair broke up in a "Missouri row."

The secret of their failure in accomplishing anything was this: A few of the brethren, learning that such a meeting was being held, met for secret prayer, and petitioned the Father to frustrate the plans of this ungodly mob, who were seeking their destruction. The Lord, in view of the fact, doubtless, that this people were partially repenting of the evils for which they had been reproved, in his mercy heard their prayers, and thwarted the designs of their enemies. But the angry clouds of the threatened persecution had been merely drifted aside, not driven from the horizon; and in a few months they assumed a more threatening aspect than on their first appearance.

The sectarian priests inhabiting Jackson and the surrounding counties were earnestly engaged in fanning the flames of prejudice, already burning in the public mind. The Rev. Finis Ewing, the head and front of the Cumberland Presbyterian church, published this statement: "The 'Mormons' are the common enemies of mankind and ought to be destroyed."

The Rev. Pixley, who had been sent out by the Missionary Society to Christianize the savages of the west, spent his time in going from house to house, seeking to destroy The Church by spreading slanderous falsehoods, to incite the people to acts of violence against the saints.

Early in July, a document was in circulation known as the "Secret Constitution," setting forth the alleged grievances of the mob, and binding all who signed it to assist in "removing the 'Mormons.'" The document set forth the following: The signers believed an important crisis was at hand in their civil society, because a pretended religious sect—the "Mormons"—had settled in their midst. The civil law did not afford them a sufficient guarantee against the threatening evils, and therefore they had determined to rid themselves of the "Mormons," "peaceably if they could, forcibly if they must;" and for the better accomplishment of this object, they had organized themselves into a company—pledging to each other their "bodily powers, their lives, fortunes, and sacred honors!"

The saints are represented as being the very dregs of that society from which they came; and also as being poor, "idle, lazy, and vicious." They are accused of claiming to receive direct revelation from God; to heal the sick by the laying on of hands; to speak in unknown tongues by inspiration;

and, in short, "to perform all the wonder-working miracles wrought by the inspired apostles and prophets of God;" all of which, the document claims, "is derogatory of God and religion, and subversive of human reason."

The signers of this document also accuse the saints of sowing dissensions and inspiring seditions among their slaves. They further charge that the "Mormons" had invited "free people of color" to settle in Jackson County; and state that the introduction of such a caste among their slaves, would instigate them to rebel against their masters, and to bloodshed.

The "Mormons" are also charged with having openly declared that God had given them the land of Jackson County; and that sooner or later they would possess it as an inheritance. The document then concludes by saying that if after timely warning, and receiving an adequate compensation for what property they could not take with them, the saints shall refuse to leave the county, such means as might be necessary to remove them were to be employed; and calls a meeting of the signers to convene at the court-house in Independence on the twentieth of July, to consult on subsequent movements.[B]

[Footnote B: The document of which the foregoing is a summary was published in the December number (1833) of the Evening and Morning Star.]

It may not be amiss here to notice the charges made against the saints:

The statement made by the mob that the "civil law did not afford them a sufficient guarantee against the threatening evils" of which they complained, is good evidence that the saints, although they may have fallen far short of coming up to the full requirements of the high moral and spiritual laws of the gospel of Jesus Christ, had violated none of the laws of man—it is an acknowledgement that they lived above that law.

As to the saints being the dregs of the society from which they came—it is untrue; they had a respectable standing in the society from which they came, and that society was far in advance in civilization and enlightenment of the people of western Missouri. This is an old and oft repeated charge against the early members of The Church—this charge that they were of the "dregs of the society from which they came," and I repeat again that it is not true. I know the usual method of defense is to concede the charge, and then quote the well-known and, I may add also, the well-worn passage from Paul's writings, where, in speaking of the early Christians, he says: "For ye see your calling, brethren, how that not many wise men after the flesh, not many mighty, not many noble, are called: but God hath chosen the foolish things of the world, * * * the weak things of the world, * * * and base things of the world, and things which are despised, * * * and things which are not, to bring to nought things that are: that no flesh should glory in his presence." [C] But however complete such an answer may have been in the days of Paul with reference to the Christians of the first century; and however satisfying it may be now in some particulars as to the character of the early membership of The Church, so far as the charge, that the early members thereof were of the "dregs of that society from which they came," is concerned, there is a better course to pursue, a more direct and perfect answer, a more complete argument; and that better course, that more complete answer, is to deny *in toto* the charge. I do deny it. It is not true. Nobler men and women than those who first embraced the gospel of the Son of God in this last dispensation are not to be found; nobler spirits were not on earth. It counts for nothing that in the main they were poor in this world's goods. It is of little moment that they were not famous for learning in the schools of men. I care nothing about their not being regarded as constituting "polite society," having neither the leisure nor the means to cultivate the special graces supposed to go to the making of "polished" gentlemen and ladies. But honesty of heart, purity of motive, nobility of soul, righteousness of life, devotion to God—all characteristics and all attributes which go to the making of a people worthy in the sight of God, may exist quite apart from all that man considers essential to entitle certain of their fellow-men to be considered as forming "good society;" and these attributes the early members of The Church possessed. The Smiths, the Whitmers, the Cowderys, the Johnsons, the Pages, the Corrills, the Knights, the Partridges, the Pratts, the Morleys, the Rigdons, the Whitneys, the Gilberts, the Allens; and a little later, the Youngs, the Snows, the Kimballs, the Taylors, the Richardses—and a host of others whose names do not appear so prominently in the very early history of The Church, were a class of people of whom both The Church and God might well be proud. So far removed were they from being the dregs of society that they were the very choicest part of it; respected and honored because possessed of those cardinal virtues which always command respect, however fallen the material fortunes, or humble the station or calling of those who possess them. Nor is this general statement concerning the respectability of the early members of The Church to be weakened because some of them were unhappily overcome of the world, the flesh and the devil. It is not to be supposed that all who start in the way of salvation will be equal to the task of persevering to the end. The inherent weakness of human nature forbids us to hope for that. The innate weakness of many of the saints was made apparent. The gospel is calculated to do that. "If men come unto me I will show them their weakness," [D] is the word of the Lord in the Book of Mormon, and indeed it is self-evident that if men are to be perfected—and that is the mission of the gospel—then it is necessary that their defects be pointed out to them; for the first step in reformation is to learn in what particular direction reformation is needed. All that can be said, then, against some of the early saints of this dispensation is that they manifested some of the sinfulness common to humanity, and much of that weakness which is the heritage of the sons of Adam; and some of them—many of them if you will—were not quite equal to the great task of overcoming that sinful nature, that human frailty. Meantime, their future is in the hands of God, and he alone will judge them. To the world we may say: "Who art thou that judgeth another man's servants? To his own master he standeth or falleth. Yea, he shall be holden up; for God is able to make him stand." [E]

[Footnote C: I Cor. chap. I.]

[Footnote D: Ether 12:27.]

[Footnote E: Rom. 14:4.]

The charge of idleness comes with a bad grace from the slave-holders of Missouri. Especially so since the charge is made against people chiefly from New England; who, whatever other faults they may possess, can never be truthfully charged with idleness. In addition to the saints who settled in Missouri having been trained from childhood to habits of industry in their former homes, they had received an express command from God to labor, and the idler was not to eat the bread nor wear the garment of the laborer,[F] and unless the idler repented, he was to be cast out of The Church.[G]

[Foonote F: Doc. & Cov. Sec. 42:42.]

[Footnote G: Ibid, Sec. 75:28.]

The saints in Missouri, it is true, claimed to receive revelations from God through the Prophet Joseph Smith; and they also enjoyed the gifts of tongues, and of healing the sick through the anointing with oil and the prayer of faith, in fulfillment of the promises of the Lord;[H] but how all this can be "derogatory of God and true religion," when these blessings of revelation and the enjoyment of the spiritual gifts enumerated are the same as those that were possessed by the primitive Christians, which they were encouraged to "desire," [I] and have ever been regarded as a crowning glory of the early Church; or how they could be "subversive of human reason," can only be comprehended by a Missouri mob, seeking a vain excuse for the destruction of an unoffending people.

[Footnote H: St. James 5:14, 15.]

[Footnote I: 1 Cor. 14:1.]

The charge of sowing dissensions and inspiring seditions among the slaves, and inviting free people of color to settle in Jackson County, has no foundation in truth. The July number of the *Evening and Morning Star*, for 1833, contains an article on "Free People of Color," and publishes the laws of Missouri relating to that class of people. "Free people of color" were negroes or mulattoes who were set free through the kindness of their masters, or who, by working extra hours, for which they were sometimes allowed pay, were able at last to purchase their liberty. Concerning such people the Missouri laws provided that: If any negro or mulatto come into the State of Missouri, without a certificate from a court of record in some one of the United States, evidencing that he was a citizen of such State, on complaint before any justice of the peace, such negro or mulatto could be commanded by the justice to leave the State; and if the colored person so ordered did not leave the State within thirty days, on complaint of any citizen, such person could be again brought before the justice who might commit him to the common jail of the county, until the convening of the circuit court, when it became the duty of the judge of the circuit court to inquire into the cause of commitment; and if it was found that the negro or mulatto had remained in the State contrary to the provisions of this statute, the court was authorized to sentence such person to receive ten lashes on his or her bare back, and then order him or her to depart from the State; if the person so treated should still refuse to go, then the same proceedings were to be repeated, and punishment inflicted as often as was necessary until such person departed.

And further: If any person brought into the State of Missouri a free negro or mulatto, without the aforesaid certificate of citizenship, for every such negro or mulatto the person offending was liable to a forfeit of five hundred dollars; to be recovered by action of debt in the name of the State. The editor of the *Star* commenting upon this law said:

> Slaves are real estate in this and other states, and wisdom would dictate great care among the branches of The Church of Christ on this subject. So long as we have no special rule in The Church, as to people of color, let prudence guide; and while they, as well as we, are in the hands of a merciful God, we say: shun every appearance of evil.

Publishing this law, and the above comment, was construed, by the old settlers, to be an invitation to free people of color to settle in Jackson County! Whereupon an extra was published to the July number of the *Star* on the sixteenth of the month, which said:

The intention in publishing the article, "Free People of Color," was not only to stop free people of color from emigrating to Missouri, but to prevent them from being admitted as members of The Church.[J] * * * * To be short, we are opposed to having free people of color admitted into the State.

[Footnote J: In making the statement that it was the intention of the *Star* article not only to stop "free people of color" emigrating to Missouri, but also to "prevent them from being admitted as members of The Church," the editor of the *Star* goes too far; if not in his second article, explaining the scope and meaning of the first, then in the first article; for he had no business to seek to prevent "free people of color" from being admitted members of The Church. And in forming a judgment of this matter the reader must remember that it is the statement of the editor of the *Star,* and by no means represents the policy of The Church. As a matter of fact there were very few if any "free people of color" in The Church at that time. The "fears" of the Missourians on that head were sheer fabrications of evil-disposed minds.]

But in the face of all this the mob still claimed that the article was merely published to give directions and cautions to be observed by colored brethren, to enable them upon their arrival in Missouri, to "claim and exercise the rights of citizenship." "Contemporaneous with the appearance of this article"— the above article in the *Star*—continued the charge published in the *Western Monitor*—"was the expectation among the brethren, that a considerable number of this degraded caste were only waiting this information before they should set out on their journey." [K] And this base falsehood was used to inflame the minds of the old settlers against the saints.

[Footnote K: Western Monitor for the 2nd of August, 1833.]

That the saints may have said the Lord would yet give them the land of Missouri for their inheritance, is doubtless true; but that they were to obtain it in any other than a legal way never entered their minds. They had been commanded of the Lord to purchase [L] the land for an inheritance. Besides, the elders stationed in Zion about this time, addressed an epistle to the churches abroad, in which they alluded to the gathering of ancient Israel, and pointing out the difference in their circumstances and those by which the saints now were surrounded. Ancient Israel had been compelled to obtain the lands of their inheritance by the sword. "But," the address adds, "to suppose that we can come up here, and take possession of this land by the shedding of blood, would be setting at naught the law of the glorious gospel and also the word of our Great Redeemer: and to suppose that we can take possession of this country without making regular purchases of the same, according to the laws of our nation, would be reproaching this great republic, in which most of us were born, and under whose auspices we all have protection." [M] Nothing then can be clearer than that while the saints may have said that Missouri would eventually be the land of their inheritance, they were expecting to obtain it in a perfectly legitimate manner—by purchase.

[Footnote L: Doc. & Cov. Sec. 57:3, 5.]

[Footnote M: Evening and Morning Star, July, 1833.]

I have been particular in examining the charges made against the saints by their enemies in Jackson County, in order that my readers may know that wherein the things charged were not in and of themselves innocent, and no cause for offense whatever, they were utterly without foundation in truth.

CHAPTER VII
THE STORM BREAKS

In answer to the call made for the citizens of Jackson County to assemble at the court house on the twentieth of July, 1833, to devise means to rid the county of the "Mormons," between four and five hundred gathered in from all parts of the county. Colonel Richard Simpson was elected chairman of the meeting, and James H. Flournoy and Colonel S. D. Lucas were chosen secretaries. A committee of seven was appointed by the chair to draft an address to the public, in relation to the object of the meeting; the following was the committee: Russel Hicks, Esq., Robert Johnson, Henry Childs, Esq., Colonel Jas. Hambright, Thomas Hudspeth, Joel F. Childs and Jas. M. Hunter.

The address this committee reported repeated the falsehoods concerning the saints interfering with slaves, inviting free people of color to settle in Jackson County; and of the saints being the very dregs of the society from which they had emigrated; again charged them with most abject poverty, idleness, and of coming to obtain inheritances in Jackson County, "without money and without price." It declared that the evils which threatened their community, by the "Mormons" settling among them, were such as no one could have foreseen, and therefore they were unprovided for by the laws; and the delays incident to legislation would put the mischief beyond all remedy. It expressed the fear that if the saints were not interfered with, the day would not be far distant when the civil government of the county would be in their hands; when the sheriff, the justices, and the county judges would be "Mormons" or persons wishing to court their favor from motives of interest or ambition; and then the following:

> What would be the fate of our lives and property in the hands of jurors and witnesses who do not blush to declare, and would not, upon occasion, hesitate to swear, that they have wrought miracles, and have been the subjects of miraculous and supernatural cures, have conversed with God and his angels, and possess and exercise the gifts of divination,

and of unknown tongues, and fired with the prospects of obtaining inheritances without money and without price—may be better imagined than described.[A]

[Footnote A: Western Monitor, August 2, 1833.]

However, in speaking of the gifts of the Spirit which the saints enjoyed—revelation, prophecy, speaking in tongues, healing the sick, etc., the committee proposed to have nothing to say, but piously close the clause which refers to these things with the words: *"Vengeance belongs to God alone!"* For the other things with which they charged the saints—each and all of them were utterly false except it might be in the matter of poverty. But even in this the truth was not stated. A few cases aside, the "poverty" in question was that poverty of the pioneer newly arrived in the wilderness which is to be the subsequent field of his enterprises and triumphs. Quite generally the saints went into Jackson County prepared to purchase lands and build homes; but pending the accomplishment of that, there was much inconvenience and some suffering for want of shelter and clothing; but "abject poverty," apart from this, there was none.

The conclusion of the mob in the whole matter was thus stated:

That no Mormon shall in future move to or settle in this (Jackson) county; that those now here, who shall give a definite pledge of their intention, within a reasonable time, to remove out of the county, shall be allowed to remain unmolested, until they have sufficient time to sell their property, and close their business without material sacrifice; that the editor of the *Star* be required forthwith to close his office, and discontinue the business of printing in this county; and as to all other stores and shops belonging to the sect, their owners must, in every case, strictly comply with the terms of the second article of this declaration, and upon failure, prompt and efficient measures will be taken to close the same; that the Mormon leaders here are required to use their influence in preventing any further immigration of their distant brethren to this county, and to counsel and advise their brethren here to comply with the above requisitions; that those who fail to comply with these requisitions be referred to those of their brethren who have the gifts of divination, and of unknown tongues, to inform them of the lot that awaits them.[B]

[Footnote B: Western Monitor, August 2, 1833.]

This address was unanimously adopted by the meeting, and a committee of twelve appointed to wait upon the "Mormon" leaders, and see that the foregoing requisitions were assented to by them. In case of a refusal on the part of the "Mormons" to comply with these demands, the committee, acting as the organ of Jackson County, were to inform them that it was the fixed determination of the mob to adopt such means as would enforce their removal.

The committee called upon Edward Partridge, A. S. Gilbert, John Corrill, Isaac Morley, John Whitmer, and W. W. Phelps, and demanded that they cease publishing the *Star* and close the printing office, and that, as elders of the "Mormon Church," they agree to move out of the county forthwith. Three months was asked for by these elders in which to consider the proposition, and to give them time to counsel with The Church authorities in Ohio; as closing a printing office and removing twelve hundred people from their homes was a work of no small moment. But this time was denied them. They asked for ten days; but that was not granted; fifteen minutes only was allowed them in which to decide. At this the conference broke up, and the mob returned to the courthouse and reported to the meeting that they had called upon the "Mormon" leaders and that they refused to give a direct answer, but asked for time to consider the propositions and counsel with their brethren in Ohio. The meeting then resolved that the printing office be razed to the ground, and the type and press destroyed.

With demoniac yells the mob surrounded the printing office and house of W. W. Phelps. Mrs. Phelps, with a sick infant in her arms, and the rest of the children, were forced out of their home, the furniture was thrown into the street and garden, the press was broken, the type pied; the revelations, book-work and papers were nearly all destroyed or kept by the mob; and the printing office and house of W. W. Phelps were razed to the ground. Having reduced these buildings to a mass of ruins, the mob proceeded to demolish the mercantile establishment of Gilbert, Whitney & Co., and destroy the goods; but when Mr. Gilbert assured them that the goods would be packed by the twenty-third, they desisted from their work of destruction.

But their fiendish hate had not spent its force. With horrible yells and cursings loud, they sought for the leading elders. Men, women and children ran in all directions, not knowing what would befall them. The mob caught Bishop Edward Partridge and Charles Allen, and dragged them through the maddened crowd, which insulted and abused them along the road to the public square. Here two alternatives were presented them: either they must renounce their faith in the Book of Mormon, or leave the county. The Book of Mormon they would not deny, nor consent to leave the county. Bishop Partridge, being permitted to speak, said that the saints had to suffer persecution in all ages of the world, and that he was willing to suffer for the sake of Christ, as the saints in former ages had done; that he had done nothing which ought to offend anyone, and that if they abused him, they would injure an innocent man. Here his voice was drowned by the tumult of the crowd, many of whom were shouting: "Call upon your God to deliver you—pretty Jesus you worship!" These expressions, intermingled as they were with the vile oaths of the mob, were enough to put hell itself to shame. The two brethren, Partridge and Allen, were stripped of their outer clothing, and daubed with tar, mixed with lime, or pearlash, or some other flesh-eating acid, and a quantity of feathers scattered over them. They bore this cruel indignity and abuse with so much resignation and meekness that the crowd grew still, and appeared astonished at what they witnessed. The brethren were permitted to retire in silence—in silence, except when it was broken by the voice of a sister, crying aloud:

> While you who have done this wicked deed must suffer the vengeance of God, they, having endured persecution, *can rejoice,* for henceforth for them is laid up a crown eternal in the heavens!

By this time it was getting late and the mob suddenly dispersed. As night drew her sable mantle over the scene of ruin, those who had escaped to the woods and corn fields began to return, to learn what had befallen their friends. Wives anxiously inquired of the fate of their husbands, and children of the fate of their parents. There can be nothing more sad than this seeking to remove uncertainty in such cases. It is like seeking the dead and wounded on the battlefield, or the missing, the maimed or the dead after an earthquake, or some devouring tempest or flood—so much alike, at least in their results, are the eruptions of the elements and the fierce, uncontrolled passions of man. Before each the timid and the helpless fly to such shelter as they find at hand. Some seek safety in flight, others in hiding from the storm or from wrath. Then when temporary safety is seemingly assured, thoughts for the safety of others assert themselves. The desire for the safety of the loved ones—a wife, a husband, a child, a parent, a brother, a friend— becomes an agony. Love by degrees conquers fear, and at last prompts the facing of danger much greater than those from which at first they fled, and the loved ones are sought despite of all risks to personal safety. So it was with the saints who had been so unexpectedly assailed. On this occasion, however, those returning from flight or hiding had nothing to discover beyond the destruction of the printing press, the wrecking of the Phelps home, the looting of Gilbert's store, and the abuse of Partridge and Allen. Enough surely for one day of persecution, but not to be compared with scenes they yet would witness!

The outrages of this day were the more reprehensible because of the character of the leaders of the mob. In the main they were the county officers—the county judge, the constables, clerks of the court and justices of the peace; while Lilburn W. Boggs, the lieutenant-governor, the second officer in the state, was there quietly looking on and secretly aiding every measure of the mob—who, walking among the ruins of the printing office and house of W. W. Phelps, remarked to some of the saints, "You now know what our Jackson boys can do, and you must leave the country!"

CHAPTER VIII
THREATS OF THE MOB—
APPEAL OF THE SAINTS

The third day after the events related in the preceding chapter, the mob, to the number of some five hundred, again came dashing into Independence bearing a red flag, and armed with rifles, pistols, dirks, whips and clubs. They rode in every direction in search of the leading elders, making the day hideous with their inhuman yells and wicked oaths. They declared it to be their intention to whip those whom they captured with from fifty to five hundred lashes each, allow their negroes to destroy their crops, and demolish their dwellings. Said they:

"We will rid Jackson County of the 'Mormons,' peaceably if we can, forcibly if we must. If they will not go without, we will whip and kill the men; we will destroy their children, *and ravish their women!*"

"WE WILL RAVISH THEIR WOMEN!"

A threat most horrible. Worse than murder; for murder has in it yet some mercy as compared with ravishment, that worst exercise of brute force against helpless innocence. Murder when it has completed its work leaves its victim senseless and peaceful in death; "after life's fitful dream is over," he may sleep well. But what damning torments must that breast suffer which is robbed of its peace by brutal force! How deep the woe that bears the burden of an outraged modesty! How agonizing to be an object of pity! How much more cruel the living tortures of a life so humiliated than the calmness and the peace of death! When devils would with their direst terrors shake a people they say,

We will ravish your women!

The leading elders, seeing their own lives, and the property and lives of those over whom they presided in jeopardy, resolved to offer themselves as a ransom for The Church—willing to be scourged, or even put to death if that would satisfy their tormentors, and stop their inhuman cruelties practiced toward the flock of which the Holy Ghost had made them overseers. The men who thus offered their own lives for the lives of their friends were:

JOHN CORRILL,
JOHN WHITMER,
W. W. PHELPS,
A. S. GILBERT,
EDWARD PARTRIDGE,
ISAAC MORLEY.

Forever let their names be known throughout all Israel as men who have given the greatest evidence within the power of man to give, that they loved the brethren. "Greater love hath no man than this, that a man lay down his life for his friends;" and that faith which will inspire in man a love for his fellows; that will lead him to offer his life as a ransom for his brethren, is so nearly akin to that faith and love which glowed within the breast of the Divine Master, that its source cannot be mistaken. But the inhuman wretches who had combined to drive the saints from their homes in Jackson County, were insensible to the sublime manifestations of love they witnessed. It appealed not to their adamantine hearts. With brutal imprecations they told these men that not only they, but every man, woman and child would be whipped or scourged until they consented to leave the county, as they had decreed that the "Mormons" should leave the county, or they "or the 'Mormons' must *die*."

The presiding brethren, finding that there was no alternative but for them to leave speedily or witness innocent blood shed by fiends incarnate, concluded to leave Jackson County. A new committee was selected by the mob to confer with the brethren, and the following agreement was entered into:

The leading elders with their families were to move from the county by the first of January following; and to use their influence to induce all their brethren to leave as soon as possible, one half by the first of January, 1834, and the remainder by April, 1834. They were also to use all the means in their power to stop any more of their brethren moving into the county; and also to use their influence to prevent the saints then enroute for Missouri settling permanently in Jackson County, but for those then on the way they were to be permitted to make temporary arrangements for shelter until a new location was agreed upon by the society. John Corrill and A. S. Gilbert were to be allowed to remain as general agents to settle up the business of The Church, so long as necessity required. Gilbert, Whitney & Co. were to be permitted to sell out their merchandise then on hand, but no more was to be imported. The *Evening and Morning Star* was not again to be published, nor a press established by any member of The Church in the county. Edward Partridge and W. W. Phelps were to be allowed to pass to and from the county to wind up their business affairs, provided they moved their families from the county by the first of January following. On the part of the mob, the committee pledged themselves to use all their influence to prevent any violence being used against the saints, so long as the foregoing stipulations were complied with on the part of The Church.[A]

[Footnote A: Evening and Morning Star, p. 229.]

A day or two after this treaty was entered into, The Church in Zion dispatched Oliver Cowdery to Ohio to confer with the general Church authorities on the situation of the saints in Missouri. This conference resulted in the general authorities sending as special messengers Elders Orson Hyde and John Gould to Jackson County, with instructions to the saints not to dispose of their lands or other property, nor remove from the county, except those who had signed the agreement to do so.

Meantime the saints attempted to settle in Van Buren, the county joining Jackson on the south (the name has since been changed to Cass), but the people of that county, after the saints commenced a settlement, drew up an agreement to drive them from there, and destroy the fruits of their labors; so they were obliged to return to their former homes.

While the saints were making efforts to carry out the first part of the stipulation entered into with the mob of Jackson County, the mob on their part failed to refrain from acts of violence. Daily the saints were insulted. Houses were broken into, and the inmate threatened with being mobbed if they stirred in their defense. But Truth began to make herself heard. As the fiendish acts of the mob became known, they called forth execrations from various quarters. A number of articles published in the *Western Monitor*, printed at Fayette, Howard County, Missouri, censured the conduct of the mob, and suggested that the saints seek redress of the State authorities for the wrongs they had suffered. Whereupon the leaders of the mob began to threaten life, and declared that if any "Mormon" attempted to seek redress by law or otherwise, for defamation of character, or loss of property, he should die.

These threats, however, did not deter the saints from appealing to the chief executive of the State for a redress of grievances. A petition setting forth their suffering, and denying the allegations of the mob, was presented by Orson Hyde and W. W. Phelps to Daniel Dunklin, who, at the time, was governor of the State. In addition to relating the story of their wrongs, and denying the charges made by the mob, upon which the old settlers of Jackson County depended to excuse or defend their acts of cruelty toward the saints, the petition set forth that whenever that fatal hour arrived that the poorest citizen's person, property, or rights and privileges shall be trampled upon by lawless mobs with impunity, "that moment a dagger is plunged into the heart of the Constitution of the country, and the Union must tremble * * * We solicit," said they, "assistance to obtain our rights; holding ourselves amenable to the laws of our country, whenever we transgress them." They asked the governor by express proclamation or otherwise to raise a sufficient number of troops, who, with themselves, might be empowered to defend their rights; that they might sue for damages for the loss of property, for abuse, for defamation of character, and, if advisable, try for treason those who had trampled upon law and government, that the law of the land might not be defied, nor nullified, but peace restored to the country.

To this very reasonable request Governor Dunklin made a patriotic reply. He stated he would think himself unworthy the confidence with which he had been honored by his fellow citizens, did he not promptly employ all the means which the Constitution and laws had placed at his disposal to avert the calamities with which the saints were threatened, and added:

> Ours is a government of laws, to them we all owe obedience, and their faithful administration is the best guarantee for the enjoyment of our rights. No citizen, nor number of citizens, have a right to take the redress of their grievances, whether real or imaginary, into their own hands. Such conduct strikes at the very existence of society, and subverts the very foundation on which it is based. I am not willing to persuade myself that any portion of the citizens of the State of Missouri are so lost to a sense of these truths as to require the exercise of *force,* in order to insure respect for them.

He advised the threatened saints, therefore, to make a trial of the efficacy of the laws; that wherein their lives had been threatened, they make affidavit to that effect before the circuit judge, or the justices of the peace in their respective districts, whose duty it then became to bind the threatening parties to keep the peace. By this experiment it would be proven whether the laws could be executed or not; and in the event that they could not be peacefully executed, the governor pledged himself, on being officially notified of that fact, to take such steps as would insure a favorable execution of them.

As to the injuries the saints had sustained in the loss of property, the governor advised them to seek redress by civil process—expressing the opinion that the courts would grant them relief.[B]

I do not doubt the sincerity of Governor Dunklin in giving this counsel to the saints, and under ordinary circumstances to seek redress at the hands of the civil authorities would be the proper thing to do. But in this case the officers of the law had been the head and front of this high-handed and infamous proceeding. In proof of this statement I give the names and offices held by those who were most active in the lawless proceeding related:

S. D. LUCAS, *colonel, and judge of the county court;*
SAMUEL C. OWENS, *county clerk;*
RUSSEL HICKS, *deputy clerk;*
JOHN SMITH, *justice of the peace;*
SAMUEL WESTON, *justice of the peace;*
WILLIAM BROWN, *constable;*
THOMAS PITCHER, *deputy constable.*

Besides these there were Indian agents, postmasters, doctors, lawyers and merchants.

These were the men who had despoiled the saints—these the ones, in connection with the secret assistance of the lieutenant governor of the State, LILBURN W. BOGGS, who inflamed the minds of the ignorant frontier settlers against an innocent people, and encouraged the vicious to maltreat the virtuous. These were the men who on the 23rd of July of the same year had said:

"We will rid Jackson County of the 'Mormons' peaceably if we can, forcibly if we must. If they will not go without, we will whip and kill the men; we will destroy the lives of their children, and ravish their women!" And these were the men— the officers of *justice,* to whom the "Mormons" were to appeal for a redress of grievances! To say the least, does it not smack of "going to law with the devil, when court is to convene in hell?" Surely it was only a forlorn hope the saints could entertain of being redressed for their wrongs by appealing to the very parties who inflicted those wrongs upon them; and yet it was about the only course open to the governor to suggest at that time. Being willing to magnify the law, the saints acted upon the governor's advice. For this purpose they engaged the services of four lawyers from Clay County, then attending court at Independence, viz.: Messrs. Wood, Reese, Doniphan and Atchison. These gentlemen engaged to plant all the suits the saints might wish to present before the courts, and agreed to attend to them jointly throughout for one thousand dollars. W. W. Phelps and Bishop Partridge gave their notes for that sum, endorsed by Gilbert & Whitney.

No sooner did the mob witness these movements than they began to prepare for further hostilities. The red right hand of persecution was again armed to plague the saints.

CHAPTER IX
AGAIN THE STORM

Having made all necessary preparations for obtaining by civil process redress for the wrongs inflicted upon them by the mob, Sunday, the twentieth day of October, 1833, the saints declared publicly that as a people they intended to defend their lands and homes. The next day the leaders of the mob began to prepare to inflict further violence upon them. Strict orders were circulated among the saints not to be the aggressors, but to warn the mob not to come upon them. Court was to convene on Monday, the 28th of October, and it was expected that some of the leaders of the mob would be required to file bonds to keep the peace.

While these preparations were progressing among the saints, the mob were not idle. They resorted to their old method of circulating false rumors about the "Mormons." The blasphemy of their doctrines; their intentions to take possession of Jackson County by force; the incompatibility between the old settlers and the "Mormons," were all urged, and the conclusion reached that a war of extermination must be waged against the saints in the name of self-preservation.

Saturday, the 26th, about fifty of the mob met in counsel, and "voted to a hand to move the 'Mormons;'" and as an earnest of their intentions, attacked a number of families who had but lately arrived from Ohio and Indiana, but without inflicting much injury. Monday, the 28th, the circuit court convened, but very few people were in attendance. There was no mob there, but threats of the most violent character were made.

The night of October 31st, however, may be regarded as the time when hostilities recommenced in earnest. That night the mob to the number of forty or fifty proceeded against a branch of The Church located on the stream called Big Blue, known as the Whitmer settlement. They shamefully whipped nearly to death several of the brethren, among whom was Hiram Page. With brutal threats they frightened helpless women and children and drove them into the wilderness in the middle of the night, and then unroofed and demolished ten or twelve houses.

This outrage was followed up the next night, November 1st, by an attack upon the saints living in Independence and vicinity. Their houses were brickbatted, doors broken down, and long poles thrust through their windows. A party of the brethren had gathered for protection about half a mile west of Independence, and to them word was sent that the mob were tearing down the store of Gilbert, Whitney & Co., and destroying their goods. Whereupon these brethren went in a body to the store. At their approach the main body of the mob fled. One of their number, bolder than his fellows, remained, however, and continued sending brickbats and stones through the shattered doors and windows, while the goods were scattered around him in the street. This man the brethren took prisoner, and brought him immediately before Samuel Weston, justice of the peace, entered a complaint, and asked that a warrant be issued that he, Richard McCarty, might be secured. But the justice refused to make out the warrant, or do anything in the matter, and McCarty was turned loose.

The same night an attack was projected upon another branch of The Church, known as the Colesville branch, located in Kaw Township, about twelve miles west of Independence. The mob sent two of their number, Robert Johnson and one Harris, as spies, armed with two guns and three pistols. They were discovered by some of the brethren, among whom was Parley P. Pratt. Without provocation Johnson struck Pratt over the head with the breech of his gun, which staggered him for a moment, and made the blood flow in streams down his face. These two men were taken and detained as prisoners through the night. The spies not returning rather disconcerted the mob, and it is generally supposed prevented an attack that night upon the Colesville branch. The morning following, Johnson and Harris were given their arms, and permitted to return to their companions, without receiving injury from the hands of those whom they had so maliciously assaulted, and into whose power they had fallen.

On the night of November 2nd, a party of the mob went against the branch located on Big Blue, unroofed one house and destroyed some furniture. They also broke into the house of David Bennett, whom they found sick in bed. Being unable to resist them, they beat him most unmercifully, and swore they would blow out his brains. One of their number shot at him with a pistol, but the ball instead of entering his head, as evidently intended, cut a deep gash across the top of it, which, however, did not prove fatal.

While the mob were in the act of beating Bennett, a number of the brethren who had gathered in a body for mutual protection came upon the scene, and a firing of guns commenced. Both parties claim that the other began the attack, but which party began the firing does not matter here. If the brethren opened the fire, they were altogether justified in doing so under the circumstances. Women and children were running here and there screaming with terror, not knowing where to go for safety. Their piteous cries, mingled with the brutal oaths of the mob, and the firing of guns, made the night hideous. In the melee a young man acting with the mob was shot through the thigh, but by which party it is not known.

This day also the saints in Independence gathered in a body as much as possible, about half a mile west of the town, for the purpose of better defending themselves against their enemies.

The day following the events just detailed. Joshua Lewis, Hiram Page, and two others were despatched to Lexington, to see John F. Ryland, judge of the circuit court, and obtain a peace warrant. The saints had previously applied to Squire Silvens for such a warrant, but he refused to grant it. They read to him the governor's letter, which directed them to proceed in that manner, but he replied that he cared nothing for what the governor said. Either his fears of the mob were greater than his respect for the governor, or the law, or he was in hearty sympathy with the rioters. Judge Ryland issued a peace warrant on the 6th; but whether it ever reached the hands of the county sheriff or not I cannot learn. If placed in his hands, then he refused to serve it. But the most reasonable conclusion is, that in consequence of the exciting times and unsettled state of affairs in Jackson County, it never reached his hands.

CHAPTER X
THE PASSIVELY GOOD

There were a few of the citizens of Jackson County who did not take part in these shameful proceedings against The Church. They were friendly disposed towards the saints, but lacked the courage to speak out boldly in their defense, or take up arms to protect suffering innocence. This is often the case with the passively good; with "conservative" citizens. They have no sympathy with rioters, or with mob lawlessness. They are ready to say that such conduct is outrageous, and even a menace to free institutions, and incompatible with freedom; but further than this they do not go. Their conception of good citizenship does not lead them to be active in resisting aggressions upon the liberties of others; especially when those "others" are people with whom they have but little sympathy. They seem not to have learned that those who would preserve their own rights and freedom must insist upon the rights and liberty of every man being respected and assured. It is vain, and especially in a republic is it vain, for any man to suppose that the freedom of any citizen or class of citizens, however humble or even unpopular they may be, can be infringed without endangering the rights and freedom of all. Many otherwise, good citizens of the Republic—simple and fundamental to the preservation of rights and freedom as is this principle— seem so far to fail in appreciation of it, that they stand by while the rights of others are invaded, and sometimes swept away, without making so much as a protest against the injustice. They are content if only their own personal and immediate rights are not directly assailed. The result is that an active minority—often, in fact, an insignificant part of the community, and contemptible of character—are permitted to perpetrate outrages upon worthy though it may be unpopular citizens, that bring disgrace upon the State, and endanger liberty itself. Such was the case in the present instance with those who were not in sympathy with the mob; and yet so far were they from standing up for the rights of those whom they confessed were unjustly assailed, that they advised the saints to leave the State immediately, as the wounding of the young man on the night of the 2nd had enraged the whole county against them; and it was a common expression among the mob that Monday (the 4th of November), would be a "bloody day."

CHAPTER XI
"BLOODY DAY"

Early on Monday the mob took the ferry-boat on Big Blue, west of Independence, which belonged to the saints, driving the owners away with threats of violence. From thence they went to a store, about one mile west of the ferry, kept by one Wilson. Word was brought to a branch of The Church located several miles still further west from the ferry, that the mob east of the Blue were destroying property, and the saints needed assistance. Upon hearing this, nineteen of the brethren volunteered to go to their aid; but on approaching Wilson's store they learned that the mob were there, and that the report of the destruction of property east of the Blue was false. The company started to return to their homes, but two small boys passing on their way to Wilson's store saw this company, and reported to the mob that the "Mormons" were on the road west of them. At this the mob, which numbered between forty and fifty, started in pursuit, and soon came in sight of the company of volunteers, which, at the enemy's approach, fled in all directions. The mob gave hot pursuit, hunting for the brethren through the corn fields, and even searching the houses of the saints for them; at the same time threatening the women and children with violence if they did not tell where the men were hiding. They fed their horses in Christian Whitmer's corn field, and took him and pointed their guns at him, threatening his life if he did not tell them where the brethren were.

Two or three of the company who were dispersed by the mob made their way to the Colesville branch of The Church, which was but about three miles away. A company of thirty men was quickly formed, and although they were armed with but seventeen guns, and knew their enemies were more numerous than they, and better armed, they promptly marched to the assistance of their brethren. They found the mob hunting for their victims, and threatening the women and children. As the mob saw this new company approaching, some of them shouted *"Fire, God damn ye, fire!"* and then they themselves fired two or three shots at the approaching company. This fire was promptly returned by a volley from the brethren, at which the mob fled, leaving two of their number and some of their horses dead on the ground. The two killed were Hugh L. Brazeale and Thomas Linville.

Brazeale had been known to say, "with ten fellows I will wade to my knees in blood, but what I will drive the 'Mormons' from Jackson County."

The first shots fired by the mob wounded Philo Dibble in the bowels, the balls remaining in him. As he bled much inwardly his bowels became swollen, and his life was despaired of. Newel Knight, however, administered to him, by laying on hands in the name of Jesus Christ, and a purifying fire penetrated his whole system. He discharged several quarts of blood and corruption, with which was one of the balls that inflicted his wounds. He was immediately healed, and remained an able-bodied man, and performed military duty for a number of years afterwards.[A]

[Footnote A: Philo Dibble lived to take part in the defense of the city of Nauvoo, some thirteen years later; afterwards removed with The Church to the Rocky Mountains, settling finally in Springville, Utah County, where he died in full faith of the gospel at the advanced age of 90, on the sixth of June 1895.]

A brother by the name of Andrew Barber was mortally wounded—his death occurred the next day.

This battle was fought about sundown, and during the night the mob dispatched runners in all directions with the false report that the "Mormons" had "riz;" that they had been joined by the Indians, and had taken Independence; that the "'Mormons' had gone into Wilson's store and shot his son," with other rumors that were calculated to excite the people, and enrage them against the saints.

The same day, November 4th, a most extraordinary affair occurred at Independence. We have already told how a number of the brethren caught Richard McCarty on the night of November 1st, in the act of hurling stones and brickbats through the doors and windows of Gilbert, Whitney & Co.'s store, while the goods—calicoes, shawls, cambric handkerchiefs, etc.—were scattered around him in the street; and how the brethren took him before the justice of the peace, Samuel Weston, and asked for a warrant to be issued against him, and how the justice refused to issue the warrant. But on this fourth day of November, Richard McCarty obtained a warrant from this same justice of the peace for the arrest of A. S. Gilbert, Wm. E. McLellin, Isaac Morley, John Corrill, and three or four others, charging them with *assault and battery*, and *false imprisonment*. In relation to this matter Brother Corrill tersely remarks, "Although we could not obtain a warrant against him for breaking open the store, yet he had gotten one for us, for catching him at it."

The trial of these men was in progress in the courthouse at Independence, when the news of the battle west of the Blue was brought to town. But instead of being reported correctly, it was said that the "Mormons" had gone into Wilson's house and shot his son. This so enraged the crowd that were in attendance at the trial that a rush was made for the prisoners, to kill them. This, however, was prevented; and at the suggestion of Samuel C. Owens, clerk of the county court, those on trial were locked up in jail for their own safety. During the night the mob were busy collecting arms and ammunition, making every preparation for a general massacre of the saints the next day.

The brethren who were imprisoned were frequently told of these warlike preparations during the night, and that, too, by men of note; and were further informed that nothing but their leaving the county would prevent bloodshed. Whereupon the brethren consented to leave the county, and furthermore agreed to go and consult with their brethren on the subject of all the members of The Church leaving. For this purpose Gilbert, Morley, and Corrill were accompanied by the sheriff and two others to the branch of The Church some half a mile from Independence; and there held an interview with their brethren upon the subject of their moving from the county, to which the members of that branch consented.

The sheriff and his prisoners then returned to the jail—it being about two o'clock in the morning. As they approached the jail they were halted by a company of armed men, six or seven in number. The sheriff answered them, giving his own name and the names of his prisoners, at the same time exclaiming, "Don't fire, don't fire, the prisoners are in my charge!" Morley and Corrill turned and fled, and the party who had halted them fired one or two shots after them. Gilbert stood his ground, and while the sheriff held him, several guns were presented at him. Two of the men, more desperate than the rest, attempted to shoot him, but their guns missed fire; seeing that they failed to shoot him, one of the party, Thomas Wilson, knocked him down. His life, however, was preserved and his injuries were not very serious.

CHAPTER XII
THE "HONOR" OF A MOB

The morning of the 5th of November witnessed the people from all parts of the county crowding well armed into Independence. But few knew of the agreement made by the saints in and about Independence to leave the county; and the presence of the armed crowds was made the occasion of calling out the militia. This last move was at the instigation of Lieutenant Governor Boggs—at least such was the report among the people that day. The command of this militia was given to Colonel Pitcher, but the men who had formerly been the mob made up the ranks of the militia; and the only difference between the mob and the militia was that the mob organized as a militia were prepared to adopt more effective measures in driving the saints from their homes than before they were so organized. The colonels in command—Pitcher and Lucas—were known as the bitter enemies of the saints, and their names were attached to the agreement, circulated in the July previous, to drive them from the county. From such a militia, officered by such men as Pitcher and Lucas, the saints could hope for no protection.

The branches of The Church west of Independence did not hear of the agreement of the Independence branch to leave the county, but reports reached them that a number of their brethren were imprisoned, and that the mob were determined to kill them. About a hundred of the brethren gathered from the various branches, and marched in a body to assist those in peril. They halted about a mile west of Independence, to ascertain the situation of affairs. Learning that the mob had not attacked the branch at Independence, and that the militia was called out, they concluded to quietly disperse and go to their homes. But they had been seen on the road, and it was reported that the "Mormons" were on the march toward Independence, with the intention, no doubt, to do mischief.

Hearing this, the militia under Colonel Pitcher became enraged, and would only consent to grant the people peace on the condition of their agreeing to deliver up certain men, engaged in the battle the evening before, to be tried for murder and surrendering their arms. To this last proposition

Lyman Wight, who, it appears, acted as the leader of the body of brethren that had marched to Independence, would not consent, unless Colonel Pitcher would also disarm the mob. To this the colonel cheerfully agreed; and pledged his honor, with that of Lieutenant Governor Boggs, Samuel C. Owens, and others, to carry out his promise.[A]

[Footnote A: Times and Seasons, 1843, p. 263.]

Upon this treaty being made the brethren surrendered their arms—in all, forty-nine guns and one pistol. They also gave up a number of the parties who were engaged the night before in the battle, to be tried for murder. These men were detained a day and a night, during which time they were insulted, threatened, and brickbatted; and after receiving a mockery of a trial, Colonel Pitcher let them go, after taking an old watch from one of them to satisfy costs!

The agreement made by Colonel Pitcher, to disarm the mob, was never executed; but as soon as the brethren had surrendered their arms, bands of armed men were turned loose upon them. Lyman Wight was chased by one of these gangs across an open prairie for five miles, but fortunately escaped. He lay three weeks in the woods, and was without food three days and nights. He was hunted by the mob through Jackson, Lafayette, and Clay counties, and also through the Indian Territory. Some of the parties who were hounding him were asked why it was they had so much against him, to which they replied: "He believes in Joe Smith and the Book of Mormon, G—d d—-n him; and we believe Joe Smith to be a d—d rascal!"

The men who had made up the rank and file of the militia on the 5th of November, the next day were riding over the country in armed gangs threatening men, women and children with violence, searching for arms, and brutally tying up and whipping some of the men, and shooting at others. The leaders of these ruffians were some of the prominent men of the county; Colonel Pitcher and Lieutenant Governor Boggs being among the number. The priests in the county, it seems, were determined not to be outdone by the politicians, for the Reverend Isaac McCoy and other preachers of the gospel (!) were seen leading armed bands of marauders from place to place; and were the main inspirers of cowardly assaults on the defenseless.

All through this day and the day following (the 6th and 7th of November,) women and children were fleeing in every direction from the presence of the merciless mob. One company of one hundred and ninety— all women and children, except three decrepit old men—were driven thirty miles across a burnt prairie. The ground was thinly crusted with sleet, and the trail of these exiles was easily followed by the blood which flowed from their lacerated feet![B] This company and others who joined them erected some log cabins for temporary shelter, and not knowing the limits of Jackson County, built them within the borders thereof. Subsequently, in the month of January, 1834, parties of the mob again drove these people, and burned their wretched cabins, leaving them to wander without shelter in the most severe winter months. Many of them were taken suddenly ill and died.

[Footnote B: Lyman Wight's affidavit, Times and Seasons, 1843, p. 264.]

CHAPTER XIII
SCENES ON THE BANKS OF
THE MISSOURI—EXILED

Other parties during the two days mentioned flocked to the Missouri River, and crossed at the ferries into Clay County. One of the companies of distressed women and children were kindly lodged by a Mr. Bennett for the night in his house. We speak of this because acts of benevolence toward the saints were so rare that whenever they occur they should be chronicled.

In one of the companies that went to Clay County was a woman named Ann Higbee who had been sick for many months with chills and fever,—she was carried across the river, apparently a corpse. Another woman named Keziah Higbee, in the most delicate condition, lay on the banks of the river all night, while the rain descended in torrents, and under these circumstances was delivered of a male child; but the mother died a premature death through the exposure. All the pity the parties received from their relentless persecutors was this brutal expression, "G—-d d—n you, do you believe in Joe Smith now?" The scene that was witnessed on the banks of the Missouri on the seventh of November is so graphically described in the Prophet Joseph's history that I cannot forbear inserting it here:

> The shores began to be lined on both sides of the ferry with men, women and children, goods, wagons, boxes, chests, provisions, etc.; while the ferrymen were busily employed in crossing them over; and when night again closed upon the saints, the wilderness had much the appearance of a camp-meeting. Hundreds of people were seen in every direction; some in tents, and some in the open air, around their fires, while the rain descended in torrents. Husbands were inquiring for their wives, and women for their husbands; parents for children, and children for parents. Some had the good fortune to escape with their family household goods, and some provisions; while others knew

not of the fate of their friends, and had lost all their goods. The scene was indescribable, and would have melted the hearts of any people upon earth, except the blind oppressor and prejudiced and ignorant bigot. Next day the company increased, and they were chiefly engaged in felling small cottonwood trees and erecting them into temporary cabins, so that when night came on, they had the appearance of a village of wigwams, and the night being clear, the occupants began to enjoy some degree of comfort.[A]

[Footnote A: Millennial Star, Vol. 14, p. 582.]

On the night of the thirteenth of November, while large bodies of the saints were still encamped on the Missouri bottoms, exiled from their homes for the gospel's sake, one of the most wonderful meteoric showers occurred that was ever witnessed. The whole heavens and the earth were made brilliant by the streams of light which marked the course of the falling aerolites. The whole upper deep was one vast display of heaven's fireworks. The long trains of light left in the heavens by the meteors would twist into the most fantastic shapes, like writhing serpents. The grandeur of the display was far beyond the power of words to describe. I mention it because of the effect it had upon the minds of the suffering saints. The scriptures teach that one of the signs of the glorious appearing of Jesus Christ shall be the falling of stars from the heaven, as a fig tree casteth her untimely figs, when she is shaken of a mighty wind; and the shaking of the powers of heaven.[B]

[Footnote B: Mark 13:25, 26; also Revelation 6:13-17.]

It is needless to say that this sign in the heavens encouraged the exiles; that it revived their hopes; that it calmed their fears; that it seemed to herald the coming of their Deliverer, the Son of God. Nor need I say that it awed the mob, and made a pause in their cruel proceedings for a season. That pause, however, was brief; for on the twenty-third of November the mob held a meeting and appointed a committee to warn away any of the saints who might possibly be found within the borders of the county. Accordingly what few families were scattered here and there through the county were threatened and abused until they were finally forced from their homes. On the twenty-fourth of December four aged families were assaulted at Independence. The mob tore down their chimneys, broke open their doors and threw large stones into their houses.

A brother by the name of Miller, sixty-five years of age, and the youngest of the men in the four families, narrowly escaped fatal injuries. A brother Jones, who was also subjected to like inhuman treatment, served as a life-guard to General Washington in the Revolution, and had fought for the establishment of the sacred principles of liberty guaranteed in the Constitution of his country, the free exercise of which was now denied him by a gang of heartless wretches, who had conspired against the liberties of worthy citizens.

Some time later in the winter, an old man of about seventy years of age was driven from his house, after which it was thrown down. His household goods, corn, etc., were piled together and set on fire; but, fortunately, after the mob left, his son extinguished the flames. About the same time Lyman Leonard had two chairs broken to splinters over his head and body, and was dragged out of doors, where he was beaten with clubs until he was supposed to be dead. The same day Josiah Sumner and Barnet Cole received the same kind of treatment.[C]

[Footnote C: Evening and Morning Star, p. 277.]

Early in the spring the mob burned the remainder of the houses belonging to the saints. According to the testimony of Lyman Wight, two hundred and three dwelling-houses and one grist mill were so destroyed [D]—destroyed in the hope, perhaps, of discouraging the return of the exiles.

[Footnote D: Lyman Wight's affidavit, Times and Seasons, 1843, p. 264.]

CHAPTER XIV
AFTERMATH OF THE EXPULSION

The saints, exiled from their homes in Jackson County, found a temporary resting place in Clay County; though some of them were scattered through Ray, Lafayette, and Van Buren Counties. Those, however, who settled in Van Buren were again driven away, as related in a former chapter. The people in Clay County, as a rule, were kind to the exiles thrown so unceremoniously upon their hospitality. They were permitted to occupy every vacant cabin, and build others for temporary shelter. Some of the sisters obtained positions as domestics in the households of well-to-do farmers, while others taught school. For their acts of kindness the people of Clay County were well repaid in labor performed by the brethren, who were by no means idle, nor of the class who would receive a gratuity when it was within their power to give its equivalent in honest toil.

But look at the situation of the saints in the best possible light, and after all, it was a gloomy prospect! In their scattered condition no regular discipline could be enforced. Many of them were beyond the reach of their spiritual teachers; and being surrounded by wickedness, their hopes blighted, and witnessing the apparent triumph of the wicked, is it any wonder if, in their despair, many of them committed sins, and were chargeable with follies unbecoming people of their profession? But in the main the saints were immovable as the everlasting hills in their righteousness, and in their integrity. They were willing to count all things as dross for the excellency of the knowledge of God. Their very sufferings only wafted them nearer to him who permitted their enemies to chasten them for their good, their very chastisement being a witness that they were sons of God—that he loved them.[A]

[Footnote A: Hebrews 12:6-9.]

The brethren were perplexed most of all as to what course to pursue. Their return to the lands from which they had been driven looked at least unlikely. They knew not whether it would be best to lease or buy lands in Clay County; whether to prepare for permanent or only temporary residence in that land. In the midst of this uncertainty, a conference was convened on the 1st of January, 1834, at the house of P. P. Pratt, at which it was—

> Resolved, that Lyman Wight and Parley P. Pratt be sent as special messengers to represent the situation of the scattered brethren in Missouri, to the Presidency of The Church, in Kirtland, and ask their advice.

Accordingly these brethren started to perform this mission, leaving their families in a penniless condition, while they themselves faced the winds and snows of winter in the interests of their afflicted co-religionists.

Pending the saints receiving instructions from their youthful Prophet, we have many events to relate to our readers. In the latter part of December, 1833, a court of inquiry was held at Liberty, Clay County, to investigate the conduct of Colonel Pitcher, in dispossessing the "Mormons" of their arms, and driving them from their homes. The inquiry resulted in his arrest and trial before a court-martial; but the court did not convene until the 20th of February, 1834; and so remiss in the performance of his duty was General Thompson, who presided at the court-martial trial, that no report was made to the governor until the first of May; and even then it had to be solicited by the governor.

From the facts brought out in that trial, the governor decided that Colonel Pitcher had no right to dispossess the "Mormons" of their arms; and sent an order to S. D. Lucas, colonel of the thirty-third regiment, to deliver the arms taken from the "Mormons" on the 5th of December, 1833, to W. W. Phelps, John Corrill, E. Partridge, A. S. Gilbert, or their order. Lucas, in the meantime, however, had resigned his position, left Jackson County and settled in Lexington. Learning of this, the governor issued a second order for the arms, directing it this time to Colonel Pitcher. This letter was inclosed in a letter from the governor to W. W. Phelps, and sent to Pitcher on the tenth of July; but the arms were never returned. Indeed, between the issuing of the first and second orders of the governor for their restoration to their owners, the arms were distributed among the mob; and they insolently boasted that the arms should not be returned, notwithstanding the order of the executive. The determination of the mob proved to be stronger than the authority of the governor—the commander-in-chief of the militia of the State.

In the month of December, 1833, the mob permitted the firm of Davies & Kelly to take the printing press owned by The Church over to Liberty, in Clay County, where the said firm began the publication of *The Missouri Enquirer;* and in payment for the press turned over to the lawyers employed by the saints three hundred dollars on the one thousand dollar note the brethren had given their attorneys. Not much to pay for a press that, with the book-works, had cost, eighteen months before, between three and four thousand dollars.

CHAPTER XV
AN "ATTEMPTED VINDICATION" OF LAW

It would appear that as soon as the news of the expulsion of the saints reached the ears of the State officers, they were anxious to reinstate them in their possessions. R. W. Wells, the attorney-general of Missouri, wrote the lawyers employed by The Church to the effect that if the "Mormons" desired to be returned to their homes in Jackson County, an adequate force of the State militia would be sent forthwith to accomplish this object, the militia have been ordered to hold themselves in readiness for that purpose. He also promised that if the "Mormons" would organize themselves into a company of militia, they should be supplied with arms by the State. He also suggested that, "as only a certain quantity of public arms can be distributed in each county, those who first apply will be most likely to receive them." This letter was written after a conversation between the governor and the attorney-general; and by that conversation, the attorney-general believed that he was warranted in making these suggestions to the "Mormons," and one would be justified in regarding the foregoing as the sentiments of the governor, as well as the attorney-general.

John F. Ryland, the circuit judge for the district of which Jackson County was a part, wrote to Amos Reese, circuit attorney for the same district, and also counsel for The Church, saying that he had been requested by the governor to inform him "about the outrageous acts of unparalleled violence that had lately happened in Jackson County;" and had been requested by him to examine into these outrages, and to "take steps to punish the guilty and screen the innocent." He, however, (that is, Judge Ryland) could not proceed without some person was willing to give the proper information before him. He asked the circuit attorney to find out from the "Mormons" if they were willing to take legal steps against the citizens of Jackson County; and if they desired to be reinstated in their possessions. If so, he was willing to adopt measures looking toward the accomplishment of this object, saying that the military force would repair to Jackson County, and execute any order he might make respecting the subject. "It is a disgrace to the State," said he, "for such acts to happen within its limits, and the disgrace will attach to our official characters, if we neglect to take proper means to ensure the punishment due such offenders."

The order for an immediate court of inquiry had been prepared by the governor, but he waited to hear from the saints, as to whether or not they desired to be reinstated in their homes. The leading elders of The Church, learning through their attorneys of the steps taken to hold an immediate court of inquiry, at once wrote the governor, asking him not to hold an immediate court of inquiry, as at that time many of those persons whom they would want as witnesses were scattered through several of the surrounding counties, and could not be notified in time to be in attendance. Besides this they urged that many of their principal witnesses would be women and children, and so long as the rage of the mob continued unabated, it would be unsafe to take these witnesses to Independence. "An immediate court of inquiry," wrote A. S. Gilbert, "called while our people are thus situated, would give our enemies a decided advantage in point of testimony." He asked his excellency therefore, in behalf of The Church, to postpone the court of inquiry until the saints were restored to their homes, and had an equal chance with their enemies in producing testimony before the court.

Amos Reese, the circuit attorney, and one of the counsel for The Church, concurred in these very reasonable requests; and said further: "I think that at the next regular term of the court, an examination of the criminal matter cannot be gone into without a guard for the court and witnesses."

The communication which made these suggestions was followed up on the 6th of December by a petition to the governor, which set forth the outrages committed against the saints by the Jackson County mob, as already related in these pages; and asked him to restore them to their possessions in that county; and protect them when restored by the militia of the State, if legal, or by a detachment of the United States troops. The petition suggested that doubtless the latter arrangement could be effected by the governor conferring with the President of the United States on the subject. They also asked that their men be organized into companies of "Jackson Guards," and furnished with arms by the State, that they might assist in maintaining their rights. "And then," said they, "when arrangements are made to protect us in our persons and property (which cannot be done without an armed force, nor would it be prudent to risk our lives there without guards till we receive strength from our friends to protect ourselves), we wish a court of inquiry instituted, to investigate the whole matter of the mob against the 'Mormons.'"

To this petition the governor replied on the 4th of February, 1834; and said the request to be restored to their homes and lands needed no evidence to support the right to have it granted. In relation to the brethren organizing into military companies, the governor said: "Should your men organize according to law—which they have a right to do, indeed it is their duty to do so, unless exempted by religious scruples—and apply for public arms, the executive could not distinguish between their right to have them, and the right of every other description of people similarly situated."

All these answers of the governor to the petition of the exiled saints, so far, were good, and manifested a spirit to administer even-handed justice. But when he comes to consider their request to be *protected* in their possessions, as well as *reinstated* in them, his reply was not so favorable. "As to the request," said he, "for keeping up a military force to protect your people, and prevent the commission of crimes and injuries, were I to comply it would transcend the power with which the executive of this State is clothed." Still, the laws of the State empower the "commander-in-chief, in case of actual or threatened invasion, insurrection, or war, or public danger, or *other emergency,* to call forth into actual service such portion of the militia as he may deem expedient."

In my judgment, it does seem that under the powers here conferred upon the executive by this provision of the fundamental law of the State— the constitution—the governor could have granted the request of the saints to be protected in their homes, until peace was restored. Surely the clause, *"or other emergency,"* in the section of the law just quoted, was broad enough to justify him in protecting, by the State militia, twelve hundred citizens of the United States in their homes until mob violence had subsided—until respect for the civil law had been restored, and these citizens allowed to dwell in safety upon the lands they had purchased from the general government. Under this provision he could have "curbed those cruel devils of their will," without "doing even a little wrong, in order to do a great right"— without "wresting the law to his authority." But he chose to interpret the law otherwise—as follows:

> The words, "or other emergency," in our militia law, seem quite broad; but the emergency to come within the object of that provision, shall be of a public nature. Your case is certainly a very emergent one, and the consequences as important to *your society* as if the war had been waged against the whole State, yet the *public* has no other interest in it than that the laws be faithfully executed.

The sequel will show how *faithfully* the laws were executed, and how the "public" stood by, indifferent spectators, while an unoffending people were robbed of their possessions, and the laws of the State set at defiance by insolent mobs. The governor closed his answer to the petition of the exiles by saying that as then advised it would be necessary to have a military guard for the court and State witnesses, while sitting in Jackson County; and he sent an order to the captain of the Liberty Blues to comply with the requisition of the circuit attorney, in protecting the court and executing its orders during the progress of the trials arising out of the Jackson County difficulties; and said the "Mormons" could if they felt so disposed, return under the protection of this guard to their homes, and be protected in them during the progress of the trials.

It required no great wisdom, however, to foresee that for the saints to return to their homes, and then be left there without protection—left to the mercy of inhuman wretches, in whose veins ran none of the milk of human kindness—would not be far removed from suicide, as the mob greatly outnumbered the saints. To return under these circumstances would only be laying the foundation for a greater tragedy than the one already enacted; and the brethren wisely concluded not to attempt to regain possession of their homes, until some measure was adopted to protect them when there— until "God or the President ruled out the mob."

At the February term of the circuit court, which convened at Independence, about twelve of the leading elders were subpoenaed as witnesses on the part of the State, against certain citizens of Jackson County for their acts of mob violence against the "Mormons." On the twenty-third of the month these witnesses crossed the Missouri into Jackson County, under the protection of the Liberty Blues, Captain Atchison commanding. The company numbered about fifty, and were all well armed with United States muskets, bayonets fixed—presenting an outward appearance "fair and warlike." The company and witnesses commenced crossing the river about noon, but it was nearly night before the baggage wagon was taken across. While waiting for the arrival of the wagon, it was decided to camp in the woods, and not go to Independence until the next morning. Half the company and a number of the witnesses went about half a mile towards Independence and built fires for the night. While engaged in these duties the quartermaster and others, who had gone ahead to prepare quarters in town for the company, sent an express back, which was continued by Captain Atchison to Colonel Allen, for the two hundred drafted militia under his command: and also sent to Liberty for more ammunition. The night was passed around the camp fires, as the party was without tents, and the weather cold enough to snow a little.

Next morning the witnesses were marched to Independence under a strong guard and quartered in the block-house—formerly the Flourney Hotel. The attorney-general of the State, Mr. Wells, had been sent down by the governor to assist the circuit attorney, Mr. Reese, "to investigate as far as possible, the Jackson outrage." These gentlemen waited upon the witnesses in their quarters, and gave them to understand that all hope of criminal procedure against the mob was at an end. Only a few minutes afterward, Captain Atchison informed the witnesses that he had received an order from Judge Ryland that the services of his company were no longer needed in Jackson County. So the witnesses for the State were marched out of town to the tune of Yankee Doodle—quick time.

Thus ended the sickly attempt of the State authorities to "execute the law"—in which execution the 'public,' according to the governor, was interested, but no further interested in this outrage. But, "so far as a faithful execution of the laws is concerned," he presumed, "the whole community felt a deep interest; for that which is the case of the 'Mormons' today, may be the case of the Catholics tomorrow; and after them, any other sect that may become obnoxious to a majority of the people of any section of the State." [A] After this effort by the State authorities to execute the law, doubtless all other sects or parties who were likely to come under the ban of popular sentiment felt secure in their liberties—satisfied with the valor of the officers of the State who had trembled before the bold front of a mob—a mob which had boasted that if the "Mormons" were reinstated in their homes by the authority of the governor, not three months should elapse before they would drive them again! And even while the circuit court was convened at Independence, and a company of militia was in attendance to execute its mandates, and the attorney-general of the State present to assist the circuit attorney prosecute those who had violated the law—yet, in the presence of all this authority, the old citizens of Jackson gathered, and assumed such a boisterous and mobocratic appearance that their bold front overawed the officers of the court; the attorneys of the State telling the State witnesses— who were also sufferers from the previous violence of the mob—that all hopes of criminal prosecutions against the mob were at an end; while Judge Ryland issued an order for the militia to withdraw, just when they were needed to protect his court in vindicating the law!

Thus ended the only effort that was ever made by the officers of Missouri to bring to justice these violators of the law. One class of citizens had conspired against the liberties of another class, and being the stronger had, without the authority of law, or shadow of justification, driven twelve hundred of them from their possessions, and there was not virtue enough in the executive of the State and his associates to punish the offenders. The determination of the mob to resist the law was stronger than the determination of the State officers to execute it and make it honorable. And yet the constitution of the State made it the imperative duty of the executive to "take care that the laws are faithfully executed." And the laws of the State empowered the commander-in-chief of the militia (the governor) "in case of * * * insurrection, or war, or public danger, or other emergency, to call forth into actual service such portion of the militia as he might deem expedient." With this power placed in his hands by the laws of the State, Governor Dunklin permitted mobs to overawe the court of inquiry he himself had ordered, and allowed them to continue unchecked in their unhallowed deeds of devastation and violence. And while the mobocrats triumphed over the law, the governor's letters to the leading elders of The Church contained many pretty patriotic sentiments, but he lacked the courage to execute the law.

[Footnote A: Governor Dunklin's communication, Millennial Star, Vol. 14, p. 702.]

CHAPTER XVI
THE CAUSE OF EXPULSION—
FUTURE REDEMPTION

It must not be supposed that the Prophet Joseph was an uninterested spectator of the stirring events that were being enacted. The circumstances of The Church were such that his presence was necessary in Kirtland, but all the sympathy of his nature went out to his brethren in affliction; and his letters were filled with words of encouragement and wise counsels: and, so far as his embarrassing financial circumstances would permit, he rendered them material aid. There were two things, however, that he could not understand; "and," said he, "they are these: Why God has suffered so great a calamity to come upon Zion, and what the great moving cause of this persecution is. And again, by what means he will return her back to her inheritance, with everlasting joy upon her head."

He was not left long in doubt as to these matters. The words we have quoted above are taken from a letter written by Joseph on the tenth of December, 1833; and six days later the Lord in a revelation to him said:

> Verily I say unto you, concerning your brethren who have been afflicted, and persecuted and cast out from the land of their inheritance, I, the Lord, have suffered the affliction to come upon them, wherewith they have been afflicted, in consequence of their transgressions. * * * Behold, I say unto you, there were jarrings, and contentions, and envyings, and strifes, and lustful and covetous desires among them; therefore by these things they polluted their inheritances. They were slow to hearken unto the voice of the Lord their God, therefore the Lord their God is slow to hearken unto their prayers, to answer them in the day of their trouble.[A]

[Footnote A: Doc. & Cov. Sec. 101:1-7.]

This explained to the uttermost why the saints were driven away from Zion. Of the evils which were in their midst they had been made aware by the reproofs of their brethren; they had been warned time and again by the Prophet and the high council at Kirtland of impending judgments. But all these warnings had only aroused them to a partial repentance; and the Lord, true to his word at the time of giving the warning, was now pleading with the strong ones in Zion, and chastening her mighty ones, that they might overcome.[B]

[Footnote B: Doc. & Cov. Sec. 90:34-37.]

Seeing, then, that the saints were punished for neglecting to observe the counsels of God, the question may arise, are the mob to be held responsible for their acts of violence against them? Most assuredly, for it is a case where "offenses must needs come, but woe unto them by whom they come."

In relation to the other matter about which Joseph was perplexed, namely, by what means the Lord would redeem Zion, this same revelation, and one given subsequently—on the twenty-fourth of February, 1834—explained. From these two revelations we learn that Zion is to be redeemed by power. "I will raise up unto my people," said the Lord, "a man who shall lead them like as Moses led the children of Israel, for ye are the children of Israel, and of the seed of Abraham, and ye must needs be led out of bondage, with power, and with a stretched out arm: and as your fathers were led at the first, *even so shall the redemption of Zion be.* Therefore, let not your hearts faint, for I say not unto you as I said unto your fathers, mine angel shall go up before you, but not my presence; but I say unto you, mine angels shall go before you, and also my presence, and in time ye shall possess the goodly land." [C] But this great blessing, they were given to understand, was not to be granted *"until after much tribulation."* [D]

[Footnote C: Doc. & Cov. Sec. 103.]

[Footnote D: Doc. & Cov. Sec. 103:12, and Sec. 58:2-4.]

Joseph Smith was commanded to gather up the strength of the Lord's house, the young men, and the middle-aged; and they were to gather to Zion to possess the land that the Lord had appointed unto the saints, much of which they had purchased and consecrated unto him. The work of gathering was to go on. The churches of the east were to sent up money in the hands of wise men to purchase inheritances; and inasmuch as their enemies came upon them to drive them from their homes, they were to defend themselves, and avenge themselves of their enemies. They were to make every effort to obtain five hundred men to go up and redeem Zion; but if they failed to get five hundred, then they were to get three hundred; and if they failed to get three hundred, they were to get one hundred; but they were not to go if unable to obtain one hundred. The Lord told the saints, even previous to this, that "there is even now already in store a sufficient, yea, even an abundance, to redeem Zion, and establish her waste places, no more to be thrown down, were the churches, who call themselves after my name, willing to hearken to my voice." [E]

[Footnote E: Doc. & Cov. Sec. 101:75.]

CHAPTER XVII
IMPORTUNING AT THE FEET OF THE JUDGE—THE GOVERNOR—THE PRESIDENT

Pending the gathering of the strength of the Lord's house to go up to redeem Zion, the saints who had been driven from their homes were instructed to importune at the feet of the judge; and if he heed them not, then to importune at the feet of the governor; and if the governor heeded them not, then to importune at the feet of the president; and if the president heeded them not, "then will the Lord rise and come forth out of his hiding place, and in his fury vex the nation, and in his hot displeasure, and his fierce anger, in his time, will cut off these wicked, unfaithful, and unjust stewards."

The brethren now began the work of petitioning in earnest. The authorities and brethren in Kirtland petitioned the governor of Missouri in behalf of their afflicted brethren of that State, inclosing in their petition the revelation the Lord had given respecting the redemption of Zion.[A] They also sent a similar petition, and the same revelation, to the President of the United States. "And now," wrote Joseph to the brethren in Missouri, "we will act the part of the poor widow [B] to perfection, if possible, and let our rulers read their destiny if they do not lend a helping hand."

[Footnote A: Doc. & Cov. Sec. 101.]

[Footnote B: Luke 18:1-6.]

The saints in Missouri were by no means idle. They continued to keep the subject of their wrongs constantly before the authorities of the State. They also prepared a petition to the President of the nation, setting forth their wrongs at great length, enclosing in it the reply of the governor to their petition to him. And since the governor claimed that the laws of his State did not authorize him to keep a military force in Jackson County, to protect them in their homes after their restoration, they asked the President to restore them to their possessions, and protect them when so restored, by an armed force, until peace was insured. Their petition also referred to the section of the Constitution which provides that the United States shall protect each state against invasion; "and on application of the legislature, or of the executive (when the legislature cannot be convened) against domestic violence." [C] At the same time the exiles informed Governor Dunklin that they had petitioned the President for a force to protect them in their homes, and asked him to assist them by sending to the chief executive of the nation a few lines in support of their claims. Elder Phelps wrote Senator Thomas H. Benton, informing him of their having sent a petition to the President, and asked him for his co-operation in securing their rights. Governor Dunklin answered that as it was possible that the saints had asked the President to do something that he was not empowered to do, he could not consistently join with them in urging him to do it. "If you will send me a copy of your petition to the President, I will judge of his right to grant it; and if of opinion he possesses the power, I will write in favor of its exercise." But whether the saints complied with this request or not, I cannot learn.

[Footnote C: Const. Art. iv, Sec. 4.]

On the second of May, 1834, they received a communication from Washington, which, as might have been anticipated, stated that the offenses of which they complained were violations against the laws of the State of Missouri, and not the laws of the United States, and the clause in the Constitution to which they had alluded, extended only to proceedings under the laws of the United States. "Where an insurrection in any State exists, against the government thereof," said the communication from Washington, "the President is required, on the application of such State, or of the executive (when the legislature cannot be convened), to call forth such a number of the militia, as he may judge sufficient to suppress such insurrection. But this state of things does not exist in Missouri, or if it does, the fact is not shown in the mode pointed out by law. The President cannot call out a military force to aid in the execution of the State laws, until the proper requisition is made upon him by the constituted authorities." And as the "constituted authorities" would not make that requisition, all hopes of assistance from the general government, of course, were at an end.

When the State legislature convened, the governor called the attention of the body legislative to the outrages committed by the citizens of Jackson County against the "Mormons," saying: "As yet, none have been punished for these outrages, and I believe that, under our present laws, conviction for any violence committed against a 'Mormon' cannot be had in Jackson County. * * * It is for you to determine what amendment the laws may require, so as to guard against such acts of violence for the future." This notice of the question in the governor's message revived the sinking hopes of the exiles, but it was only again to have them disappointed. The portion of the governor's message which referred to the Jackson outrage was given to a special committee, and at the suggestion of Messrs. Thompson and Atchison, of the Missouri legislature, the saints petitioned that body for an enactment to reinstate them in their homes and protect them, when thus reinstated, but it availed nothing. The legislature took no action in the matter. The violators of the law went unwhipped of justice. Suffering innocence found no protector in the State.

CHAPTER XVIII
ZION'S CAMP

"When the Lord commands, do it." This is what the Prophet Joseph declared to be his rule. Therefore, when the Lord, on the twenty-fourth of February, 1834, commanded him to gather together the strength of the Lord's house—the young and middle-aged men in The Church—for the purpose of going to Missouri, to redeem Zion, two days later he was seen leaving his home for the State of New York, to fulfill this commandment.

He was accompanied by Parley P. Pratt on this mission. Other leading Elders went in various directions on the same errand. They traveled among the branches of The Church in the east pleading the cause of Zion, asking the saints to assist in her redemption by contributing of their substance to relieve the distresses of their brethren who had been driven from their homes in Missouri, who now were exiles and largely dependent upon the kindness of strangers for means of living. They called upon the saints to send money to Missouri with which to purchase inheritances for themselves; they also asked the young and the middle-aged men to volunteer to go to Zion for the purpose of assisting their brethren to maintain their possessions in Jackson County, when the State authorities should reinstate them in their homes. We have none of the speeches of these elders in print, we cannot tell how well they told the story of Zion's wrongs; but surely the plain, unvarnished statement of her woes would be sufficient to move adamantine hearts to pity; while those who held the sufferers as brethren in a common cause would weep over their affliction, and with resolution stronger than the love of life, pledge their fortunes, and themselves to bring about their restoration to their homes and secure to them the enjoyment of life, liberty, and the pursuit of happiness. It will become necessary, however, in another place, for us to tell how unsympathetic, and what a lack of faith there was among the eastern branches of The Church; and how these things justly brought upon the saints in the east the displeasure of God, and prevented, at that time, the redemption of Zion.

The village of New Portage, about fifty miles from Kirtland, Ohio, was made the place of rendezvous for the young and middle-aged brethren, who, in response to the call of the Lord and his Prophet, had volunteered to go to the assistance of their brethren in Missouri; and here, about the first of May, the volunteers began to assemble. On the sixth they were joined by their youthful prophet-leader, who, the next day, organized them as follows: F. G. Williams was appointed treasurer and pay-master of the camp. All the money was collected and given into his keeping. Zerubbabel Snow was appointed commissary general. There were also other general officers that were appointed, but what they were we have been unable to learn. The camp was divided into small companies, twelve men in each. These companies elected their own captains, who then assigned each man his duty in the respective companies, thus: two cooks; two firemen; two tent makers; two watermen; one runner, or messenger; two wagoners and horsemen; and one commissary.

In all, the company that collected at New Portage numbered one hundred and fifty, which was increased by the time the camp reached Missouri to about two hundred.

They purchased flour and baked their own bread, and cooked their own provisions, which, at times, were scarce. Their baggage wagons, about twenty in number, were so loaded with their provisions, arms, ammunition and clothing for their distressed brethren in Missouri, that nearly the whole company had to walk. Every night before retiring to sleep, the blast of the evening trumpet called them to prayers in their respective tents; and the morning trumpet summoned them to implore the assistance of Divine Providence in the day's march. Thus they made the journey, pitching their tents by the way-side, alike in the settled country and in the wilderness; stopping occasionally for a few days, to refresh their overworked teams; and always remaining in camp on the Sabbath day to hold divine service, and partake of the sacrament. On the occasion of their holding public worship, the people in the vicinity of their encampment would often attend and wonder much at the doctrines they heard, being puzzled to know what sect of men they were.

Such a company of men traveling in this manner through the country did not fail to excite the curiosity of the people; and every effort was made to learn the names of the leaders, the business, object, and destination of the expedition; but in this they failed, as it was Joseph's instructions to the members of the company not to make these things known. There were several boys in the expedition, and at times these were questioned by strangers, but with very unsatisfactory results. Among the number of boys so questioned was Geo. A. Smith, afterwards one of the counselors to President Brigham Young, in the Presidency of The Church. The questions and answers were about as follows:

"My boy, where are you from?"

"From the east."

"Where are you going?"

"To the west."

"What for?"

"To see where we can get land cheapest and best."

"Who leads the camp?"

"Sometimes one, sometimes another."

"What name?"

"Captain Wallace, Major Bruce, Orson Hyde, James Allred, etc." [A]

[Footnote A: Celebration Pioneers' Day, p. 18.]

The people not unfrequently, however, suspected they were "Mormons," and many times the little band was threatened with destruction, and spies continually harassed them by trying to get into their camp. They were foiled in these efforts though, by the vigilance of the guards, who nightly patrolled their encampment. At various points through Indiana and Illinois, they were told their passage would be resisted, but these threats nothing daunted them. The opposition was overawed more than once by the numbers in the camp being multiplied in the eyes of their enemies. The brethren of Zion's Camp knew the object of the expedition to be a noble one. They were conscious of God's approval, and of the presence in their midst of his angels; and strengthened by this knowledge, they fearlessly marched on to accomplish the work of redeeming Zion.

Joseph says: "We know that the angels were our companions, for we saw them." A circumstance in the experience of Parley P. Pratt furnishes further testimony of the presence of angels with this expedition. Elder Pratt was chiefly engaged as a recruiting officer, and on one occasion, when he had traveled all night to overtake a small company he was conducting to the main camp, he stopped at noon on a broad level plain to let his horse feed. No habitation was near. Stillness and repose reigned around him. "I sank down," he says, "overpowered with a deep sleep, and might have lain in a state of oblivion till the shades of night had gathered about me, so completely was I exhausted for the want of sleep and rest; but I had only slept a few moments till the horse had grazed sufficiently, when a voice, more loud and shrill than I had ever before heard, fell upon my ear, and thrilled through every part of my system; it said: 'Parley, it is time to be up and on your journey.' In the twinkling of an eye I was perfectly aroused, I sprang to my feet so suddenly that I could not at first recollect where I was, or what was before me to perform. I afterwards related the circumstance to Brother Joseph Smith, and he bore testimony that it was the angel of the Lord who went before the camp, who found me overpowered with sleep, and thus awoke me." [B]

[Footnote B: Autobiography of Parley P. Pratt, p. 123.]

The line of march led the camp through Indiana and the central part of Illinois. The journey was undertaken, too, at a time of year—May and June—when nature appears in her most lovely attire—when the forests were in full leaf, and filled with the resonance of birds, the hum of bees and insects; when the great prairies, which quite bewilder one with their vastness, are clothed in their variegated garments of grass and wild flowers; at a time of year when in the upper deep there is a deeper blue, when the rising sun seems to shed a brighter light upon the earth beneath, and when his parting rays paint the evening skies in splendors unsurpassed.[C]

[Footnote C: PEN-PICTURE OF THE CAMP.—In fancy I see them after a hard day's march making their encampment. The sun has just sunk behind the western horizon as Joseph and the standard bearer are choosing the place for their night's encampment They have paused on the summit of one of the gentle swells of prairie so common in their line of travel. A short distance to the south is a small wooded stream. To the north and east, as far as the eye can see, is nothing but the broad, rolling prairie; looking west, the horizon is bounded by a view of the heavy forests which marked the meandering course of the Illinois.

"Brother Joseph, would it not be better to make our camp further to the south, down on the banks of the stream where wood and water will be more convenient?" said he who bore the standard. "I think not," replies the Prophet. "You know we received word that the people intend to prevent us crossing the Illinois River, which we will reach by ten o'clock tomorrow; so that we are in the vicinity of our enemies. If we camp in the woods, they could surround us, and we not be aware of it. But by making this eminence our camp ground they can't approach without being observed by our guards; and the brethren will be willing to carry both wood and water this short distance in order to enjoy the security of this position."

And now the main company has come in full view over a hill to the east, and as they see the ensign planted they know the camp ground has been chosen. Anxious to obtain food and rest, they urge their jaded teams to make better speed, and soon the twenty wagons are arranged in two curving lines, to make an oval enclosure with openings at each end. Now is enacted a busy scene. Men are hurrying to and fro in all directions; but there is no confusion. Each knows what is required of him, and cheerfully performs his allotted part. The teamsters have unhitched and stripped the harness from their sweating horses that now quietly crop the rich grass; the firemen and watermen have brought both fuel and water, and already the sombre twilight is made cheerful by the light of the camp fire, around which the cooks are busy preparing the evening meal. The tent makers are stretching the tents within the space enclosed by the wagons. Orders are given in a cheerful, half-jesting manner. All is peace—all is union. Now you see the men quickly gathering around their respective fires, as their several cooks announce supper ready. As they quietly seat themselves around their food, heads are bared, and thanks returned to Him, who had commanded them in everything to give thanks. Pleasant conversation prevails in nearly every group. The trials of the day are turned into merriment—anecdotes and jests provoke peals of laughter, and the toils of the day are forgotten. Supper is over. Around a fire near the center of the encampment have gathered a number of brethren, and their prophet-leader is relating to them some of the visions of his early youth, interspersing his narrative with maxims of incalculable value to the hearers. As he warms under the glow of the Spirit of God, he tells them of the future glory of Zion—of the temple to be overshadowed by a pillar of cloud by day and of fire by night—of her being a place of refuge—a city of peace in which the saints of God shall safely dwell, and how the wicked shall say, "let us not go up to battle against Zion, for her inhabitants are terrible." But listen! In another part of the camp a number of the brethren are singing; and as the melody floats out on the calm stillness of the night, you recognize one of the familiar songs of Zion:—

Glorious things of thee are spoken,
Zion, city of our God
He, whose word can not be broken,
Chose thee for his own abode.

On the Rock of ages founded,
What can shake thy sure repose!

With salvation's walls surrounded,
Thou may'st smile on all thy foes.

The song was scarcely concluded when the sharp, thrilling notes of the bugle summon to prayer. All promptly retire to their tents and are engaged in solemn devotion. Few leave the tents after prayers. The guards have been notified to take their places, and their comrades stretch out their tired limbs upon their rude pallets. As the bustle in the camp ceases, and naught is heard but the whispered conversation of the guards, or their footsteps as they move back and forth upon their beats, you hear in the distance the plaintive notes of the whip-poor-will. And now the pale moon slowly rises and bathes in her soft light the sleeping camp.—*Roberts*.]

CHAPTER XIX
ZELPH

After crossing the Illinois River Zion's Camp passed many of those mysterious earth mounds so common in that section. Mysterious mounds! No, not mysterious to them, for they had with them the record of the peoples who erected them—the Nephites and Lamanites, or, more likely still, the people of Jared.

While encamped on the western bank of the Illinois, Joseph and several others ascended one of these high mounds from which they could overlook the tops of the trees, and see the prairies beyond. On the top of the mound were three stone altars, erected one above the other, "according to the ancient order," said Joseph. Human bones were scattered about on the surface of the ground; and after removing about a foot of the soil at the crown of the mound, they found the skeleton of a man nearly complete. Between his ribs was an Indian arrowhead which, doubtless, had produced his death. The visions of Joseph's mind the day following were opened, and he learned that this man whose skeleton they had found was named Zelph. He was a white Lamanite; the curse of the black skin had been taken from him because of his righteousness. He was a noted character, a warrior and chieftain under the great prophet Omandagus, who was known from the hill Cumorah to the Rocky Mountains. He was killed in the last great struggle of the Lamanites and Nephites by the arrow-head found between his ribs.[A]

[Footnotes A: President Brigham Young took possession of the arrow-head.]

CHAPTER XX
DISSENSIONS IN THE CAMP

On the seventh of June Zion's Camp reached the Allred settlement, on Salt River. This Allred settlement consisted, for the most part, of Latter-day Saints, and here Joseph resolved to refresh his men and teams by resting a few days. The day following their arrival, they were rejoined by Hyrum Smith and Lyman Wight who had parted from the main company in Ohio for the purpose of going into Michigan, to raise from among the several branches of that State, volunteers to assist in redeeming Zion. The addition of these volunteers swelled the number in the camp to two hundred and five men, and twenty-five baggage wagons, with two or three horses to each.

During this stay of several days at Salt River, a reorganization of the camp took place. Lyman Wight, who had some knowledge of military evolutions and tactics, and was, withal, a bold, fearless man, was elected general of the camp. Joseph chose a company of twenty men to be his life guard, of whom his brother Hyrum was made captain. The rest of the men were organized into companies as at New Portage. The general of the camp drilled these companies in military manoeuvres; inspected their fire-locks, and gave them target practice by platoons—in short, prepared them for effective service should the emergency arise for them to use force to retain their possessions in Zion.

I regret to say that the spirit of union and harmony depicted in my pen sketch of the camp, in the foot-note of chapter eighteen, was not always characteristic of it. There were times when a spirit of selfishness and an utter lack of brotherly love with some was manifested. Particularly was this true of one Sylvester Smith, who exhibited a selfish and at other times a quarrelsome spirit. One evening when provisions in camp were scarce, Elder P. P. Pratt called upon Sylvester Smith for something to eat; and although Smith had food, he refused to divide with Brother Pratt, and sent him to someone else. The end of it was Brother Pratt had to retire hungry. Joseph being told of this, severely reproved the offender; and whether that reproof continued to gall the feelings of Sylvester Smith or not, I cannot say. But at any rate, as soon as the camp arrived at what is known as the twenty-two mile Wockendaw Prairie, well on to two hundred miles west from the Mississippi, this same man and Lyman Wight made an effort to divide the camp. The company had first taken up quarters in the woods on the bank of the river; but being threatened by their enemies, Joseph decided that it would be better to move out into the open prairie. With this arrangement some were dissatisfied, as it took them away from firewood. Lyman Wight and Sylvester Smith turned aside with their companies and went into camp before leaving the timber; and as the other companies came along, would hail the captains and ask them if they were following General or Wight some other man.

At this some companies hesitated a moment, and then drove out to the plain where the ensign had been planted to mark the place Joseph had chosen for the encampment. Those who had turned aside, and made an effort to divide the camp, came up also, and were called upon to give an account of their conduct. They acknowledged their error, and were forgiven.

Another difficulty arose among the brethren, about a dog which had snapped at Sylvester Smith and others. Considerable anger and ill feeling existed in camp about it. At last Joseph in the presence of a number of the brethren said: "I will descend to that spirit which is in the camp, to show you the spirit you are of; for I want to drive it from the camp. *The man that kills that dog, I will whip him.*" Sylvester Smith came up just in time to hear the last part of Joseph's remarks, and said: "If that dog bites me I shall kill him."

"If you do I will whip you," replied Joseph.

"If you do, I shall defend myself the best way that I can."

To which Joseph rejoined that he would whip him in the name of the Lord. "Now," said he, "I have descended to that spirit to show you the spirit which is among you. Brethren, are you not ashamed of it? I am." Then he reproved them sharply for their murmuring and follies. As they continued in their rebellious moods and manifested but little of the spirit of repentance, he predicted that a plague would overtake the camp, and they would die like sheep with the rot.[A] Of the fulfillment of this prediction, I shall speak hereafter.

[Footnotes A: Of this prophecy Heber C. Kimball, in his journal under date of June 3rd says: "This day June 3rd, while we were refreshing ourselves and our teams, about the middle of the day, Brother Joseph got up in a wagon and said that he would deliver a prophecy. After giving the brethren much good advice, exhorting them to faithfulness and humility, he said the Lord had told him that there would be a scourge come upon the camp, in consequence of the factions and unruly spirits that appeared among them and they should die like sheep with the rot; still if they would repent and humble themselves before the Lord, the scourge in a great measure might be turned away; but as the Lord lives, this camp will suffer for giving way to their unruly temper."—Times and Seasons Vol. vi. p. 788.]

CHAPTER XXI
VIEWS CONCERNING ZION—MOB VS STORM

As soon as the camp was reorganized at Salt River, Parley P. Pratt and Orson Hyde were sent as delegates to wait upon Governor Dunklin, at Jefferson City, and request him to call out a sufficient military force to reinstate the saints in the possession of their homes. In the interview the governor frankly admitted the justice of the demand, but expressed fears that if he should so proceed, it would excite civil war, and deluge the whole country with blood. He advised these delegates to counsel their people, for the sake of peace, to sell the lands from which they had been driven. To this the delegates refused to consent, saying:

> We will hold no terms with land pirates and murderers. If we are not permitted to live on the lands we have purchased of the United States, and be protected in our rights and persons, they will at least make a good burying ground in which to lay our bones; and we shall hold on to our possessions in Jackson County, for this purpose at least.

The governor could not and did not blame them; but he trembled for the country, and dared not carry out what he admitted to be the plain, imperative duties of his office.

Elders Pratt and Hyde rejoined the camp not far from the line of Ray County. As soon as they arrived, the Prophet Joseph, his brother Hyrum, Lyman Wight, and some others repaired to a grove, and heard their report.

"After hearing our report," says Parley P. Pratt, "the President (Joseph Smith) called on the God of our fathers to witness the justice of our cause, and the sincerity of our vows, which we engaged to fulfill whether in this life or in the life to come. For, as God lives, truth, justice, and innocence shall triumph; and iniquity shall not reign."

As the brethren approached Richmond, threats were made that they should not pass through the town, and rumor had it that a force of men was in waiting to intercept them. Daylight of the nineteenth of June saw them, in spite of the threats, quietly passing through the streets of the sleeping town. When they broke camp in the morning, they designed reaching Clay

County that day; but they met with so many reverses in the day's march, such as wagons breaking down, wheels running off, etc., that they failed to accomplish it. Early in the evening they went into camp between two forks of Fishing River.

A plan had been laid for the complete destruction of "Joe Smith's army," as Zion's Camp was called by the Missourians; and now the time for its\ execution had arrived. A mob of two hundred men had been raised in Jackson County, which was to cross the Missouri into Clay County, about the mouth of Fishing River, where a man named Williams kept a ferry. This mob was to be joined at the fords of Fishing River by a party of sixty from Richmond; and still by another mob, seventy in number, from Clay County. Indeed, it looked as if Zion's Camp was to be annihilated forthwith.

While the brethren were making preparations for the night, five men armed with guns rode into camp, and insolently told the brethren they would "catch hell before morning." "And their oaths," says Joseph, "partook of all the malice of demons."

The Jackson mob assembled opposite the mouth of Fishing River, and one scow-load—forty in number—was sent over. By this time the sun was but little more than an hour high, and the camp observed a small cloud coming up from the west. "It wasn't any larger than your hat when I first saw it," said one [A] who was present, and described the occurrence to me; "but in about twenty minutes the whole heavens were inky blackness, which now and then seemed split by the vivid streams of lightning." All the artillery of heaven seemed to be in action. The wind blew and the rain and hail fell in torrents. The hailstones—unusually large ones—cut down the corn crop and other vegetation. Large limbs were wrenched from sturdy oaks and twisted into withes by the fierce wind.

[Footnote A: This was the late Judge Joseph Holbrook of Davis County, who personally related the circumstance to me.]

The tents in the camp were blown down, and the most of the brethren took refuge in an old church house near their camp ground. Big Fishing River, that was not more than six inches deep before the storm arose, was about forty feet deep the next morning; and the mob swore that Little Fishing River rose thirty feet in that many minutes.

This storm prevented the mob from collecting as arranged. The scow that had ferried over part of the Jackson mob, in returning for more, was met by the storm and only after much difficulty about dark reached the Jackson side. Those that had been shipped across were exposed to the pitiless pelting of the storm all night, which cooled their desire to "kill Joe Smith and his army."

"Instead of continuing a cannonading which they commenced, * * * they crawled under wagons, into hollow trees, and filled one old shanty." [B] The next morning they were as anxious to reach the Jackson side of the Missouri as they had been the night before to get at "Joe Smith's" camp. The other parts of the mob who were to give the brethren "hell before morning" met with a fate equally unpleasant. Their horses were frightened, broke away from their masters, and wandered over the prairies in some instances several days. Their plans for the destruction of Zion's Camp were frustrated, and the brethren rejoiced.

[Footnote B: Joseph's history under date of 19th of June, 1834.]

CHAPTER XXII
NEGOTIATIONS

The day following this providential storm the camp moved out into the prairie some five miles, where there was a better chance to defend themselves. Here, the next day, Colonel Sconce and two other leading men from Ray County called upon the camp to learn what the intentions of the brethren were. Said the colonel: "I see there is an Almighty power that protects this people, for I started from Richmond with a company of armed men having a full determination to destroy you, but was kept back by the storm, and was not able to reach you." Having said so much, he was seized with such excitement that he trembled from head to foot like an aspen-leaf, and had to take a seat in order to compose himself.

Joseph, in a lengthy speech, related the trials and persecutions of the saints, particularly the sufferings of those in Jackson County. He related the story of the travels of Zion's Camp, how they had come one thousand miles to assist their afflicted brethren by bringing them clothing, etc., and to aid them in returning to their homes and maintaining them, and denied the infamous reports circulated to arouse the anger of the people against the exiled saints. This speech was so simple, so pathetic, and yet so forcible that the strangers were melted by its spirit, so that they wept at the story of the persecutions of God's people. At the close of the speech they arose, and gave their hands to the youthful speaker; promising to use all their influence to allay the excitement and correct the false impressions that had gone out respecting the object of the expedition—a promise they faithfully kept.

It is said of the Prophet Joseph that if he could but once get the attention even of his most bitter enemies his native eloquence, inspired by the truth and the pathos of his people's sufferings, usually overwhelmed them; and in no instance was his triumph more marked than in the one just related.

The day after the visit of Colonel Sconce, Cornelius Gillium, the sheriff of Clay County, came into camp and desired a consultation. The company was marched into a grove adjacent and formed a large circle with Gillium in the center. "I have heard that Joseph Smith is in the camp, and if so, I should like to see him," commenced Gillium.

"I am the man," replied Joseph, as he rose to his feet. This was the first time Joseph was made known to strangers since leaving Kirtland, as he had gone by a fictitious name through the whole journey.

Gillium then proceeded to describe the character and disposition of the Missourians, and the course that ought to be pursued to secure their favor and protection; and concluded by requesting to know what the intentions of the company were. This brought out the statements we now give, which were published in the *Missouri Enquirer* of the first of July, 1834.

GILLIUM'S COMMUNICATION.

Being a citizen of Clay County, and knowing there is considerable excitement amongst the people thereof, and also knowing that different reports are arriving almost hourly; and being requested of the Hon. J. F. Ryland to meet the "Mormons" under arms, and obtain from the leaders thereof the correctness of the various reports in circulation, the true intent and meaning of their present movements, and their views generally regarding the difficulties existing between them and Jackson County,—I did in company with other gentlemen, call upon the said leaders of the "Mormons," at their camp in Clay County; and now give to the people of Clay County their written statement, containing the substance of what passed between us.

(Signed) CORNELIUS GILLIUM.

PROPOSITION, ETC., OF THE MORMONS.

Being called upon by the above named gentleman, at our camp in Clay County, to ascertain from the leaders of our men, our intentions, views, and designs, in approaching this county in the manner we have, we therefore the more cheerfully comply with their request, because we are called upon by gentlemen of good feelings, and who are disposed for peace and an amicable adjustment of the difficulties existing between us and the people of Jackson County. The reports of our intentions are various, and have gone abroad in a light calculated to arouse the feelings of almost every man. For instance, one report is, that we intend to demolish the printing office in Liberty; another report is, that we intend crossing the Missouri River on Sunday next, and falling upon women and children, and slaying them; another is, that our men were employed to perform this expedition, being taken from manufacturing establishments in the east, that had closed business; also that we carried a flag, bearing "peace" on one side, and "war or blood" on the other, and various others too numerous to mention, all of which a plain declaration of our intentions, from under our own hands, will show are not correct.

In the first place it is not our intention to commit hostilities against any man, or set of men; it is not our intention to injure any man's person or property, except in defending ourselves. Our flag has been exhibited to the above gentlemen, who will be able to describe it. Our men were not taken from any manufacturing establishment. It is our intention to go back upon our lands in Jackson County by order of the executive of the State, if possible. We have brought our arms with us for the purpose of self-defense, as it is well known to almost every man of the State, that we have every reason to put ourselves in an attitude of defense, considering the abuse we have suffered in Jackson County. We are anxious for a settlement of the difficulties existing between us, upon honorable and constitutional principles.

We are willing for twelve disinterested men, six to be chosen by each party, and these shall say what the possessions of these men are worth who cannot live with us in the county; and they shall have their money in one year; and none of the "Mormons" shall enter that county to reside until the money is paid. The damages that we have sustained in consequence of being driven away, shall also be left to the above twelve men, or they may all live in the county, if they choose, and we will never molest them if they let us alone, and permit us to enjoy our rights. We want to live in peace with all men; and equal rights is all we ask. We wish to become permanent citizens of this State, and wish to bear our proportion in support of the government, and to be protected by its laws. If the above propositions are complied with, we are willing to give security on our part, and we shall want the same of the people of Jackson County, for the performance of this agreement. We do not wish to settle down in a body, except where we can purchase the land with money; for to take possession by conquest or the shedding of blood, is entirely foreign to our feelings. The shedding of blood we shall not be guilty of, until all just and honorable means among men prove insufficient to restore peace.

(Signed) JOSEPH SMITH, JUN.,
F. G. WILLIAMS,
LYMAN WIGHT,
RODGER ORTON,
ORSON HYDE,
JOHN S. CARTER.

To John Lincoln, John Scone, George R. Morehead, Jas. H. Long, Jas. Collins.

After the departure of Gillium a revelation was given.[A] The Lord in this revelation declared that Zion might have been redeemed by that time, had it not been for the transgressions of his saints. They had not been obedient to the requirements made of them. They had withheld their means, and in their hearts had said: "Where is their God? Behold he will deliver them in time of trouble, otherwise we will not go up unto Zion, and we will keep our monies."

[Footnote A: Doc. & Cov. Sec. 105.]

Besides these evidences of a lack of faith, they were wanting in that unity required by the law of the celestial kingdom, and it is only through the observance of that law that Zion can be redeemed. The Lord, therefore, commanded the elders to wait a season for the redemption of Zion, until the saints should obtain more experience, learn obedience, and until means could be raised to purchase all the lands in Jackson County that could be purchased, and also in the surrounding counties; and until the Lord's army had become very great, and sanctified before him. And when this was done the Lord promised to hold his people guiltless in taking possession of that which was their own; and they should possess it forever. He had permitted the elders composing the camp to come thus far, for a trial of their faith; and now he had prepared a great endowment for them in the house which he had commanded to be built in Kirtland. Those who could stay in Missouri were to do so, but those who had left their families in the east, were at liberty to return.

The saints who had been driven from their lands in Jackson were instructed to carefully gather together in one region as much as could be, without exciting the fears of the people. They were to be very faithful and humble; boasting neither of faith nor judgments. By following this counsel, the Lord promised to give them favor in the eyes of the people, that they might rest in peace while they were saying to the people: "Execute judgment and justice for us according to the law, and redress us of our wrongs."

CHAPTER XXIII
THREATENED JUDGMENT—IF—!

The day following this revelation the camp left Fishing River and approached Liberty, Clay County; but when within five or six miles of that place they were met by General Atchison and others who requested them not to go to Liberty, as the people were very greatly enraged at them. As this request was made by men of influence, and those who desired peace, and who felt an interest in the execution of justice, Joseph consented not to go to Liberty; and turning aside, camped on Rush Creek, near the residence of Sydney Gilbert, and in a Brother Burghart's field.

The day before, three of the brethren had suffered some with the cholera but it was not until the camp came to Rush Creek that the disease broke out among them in its fury. The night of the twenty-fourth of June will long be remembered by the members of Zion's Camp. All night long they heard the moans and piteous cries of the sufferers, and loud lamentations of those who lost their loved ones by the ravages of this dreadful disease.

When it first made its appearance Elder John S. Carter attempted to rebuke it, but he became its first victim. Joseph also undertook to stay its ravages by the laying on of hands. He administered to his brother Hyrum. "The moment I attempted to rebuke the disease, that moment I was attacked," he writes; "and had I not desisted, I must have saved the life of my brother by the sacrifice of my own, for when I rebuked the disease, it left him and seized upon me. I quickly learned by painful experience that when the great Jehovah decrees destruction upon any people, and makes known his determination, man must not attempt to stay his hand."

The brethren unitedly covenanted and prayed, hoping that they might have power with the heavens to stay the ravages of the plague; but to no purpose; for while they were engaged in prayer Elder Wilcox died. The deaths occurred so rapidly that coffins could not be prepared, so the dead were rolled up in blankets and put hurriedly into their graves; and while part of the brethren were engaged in digging the graves, others had to stand guard, musket in hand. After the plague had continued for two or three days, an effectual remedy was found for it by dipping those afflicted in cold water, or pouring it upon them. In all about seventy suffered from the cholera, and out of that number thirteen died.

The camp was dispersed early on the morning of the 25th, and Joseph sent by express to Messrs. Thornton, Doniphan, and Atchison, the following note:

> *Gentlemen:*—Our company of men advanced yesterday from their encampment beyond Fishing River to Rush Creek, where their tents are again pitched. But feeling disposed to adopt every specific measure that can be done without jeopardizing our lives, to quiet the prejudices and fears of some part of the citizens of this county, we have concluded that our company shall be immediately dispersed and continue so till every effort for an adjustment of differences between us and the people of Jackson has been made on our part, that would in anywise be required of us by disinterested men of republican principles.
>
> I am respectfully,
> Your obedient servant,
> JOSEPH SMITH, JR.

Thus Zion's Camp was disbanded. Had Governor Dunklin possessed the courage to enforce the law of the State; had he called out the militia of Missouri to reinstate the exiles in their homes, as at one time he expressed a willingness to do, the history of the camp might have been different. But Governor Dunklin lacked that courage, and without that assistance the camp itself was powerless.

Perhaps another view is also admissible. Had the members of Zion's Camp been more faithful—less contentious—more united; and had the saints in the eastern branches had more faith—faith to send up to Zion more men and more money with which to strengthen the hands of the saints on the land of Zion—the history of Zion's Camp might have been different. But thus it is: what men and great movements might attain to is often defeated, sometimes by the actions of enemies, sometimes by the lack of devotion and faith and energy on the part of those into whose hands great enterprises are committed. While God's general purposes will never ultimately be defeated by man, still upon each side of the general purposes of God a margin somewhat wide seems to have been left in which those both for and against those purposes may write what history they please—one that will meet with the approval of God, or one that will meet only with condemnation—herein is the agency of man. But in the exercise of that agency God's purposes will not be thwarted, for man's agency will not extend so far as that—if it did it would interfere with God's agency and decrees.

Joseph Smith and his brethren, on hearing that the governor of Missouri was afraid to execute the laws by returning the exiled saints to their homes, again covenanted that they would never cease their exertions until Zion was redeemed, and truth, justice and law should triumph over falsehood, injustice, and mobocracy,—a covenant which they called upon the God of their fathers to witness, and which they engaged to fulfill either in this life or the life to come.

But standing above all human resolutions, as the heavens stand above the earth, is Jehovah's own decree that he will execute justice and judgment, and that he will not give to wickedness a lasting victory. Zion will be redeemed. God has decreed it. "Behold, I say unto you, the redemption of Zion must needs come by power; therefore, I will raise up unto my people a man, who shall lead them like as Moses led the children of Israel, for ye are the children of Israel, and of the seed of Abraham, and ye must needs be led out of bondage with power, and with a stretched out arm: and as your fathers were led at the first, even so shall the redemption of Zion be." [A]

[Footnotes A Doc. & Cov. Sec. 103:15-18.]

CHAPTER XXIV
ATTEMPT AT ARBITRATION

Whether it was the fear of popular censure or the approach of Zion's Camp that awed the Jackson County mob into suggesting a peaceable adjustment of their difficulties with the saints, we cannot say. Perhaps both considerations had their weight. At any rate the month of May, 1834, found them suggesting to Governor Dunklin, through some influential gentlemen of Clay County, the propriety of dividing Jackson County so that the old settlers and the saints could occupy separate territory, and confine themselves within their respective limits, with the exception of the public right of ingress and egress upon the highway.

This plan of settling the Jackson County trouble was suggested by Colonel J. Thornton, and concurred in by Messrs. Reese, Atchison and Doniphan. Their communication brought out a reply from the governor in which he expressed his pleasure at these gentlemen making an effort to bring about a compromise of the difficulties. He told them that had he not been afraid of embarrassing himself as an officer of the State he should have exerted himself to have brought about a compromise even before then; but he was fearful of traveling out of the strict line of his duty as the chief executive of the State, should he do so. Said he:

> My first advice would be to the "Mormons" to sell out their lands in Jackson County, and to settle somewhere else, where they could live in peace, provided they could get a fair price for their lands, and reasonable damages for injuries received. If this failed, I would try the citizens, and advise them to meet and rescind their illegal resolves of last summer, and agree to conform to the laws in every particular, in respect to the "Mormons."

Should success attend neither of these plans, he would then try the plan of dividing the county as suggested by Colonel Thornton. "If all these failed," said the governor, "then the simple question of legal right would have to settle it. It is this last that I am afraid I shall have to conform my action to in the end." From the whole tenor of this communication, we learn that even the governor understood that the "simple question of *legal right*" would reinstate the saints on the lands from which they had been driven. Here is an extract from the letter which confirms this statement:

> A more clear and indisputable right does not exist, than that the "Mormon" people who were expelled from their homes in Jackson County, should return and live on their lands; and if they cannot be persuaded as a matter of policy to give up that right, or to qualify it, my course as the chief executive officer of the State is a plain one. * * * The Constitution of the United States declares: "that the citizens of each State shall be entitled to all privileges and immunities of citizens in the several States." Then we cannot interdict any people who have a political franchise in the United States, from emigrating to this State, nor from choosing what part of the State they will settle in, provided they do not trespass on the property or rights of others. * * * And again, our Constitution says, "that all men have a natural and indefeasible right to worship Almighty God according to the dictates of their own conscience." *I am fully persuaded that the eccentricity of the religious opinions and practices of the "Mormons," is at the bottom of the outrages committed against them.* They have the right constitutionally guaranteed to them, and it is indefeasible, to believe and worship JOE SMITH as a man, an angel or even as the only true and living God, and to call their habitation Zion, the Holy Land, or even Heaven itself. Indeed there is nothing so absurd or ridiculous that they have not a right to adopt as their religion so that in its exercise they do not interfere with the rights of others.

Surely this is a liberal statement of the rights of the Latter-day Saints, and, indeed, of any other people; for the rights, privileges, and immunities of the saints under the government of the United States are no more than those belonging to other people—certainly they are no less. Still the governor was loath to perform what he admits to be his plain duty in restoring the "Mormons" to their homes. Indeed, he at length refused to do it; fearing that in executing the law, by returning the saints to their homes, he would involve the State in a civil war. He came the easier to this conclusion, doubtless, because the sufferers were an unpopular religious community. But if the execution of law must be abandoned because the violators thereof threaten to resist its execution, or because a reckless mob led by desperate men threaten that if the law is enforced they will plunge the country into civil war—what a burlesque on government it would be to refrain from the execution of law on that account!

On the tenth of June, 1834, the district judge, John F. Ryland, wrote a letter to Elder A. S. Gilbert, asking him to use his influence in gathering his brethren at Liberty, in Clay County, on the sixteenth of the month; saying that he expected to meet a delegation of citizens from Jackson County there, and he was desirous of giving his views upon the present situation of the parties concerned in the Jackson troubles, with the hope of bringing about a peaceable adjustment of them. This letter was read in a public meeting of the saints, and a respectful answer given, promising that as many of the exiles and their friends as conveniently could attend the meeting on the sixteenth would be present. Knowing there had been some talk about the propriety of the saints selling out their lands in Jackson County, and fearing the judge would advise them to do so, the brethren took occasion to say in this communication to him that no such proposition could possibly be acceded to by them, and concluded by saying: "Home is home, and we want possession of our homes from which we have been wickedly expelled—and those rights which belong to us as native free born citizens of the United States."

About one thousand people were in attendance at the meeting at the courthouse in Liberty on the sixteenth of June; and among them were many of the brethren and a deputation of citizens from Jackson County, who made the following proposition for the settlement of the Jackson difficulties:

The people of Jackson County will buy all the land the "Mormons" own in the County of Jackson, and also all the improvements which the "Mormons" had on any of the public lands as they existed before the first disturbance between the people of Jackson and the "Mormons," and for such improvements as they have made since. The valuation of the land and improvements shall be ascertained by three disinterested arbitrators, to be chosen and agreed upon by both parties; should the parties disagree in the choice of arbitrators, then——is to choose them.

Twelve Mormons shall be permitted to go with the arbitrators to show them their lands and improvements while they are being valued; and any other "Mormons" may accompany the arbitrators whom they may desire in order to give them information; and the people of Jackson guarantee their entire safety while doing so.

When the arbitrators report the value of the land and improvements, the people of Jackson will pay to the "Mormons" the valuation, *with one hundred per cent added thereon,* within thirty days thereafter; the Mormons are to agree not to make any effort ever after to settle, either collectively or individually, within the limits of Jackson County; and are to enter into bonds to insure the conveyance of their lands in Jackson County, according to these terms, when the payment shall be made, and the committee will enter into a like bond, with such security as shall be sufficient, for the payment of the money according to this proposition. While the arbitrators are investigating and deciding upon the matters referred to them, the "Mormons" are not to attempt to enter into Jackson County, or to settle there, except such as are by these propositions permitted to go there.

Or——

The people of Jackson will sell all their lands and improvements on public lands in Jackson County to the "Mormons," the valuation to be obtained in the same manner, the same per cent to be added, and thirty days allowed for payment as in our proposition to buy: the "Mormons" to give good security for the payment of the money, and this delegation will give security that the land will be conveyed to the "Mormons." All parties to remain as they are till the payment is made, at which time the people of Jackson will give possession.[A]

[Footnote A: Abridged from Millennial Star, Volume 15, p. 81.]

After these propositions were submitted to the meeting, a number of speeches were made in which much bitterness was manifested against the saints. The Rev. M. Riley, a Baptist minister, said: "The 'Mormons' have lived long enough in Clay County; and they must either clear out, or be cleared out."

To which the chairman of the meeting, Mr. Turnham, replied: "Let us be republicans, let us honor our country, and not disgrace it like Jackson County. For God's sake don't disfranchise or drive away the 'Mormons.' They are better citizens than many of the old inhabitants."

General Doniphan:—"That's a fact, and as the 'Mormons' have armed themselves, if they don't fight they are cowards. I love to hear that they have brethren coming to their assistance. Greater love can no man show, than he who lays down his life for his brother."

Cries of "adjourn," and "no, no, go on!" were now heard, mingled with curses loud and deep, and the ominous gleaming of knives, and cocking of pistols. To add to the excitement a man by the door yelled out—"A man stabbed!" At this, those in the court room rushed out to learn what had happened. It turned out that a blacksmith by the name of Calbert had stabbed a man by the name of Wales, who had boasted of having whipped many of the "Mormons" — one of whom had nearly lost his life through the injuries received. The meeting broke up without further bloodshed.

In the midst of this excitement a few of the brethren retired and addressed a communication to the Jackson County delegation in attendance at the meeting, to the effect that their proposition for a settlement of the Jackson difficulties would be presented to the saints, and an answer to it would be handed to Judge Turnham by the twentieth, sooner if possible. The brethren assured the Jackson delegation that peace was what they desired, and promised to use all their influence to establish it, and disclaimed any design to commence hostilities against the inhabitants of Jackson County; and further pledged themselves to use their influence to prevent the large company of their men (Zion's Camp) then en route for Missouri, going into Jackson County until the citizens of Jackson should receive an authoritative answer to their proposition to "buy or sell."

The Jackson delegation, in a very bad humor, started for Independence. One of the leaders, James Campbell, as he adjusted his pistols in his holsters, exclaimed: "The eagles and buzzards shall eat my flesh, if I don't fix Joe Smith and his army [meaning Zion's Camp,] so that their skins won't hold shucks before two days are passed."

The Jackson delegation went to Ducker's ferry and started to cross the Missouri, but when about the middle of the river, their boat suddenly went down as if made of lead. There was no storm — the river was calm, and no natural explanation could be given for the sinking of the boat. Joseph declared that the angel of the Lord sank it.[B] Indeed the circumstances are such as to go very far toward strengthening the statement. It is supposed that about twelve men were in the boat, and of this number seven [C] were drowned. Of the number drowned the names of three are all that have been learned — Ike Job, — — Everett and James Campbell. The body of Campbell was found by a Mr. Purtle, about three weeks after the occurrence, on a pile of drift-wood, some four or five miles below where the boat sank. But little more than the skeleton of the man remained. His flesh had been eaten by the eagles and buzzards. His fate points a fearful warning to those who raise their hands against God's anointed. It gives us reason to believe that the day is not distant when the command of Jehovah — "Touch not mine anointed, and do my prophets no harm" — must be obeyed.

[Footnote B: Millennial Star, Volume 15, p. 83.]

[Footnote C: Joseph states that seven were drowned, (see History of Joseph Smith, Millennial Star, Volume 15, p. 83); but the History of Clay County, published in St. Louis by the National Historical Society, says that only five were drowned.]

The fate of Owens was more ludicrous—a comedy rather than a tragedy. He floated down the stream until he landed on an island, where he remained all night. The next morning he stripped off his clothes and swam ashore and laid down by the side of a log, close to the road. A lady passing on horse-back, learning of his condition, dropped him her shawl to cover his nakedness, until he could secure clothing.

CHAPTER XXV
THE PROS AND CONS OF
ARBITRATION PROPOSITION

Having related the principal events connected with the meeting held at Liberty, we must consider the propositions made by the Jackson people to the saints, for the peaceful adjustment of their difficulties. To have the lands owned by the saints and the improvements thereon valued by disinterested arbitrators, and the amount paid with *one hundred per cent added* within thirty days, looks like a very fair proposition; but still the saints could not accept such terms; as the condition upon which the proposition was made required the surrender of some of their rights as citizens of the United States and freemen.

The Constitution of the United States says expressly: "The citizens of each State shall be entitled to all privileges and immunities of citizens in the several States." [A] The saints were citizens of the United States, possessing all the rights and franchises thereof, and they had a right—an indefeasible one, too—to settle in whatever State they saw proper to choose for their abode; and they had a right to settle in whatever part of the State pleased them best; and, as Governor Dunklin admitted, they had a right to call their habitation "ZION, the Holy Land, or Heaven itself," so long as in doing so, they interfered not with the property and rights of others. To accept the proposition of the Jackson people, therefore, and bind themselves never again to make any effort to settle collectively or individually within the limits of Jackson County, would be a surrender of their dearest rights of citizenship; and would be permitting mobocrats and murderers to dictate them in the exercise of their liberties; binding not only themselves, but their children as well, to the dictum of these wretches. To accept such a settlement of their troubles, would have been a covenant with death, an agreement with hell! To their honor be it said, they spurned the proposition with the contempt it deserved.

[Footnote A: Const. Art. IV, Section 2.]

But the surrender of some of their rights as citizens of the United States was not the only difficulty involved in the settlement of the Jackson troubles by the saints selling their possessions. God had revealed it to them that Jackson County was the place where is to be built the Zion of their God. For them to sell their lands then, and agree never after to make a settlement there, collectively or individually, would be a denial of their faith and bring upon them the displeasure of their God. For them to sell their lands was entirely out of the question.

But the mob offered not only to buy, but to sell upon the same conditions that they proposed to buy. Why did not the saints accept this offer? Simply because they could not, and the citizens of Jackson knew very well they could not. The old settlers of Jackson owned many times more the amount of land than was possessed by the saints, say thirty acres to one. The saints were not wealthy to begin with; and now, after they had been driven from their homes, robbed of their goods, their cattle driven away, their houses, stables, and stacks of grain burned, they are asked to buy nearly the whole of Jackson County, for which they must pay double price, because they were to add *one hundred per cent* to the appraised value—in *thirty days!* I don't believe the people of Jackson County were sincere in making the proposition. They knew the saints could not sell their lands without surrendering many of their rights as free men and citizens of the United States; and without being untrue to their God, by virtually denying their faith in the revelations he had given regarding the building up of Zion in Jackson County. This the old settlers knew the Mormons would not do. They had tried to whip and frighten too many of them into a denial of their religious convictions, to think for one moment that money would be any inducement for them to deny that faith. On the other hand, they determined to put the price of their own land beyond the possibility of the saints purchasing it.

The whole scheme was concocted with a view of covering up their outrages against the people of God, under an appearance of fairness. "In the corrupted currents of this world, where Offense's gilded hand may shove by justice," where hypocrisy is often mistaken for piety, and cunning for fairness, the subterfuge may have served its purpose; but when the wretches who would have murdered the saints and plundered them of their goods shall stand before the bar of God where there is "no shuffling," but where the actions of men "lie in their true light," they will find their refuge of deceit will not shield them from the justice of Him who has declared, "vengeance is mine, I will repay!"

The saints refused to accept the terms of settlement made by the people of Jackson, but they themselves proposed terms of adjustment, as follows:

Twelve disinterested men were to be chosen, six by the exiles, six by the people of Jackson County. These twelve men were to say what the possessions of those men were worth that would not consent to live with the "Mormon" people, and they should receive the money for the same in one year from the time the treaty was made, none of the saints to enter Jackson County to reside until the money was paid.

This same company of twelve men was to be empowered to say what the damage was which the "Mormons" sustained in being driven from their homes and in the destruction of their property, the said amount allowed for damages to be deducted from the amount paid for the lands of those who would not consent to live with the saints.

The only reply received to this proposition was in a letter from S. C. Owens to Mr. Amos Reese, which plainly said the Jackson people would listen to nothing like the proposition made by the "Mormons;" and here the hopes of settling the Jackson County trouble by arbitration ended.

CHAPTER XXVI
AN INTERIM—BLIGHTED HOPES

The work accomplished by the Prophet Joseph was considerable during his stay in Missouri. On the first of July, with a few of the brethren, he crossed the Missouri into Jackson County, "once more," he remarked, "to set my foot on this 'goodly land.'" What contending emotions would be awakened by such a visit! There, just to the west of the courthouse in Independence, three years before, he had assembled with his brethren, and dedicated a site for the temple of the Lord. Now and then they would come to the ruined homes of the brethren; now in vision he might, for a moment, see the future glory of Zion; then he would weep to think of the saints stripped of all their earthly goods, and in the midst of strangers whose bond of friendship was not strong.

On the third of July a High Council was organized by the Prophet, in Clay County, of which David Whitmer was made president and W. W. Phelps and John Whitmer, counselors. This council proceeded to discuss a variety of subjects pertaining to the situation of The Church and its members. They made a direct appeal to the people of the United States, and to mankind everywhere, stating their wrongs and imploring their assistance in securing and maintaining their rights. They declared their devotion to the laws of their country, and their faith in God, and the final establishment of Zion in Jackson County, and expressed a desire to be at peace with all mankind.[A]

[Footnote A: History of Joseph Smith, Millennial Star, Vol. 15, p. 121.]

This High Council investigated some matters arising between the members in The Church, and busied itself in setting in order The Church in Missouri generally. On the twelfth of July the council appointed Edward Partridge, Orson Pratt, Isaac Morley and Zebedee Coltrin to visit the afflicted and scattered brethren in Missouri. They were not to hold public meetings, as that would arouse too much popular prejudice; but they were to work quietly, setting the saints in order and teaching them the way of holiness, as the Lord by his Spirit might direct. Subsequently a few elders were sent out to hold public meetings, "to teach the disciples how to escape the indignation of their enemies, and keep in favor with those who were friendly disposed." On the seventh of August the council sent out about twenty elders to preach the gospel to the world; and thus in these trying circumstances, these faithful men continued to preach the Gospel of Jesus Christ.

In the meantime, Joseph and a few of his brethren who had accompanied him had arrived in Kirtland, having left the brethren in Missouri on the ninth of July. On his return to Kirtland, the Prophet was charged with aspiring to be "tyrant, pope, king, usurper of men, false prophet, prophesying lies in the name of the Lord, taking consecrated moneys," etc., etc., "a catalogue," said Joseph, "as black as the author of it." But High Council meetings were called, investigations were inaugurated; the accusers were brought face to face with the accused; the character of God's Prophet was vindicated, his accusers were made to hang their heads in shame, and in the most public manner made known their errors so that shortly the Prophet was, as he himself stated it, "swimming in good, clear water with his head out."

No sooner had these difficulties been settled than the Prophet again turned his attention to Zion. On the eleventh of August, 1834, he wrote the brethren in Missouri concerning what had befallen him in Kirtland, and also requested that another petition be written such as the High Council would approve, asking the governor of Missouri to call on the President of the United States to furnish a guard to protect the saints in their homes in Jackson County (when they should be restored) from the insults and violence of the mob. Copies of this petition were to be placed in the hands of the elders going on missions through the United States, and every effort was to be made to get signers; "that peradventure," wrote Joseph, "we may learn whether we have friends or not in these United States."

Lyman Wight was instructed to enter complaints to Governor Dunklin as often as he should receive insults or injuries; and should mobs take life or burn houses, and the people of Clay County refuse to protect the saints, he was to collect the little army of brethren scattered through Clay County, be sent over into Jackson County—it will be remembered that the governor had expressed his willingness to escort the saints back to their lands by aid of the State militia, though holding that he had no authority of law to keep a military force under arms for their protection—and do the best he could in maintaining the ground. If the excitement continued to abate, then the saints were to gather quietly together in the regions surrounding, and be in "readiness to move into Jackson County *in two years from the eleventh of September next* [1836], *which is the appointed time for the redemption of Zion.* IF—verily I say unto you—IF The Church, with one united effort, perform their duties—if they do this, the work shall be complete." [B] If, on the other hand, The Church failed to gather up the young men and means to redeem Zion by the appointed time, "behold," said the Prophet, "there remaineth a scourge for The Church, even that they shall be driven from city to city, and but few shall remain to receive an inheritance," [C]

[Footnote B: History of Joseph, Millennial Star, Vol. 15, p. 140.]

[Footnote C: Ibid.]

During the two years following, the Prophet was busily engaged in setting in order the various quorums of the priesthood.

In the winter of 1834-5 the quorum of Twelve Apostles and the first quorum of Seventies were organized, being chosen principally from among those brethren who had gone up to Missouri in Zion's Camp.

But amid the busy scenes at Kirtland—while organizing these quorums and instructing them in the duties of their respective callings; attending the school for the elders; studying Hebrew under Professor Sexias; translating some rolls of Egyptian papyrus containing the precious Book of Abraham, which he purchased from M. H. Chandler; attending to general duties and correspondence—amid all these busy scenes, Joseph still had time to think of Zion and her redemption. On the occasion of a large body of the priesthood being present at a meeting in Kirtland, on the second of May, 1835, he moved that they never give up the struggle for the redemption of Zion, so long as life should last.

September following, the High Council met at the house of the Prophet to take into consideration the redemption of Zion. It was the decision of the council that the saints who had been expelled from Zion, petition the governor of the State to reinstate them the following spring, and they would either live or die on their lands, and Joseph prayed that they might be successful in getting eight hundred or a thousand emigrants to go up to settle in Zion. Still later, viz: thirteenth of March, 1836, the First Presidency resolved to remove on or before the fifteenth of May next to Zion; that their influence might be more effectual in encouraging the saints to gather there. But events of a strange character were to occur that would prevent the carrying out of these resolutions. The saints did not comply with the conditions upon which Zion was to be redeemed. They did not with a united effort do their duty. They did not give of their means liberally, nor did their young men volunteer readily to go up to Zion. Hence, they were not entitled to the fulfillment of God's promise to redeem Zion; but instead of this blessing, there was suspended over them the promised scourge of being driven from city to city, because they failed to keep the commandments; a scourge that has been executed to the uttermost—but I will not anticipate the story.

The petitions the elders circulated throughout the States in their travels, asking the people to petition the governor of Missouri to reinstate the saints in their homes, met with a response that was considerable. I cannot learn how many names were attached to this petition, but when it was mailed on the ninth of December, 1835, the package was large, the postage amounting to five dollars. But all these efforts failed to move the State officials of Missouri to make any effectual effort towards restoring the exiles to their own and protecting them in the quiet possession of their property and lives.

CHAPTER XXVII
PEACEFUL EXODUS FROM CLAY COUNTY

Meantime the presence of the saints in Clay County began to be a cause of uneasiness among the non-"Mormons" of the community. The leading citizens of the county assembled at the courthouse in Liberty on the twenty-ninth of June, 1836, to consider the difficulties threatening the people of Clay County in consequence of the presence of the "Mormons." After the usual organization at such meetings, the committee on resolutions reported a document that briefly stated the circumstances under which the "Mormons" flocked into Clay County; without money; without property; without food for their wives and children; and, like Noah's dove, without a resting place for their feet; and how the people of Clay County in face of the thousand reports accusing them of every crime known to the laws of the country, had treated them with toleration, and often with peculiar kindness. The document referred to the statements of the leading brethren who had said they did not regard Clay County as their permanent home, but merely as a temporary asylum which they would promptly leave whenever a respectable portion of the citizens of the county should request it; and now the best interest of the county demanded the fulfillment of that pledge.

The reasons why the saints had become objectionable as permanent citizens to many of the people of Clay County were stated to be:

1. Their religious tenets were so different from the present churches of the age, that this always had and always would excite deep prejudice against them in any populous country where they might locate.

2. They were eastern men whose manners, habits, customs, and even dialect were essentially different from the Missourians.

3. They were *non*-slave holders, and opposed to slavery, which excited deep and abiding prejudices in a community which tolerated and protected slavery.

4. Common report had it that they kept up a constant communication with the Indian tribes on the frontier; and declared from the pulpit that the

Indians were a part of God's chosen people, destined by heaven to inherit with them the land of Missouri.

"We do not vouch for the correctness of these statements," said the committee in their report, "but whether they are true or false, their effect has been the same in exciting our community."

The causes named are represented as having raised a prejudice against the saints, and a feeling of hostility, that the first spark might, and the committee deeply feared would, ignite into all the horrors and desolations of a civil war, and it was

> Resolved: That it is the fixed and settled conviction of this meeting, that unless the people commonly called Mormons, will agree to stop immediately the immigration of their people to this country, and take measures to remove themselves from it, a civil war is inevitable.
>
> We do not contend that we have the least right under the constitution and laws of the country to expel them by force. But we would indeed be blind, if we did not foresee that the first blow that is struck at this moment of deep excitement, must and will speedily involve every individual in a war, bearing ruin, woe, and desolation in its course. It matters but little how, where, or by whom the war may begin, when the work of destruction commences, we must all be borne onward by the storm, or crushed beneath its fury.

The saints were told that if they had one spark of gratitude they would not willingly plunge a people into civil war who had held out to them the friendly hand of assistance in the dark hour of their distress. A committee of ten were appointed to present these views to the leading elders among the "Mormons" with the understanding that if the saints would consent to move as requested, the gentlemen who had called the meeting, and now asked them to leave Clay County, would use all their influence to allay the excitement among the citizens of the county.

The reply of the Saints to the request to remove from Clay County was adopted at a general mass meeting. In their reply they expressed their appreciation of the kindness shown them by the people of Clay County. They denied having any disposition to meddle with slavery. They also denied holding communication with the Indians, and said they held themselves as ready to defend their country against their barbarous ravages as any other people. After making these denials they resolved that

> For the sake of friendship, and to be in a covenant of peace with the citizens of Clay County, and they to be in a covenant of peace with us, notwithstanding the necessary loss of property, and expense we incur in moving, we comply with the requisitions of their resolutions in leaving the county of Clay, as explained by the preamble accompanying the same; and that we will use our exertions to have The Church do the same.

It appears that the committee who had presented the resolutions of the Clay County citizens, had tendered their services to assist the saints in selecting a new location, and the latter resolved to accept that assistance. The reply from the saints was perfectly satisfactory to the people of Clay County, and the latter made some arrangements to assist the former in complying with their request; that is, two persons from each township were appointed to raise money by subscription to aid the "Mormons" who might need assistance to leave the county, and also arrange for some suitable person to assist them in selecting a new location for settlement; and recommended the "Mormons" to the good treatment of the citizens in surrounding counties; and asked them to assist the exiles in selecting some abiding place, where they would be, in a measure, the only occupants of the land; and where none would be anxious to molest them.

On the twenty-fifth of July, 1834, the brethren received a letter from Governor Dunklin that was the funeral knell to their hopes of executive interference in their behalf. He informed them their cases were individual cases, and as such, were subjects for judicial interference, and not for the special cognizance of the executive, and to this the governor added:—

> And there are cases, some times, of individual outrage which may be so popular as to render the actions of the courts of justice nugatory, in endeavoring to afford a remedy. * * * * * A public sentiment may become paramount law, and when one man, or society of men become so obnoxious to that sentiment, as to determine the people to be rid of him or them, it is useless to run counter to it. * * * Your neighbors accuse your people of holding illicit communication with the Indians, and of being opposed to slavery. You deny. Whether the charge or the denial is true I cannot tell. The

fact exists, and your neighbors seem to believe it true; and whether true or false, the consequences will be the same, unless you can, by your conduct and arguments, convince them of your innocence. If you cannot do this, all *I* can *say* to you is, that in *this republic* the *vox populi* is the *vox Dei.*

What a mockery then is such government! Under it none may hope to enjoy liberty but those who are willing to swim in the stream of popular sentiment—a stream oftener filthy than clean! oftener wrong than right!—influenced by passion rather than reason! How precarious is the hold of the inhabitants of such a government upon their liberties—depending upon the changing whims of the populace—the populace, which "to-day will weep a Caesar slain; to-morrow vote a monument to Brutus!" Under such a government what is to become of reformers? Perhaps the fate of reformers of other ages, who have fallen victims to the hatred of popular sentiment will answer the question. What is to become of the weaker parties if all are to be crushed or banished that popular sentiment condemns? For what are governments established if not to protect *all*, the weak as well as the strong, the despised as well as the favored in the enjoyment of life, liberty, and the pursuit of happiness?

What do constitutions amount to if they are not recognized as conservators of liberty, by acting as restraints upon these rash acts of injustice, so frequently prompted by the frenzy of popular sentiment—a sentiment often manufactured by a misrepresentation of the principles and motives of those against whom the injustice is levelled? In popular governments constitutions are adopted for the express purpose of restraining the majority in the exercise of its power, and to guarantee the enjoyment of rights and liberties to the minority—to those out of favor with the popular sentiment of the hour. The tyranny of a majority is known and feared, and hence it is restrained by constitutional provisions, which thus become the bulwarks of freedom, by especially guarding the weak against the strong.

It may be held that in popular governments the constitutions and laws enacted in accordance therewith are but the expressions of popular sentiment. Grant it. But the popular sentiment as expressed in constitutions and laws, is very different from that expressed by an excited populace, not unfrequently controlled by demagogues. Popular sentiment is often created by intemperate speeches, and sustained by misrepresentation. But the popular sentiment as expressed by laws and constitutions is adopted in legislative halls where *right reason* has a chance to assist in forming the sentiment; and where a decent respect for the long established maxims of justice and liberty will be taken into consideration, and will influence the legislature in forming the rules for the action of the people. When popular sentiment is expressed in constitutions and laws, and they are enforced, the citizens are, in a measure at least, secure from oppression and sudden destruction; but what guarantee have the people against injustice being done, if an inconsiderate, frenzied, popular sentiment is to be enforced—a sentiment that falsehood creates and that passion directs? None whatever. And when the citizens of the American Republic regard the prejudiced and excited voice of the populace as the voice of God—as Governor Dunklin of Missouri did—let them bid an everlasting farewell to freedom!

CHAPTER XXVIII
FAR WEST

At the time the saints were requested to leave their homes in Clay County, the whole northern part of Missouri was very sparsely settled; and but few counties were organized. As it was desirable on the part of the saints to obtain a location where they would be the principal settlers and occupants of the lands, where they would be free from injustice and violence of mobs, where they might quietly gather together and be taught to observe the principles of truth in the Gospel of Christ, that they might be prepared in all things for the redemption of Zion—upper Missouri, with its boundless prairies, wooded streams, and sparse population, seemed admirably adapted for their home until Zion could be redeemed.

W. W. Phelps and others had traveled through it, and had described it to the saints some two years before. It was recommended to the attention of the brethren by their influential friends in Clay County, and so the month of October, 1836, found a number of them settling on Shoal Creek. They soon petitioned for an enactment organizing a new county, which was granted. The new county was organized on the 26th of December, 1836, and was named Caldwell, with the county seat at Far West.

The town plat of Far West as first laid off embraced a square mile, but afterwards additions were made as the population increased. In the center of the town a large public square was laid off, approached by four main roads running east and west, north and south, each a hundred feet wide. Eventually the blocks were so laid off that each block contained four acres, divided into four lots. Far West was located in the western part of Caldwell County, about eight miles west of the present county seat—Kingston. The town site is the highest swell in that high rolling prairie country, and is visible from a long distance.

Standing on what used to be the public square of Far West, on the occasion of my visit there in 1884, I obtained an excellent view of all the surrounding country. Vast fields of waving corn and meadow land were stretched out on all sides, as far as the eye could see. Several towns and villages, with their white church spires gleaming in the sun-light, were in plain view, though from five to ten miles distant. Away to the east is Kingston, the present county seat of Caldwell; further to the northeast is Breckenridge, Hamilton and Kidder; to the west is Plattsburg, and south is the quaint village of Polo. All these places are within easy vision from the site of Far West, and increase the grandeur of the scene.

The site chosen for Far West is the finest location for a city in the county, but notwithstanding all the advantages of the location, Far West has been abandoned. In the fall of 1838 it was a thriving town of some three thousand inhabitants, but today nothing remains except the house of the Prophet Joseph, now owned by D. F. Kerr,[A] and one portion of the Whitmer Hotel, now used as a stable. This is all that remains of the buildings, at Far West, erected by the hands of the saints. A few farm houses have been built in the vicinity since their expulsion from Missouri, and a quarter of a mile from the public square stands a neat white Methodist church.

[Footnote A: At least it was owned by him in 1884.]

Nothing but an excavation one hundred and ten feet by eighty, enclosed in an old field, with a large rough, unhewn stone in each corner, now marks the spot that was once the pretentious public square of Far West. This excavation was made on the 3rd of July, 1837, and was intended for the basement of the temple the saints expected to erect there. There are several very interesting circumstances connected with this old excavation and the rough corner stones, that will be related as the circumstances of which I am writing, shall bring them due.

Standing on this consecrated ground and viewing the few relics that are left to remind us that the saints once lived here, one naturally falls into a sad reverie. It is true we are not surrounded by the fallen columns of ruined temples; or the ruins of splendid palaces, or massive walls, such as one would meet with at Babylon, Jerusalem, Rome or Athens. It is not the ruins of an antique or celebrated civilization that inspires one's sadness over Far West. But there one sits in the midst of the ruined prospects and blighted hopes of the saints of God, instead of in the midst of broken columns, ponderous arches, and crumbling walls.

The chief interest about Far West, of course, is the fact that it was the theatre where was enacted those stirring scenes which add another black page to the history of Missouri.

"If that strange people," says Crosby Jackson in his history of Caldwell County, "who built Nauvoo and Salt Lake, who uncomplainingly toiled across the American desert, and made the wilderness of Utah to bloom like a garden, had been permitted to remain and perfect the work which they had begun here, how different would have been the history of Far West! Instead of being a farm with scarcely sufficient ruins to mark the spot where once it stood, there would have been a rich, populous city, along the streets of which would be pouring the wealth of the world; and instead of an old dilapidated farmhouse, there would have been magnificent temples to which the devout saints from the further corners of the world would have made their yearly pilgrimage. But the bigotry and intolerance of the saints towards the gentiles, and especially toward dissenters from the new revelations of Joe Smith, rendered such a consummation impossible!"

It now becomes my duty to relate those circumstances which prevented the saints from building up Far West, and which at last drove them as exiles from the State of Missouri; and we shall, in the course of our narrative, see whether it was the "bigotry and intolerance of the saints towards the gentiles and dissenters," that brought about the fate of Far West, or whether it was the brutal savagery of pretended "Christians" incited to deeds of cruelty by jealous sectarian ministers, and unscrupulous demagogues fearful of the growing political power of the "Mormons."

The first settlement in the vicinity of Far West was made in October, 1836; by July following, about one hundred buildings had been erected, eight of which were stores. This same month the school section of land was sold at auction, and although entirely a prairie it sold, on a year's credit, for seven dollars and ninety cents per acre, making the settlers' school fund about five thousand dollars. Some non-members of The Church expressed a desire to establish saloons in the growing town, and endeavored to induce some of the brethren to sell intoxicants on commission for them, but the High Council resolved not to sustain any persons as members of The Church, who would become retailers of spirituous liquors, and the liquor business was dropped.

In September, 1837, The Church at Kirtland appointed Joseph Smith and Sidney Rigdon to seek out new places for the gathering of the saints and lay off other stakes of Zion, than those of Far West and Kirtland. On this mission Joseph and Sidney arrived at Far West in the latter part of October. A council of the Priesthood was called at which it was decided that there was sufficient room in the vicinity of Far West for the gathering of the saints from abroad; and hence it was decided that it was not necessary for the present to select other places.

At a general conference convened in October, 1837, the several quorums of the Priesthood were set in order. Men and measures were thoroughly discussed. Difficulties were adjusted and covenants of brotherly love renewed. Twenty-three Elders were started out to preach the gospel. It was voted to enlarge the town plat of Far West so that it would contain four sections—two miles square. The conference also voted not to support any stores or shops selling spirituous liquors, tea, coffee or tobacco.

CHAPTER XXIX
THE FALL OF DAVID WHITMER
AND OLIVER COWDERY

Thus Far West was founded; and the impediments to her growth as a strictly moral and temperance city removed. And yet, causes were at work that were undermining the spiritual strength of many of the saints, and killing the influence of a number of the elders in high positions. A wave of speculation, especially in lands, swept over the entire country, and the brethren partook largely of this spirit, which proved ruinous to their spiritual life. Among those who were affected by this spirit of wild speculation to their injury were John Whitmer and W. W. Phelps. Shortly afterwards Oliver Cowdery and David Whitmer, two of the three witnesses to the truth of the Book of Mormon, were excommunicated. The charges sustained before the High Council against Oliver Cowdery were:

1. Persecuting the brethren by urging on vexatious law suits against them, and thus distressing the innocent.

2. Seeking to destroy the character of Joseph Smith, Jr., by falsely insinuating that he was guilty of adultery.

3. Treating The Church with contempt by not attending meetings.

4. Leaving his calling, to which God had appointed him by revelation, for the sake of filthy lucre, and turning to the practice of law.

5. Disgracing The Church by being connected in the "bogus" business, as common report says.[A]

[Footnote A: Upper Missouri was infested with sharps engaged in counterfeiting the currency of the United States, and common rumor connected Oliver Cowdery with them.]

6. Dishonestly retaining notes after they had been paid; and finally forsaking the cause of God and returning to the beggarly elements of the world, and neglecting his high and holy calling, according to his profession.

The charges sustained against David Whitmer were:

1. Not observing the word of wisdom.

2. Unchristian-like conduct in neglecting to attend meetings, and in uniting with and possessing the same spirit as the dissenters.

3. Writing letters to the dissenters in Kirtland, unfavorable to the cause and to the character of Joseph Smith, Jr.

4. Neglecting the duties of his calling, and separating himself from The Church.

5. Signing himself president of the Church of Christ in an insulting letter to the High Council, after he had been cut off from the presidency [B]

[Footnote B: In reorganizing the quorums of the Priesthood at Far West, in November, 1836, to which we have alluded, David Whitmer was made president of The Church in Missouri, and W. W. Phelps and John Whitmer, counselors; but the whole Church under the leadership of Thomas B. Marsh, Lyman Wight, David Patten, and others, on February 5, 1838, met as a committee of the whole, and preferred serious charges of wickedness against the three presidents, and refused to sustain them in their office. The vote which deposed them was unanimous, but the presidents refused to acknowledge the authority of The Church and continued to sign documents as presidents of The Church. It is this to which the fifth charge against David Whitmer refers.]

As before stated, these two men, Oliver Cowdery and David Whitmer, were two of the three special witnesses to the Book of Mormon. It was, therefore, a bold move to excommunicate them. Although it may be thought outside the theme I am following in these pages to make such a digression, still I cannot refrain from indulging in the following reflections: Suppose for a moment that the theory of the world relative to the origin of the Book of Mormon be true: that is, that it was the production of Solomon Spaulding or Sidney Rigdon; that Joseph Smith was put forward as a figure-head; and the three witnesses were induced to become parties to the fraud that was to be perpetrated on mankind—if this supposition were true, would Joseph Smith and Sidney Rigdon, under such circumstances, have dared to withdraw their fellowship from these men? If the Book of Mormon were a huge scheme to deceive mankind, and Cowdery and Whitmer were parties with Smith and Rigdon to the deception, the latter would hardly venture to cast away the former, for fear they might deny their testimony, expose the fraud, and cause the whole Mormon Church fabric to collapse. If the Book of Mormon had been a fraudulent production, Joseph Smith and Sidney Rigdon would never have dared to break with these two important witnesses, whatever their wickedness might be. But the bold, independent course pursued in excommunicating them, when their conduct warranted the action, supplies good evidence that Joseph Smith knew that the existence of The Church did not depend on the testimony of Oliver Cowdery and David Whitmer. The Book of Mormon being true, it would stand independent of these witnesses, and Joseph knew it. But the most gratifying part of it is, these witnesses to the Book of Mormon, though separated from The Church—excommunicated for unrighteousness—never denied their testimony or changed it in the least. But the fact of their having uniformly adhered to their testimony while disconnected with The Church, doubtless adds strength to that testimony, as they stand in the light of disinterested witnesses.

Oliver Cowdery, after his excommunication, became a wanderer for a number of years, unsettled and restless, though following the profession of the law. It was impossible for a man who had once tasted the glories of the Celestial Kingdom of God, as Oliver Cowdery had, to be satisfied with the dry husks of the beggarly elements of the world; and hence after some ten years of wandering outside The Church of Christ he at last found his way back to the fold of God, to the house of his father, and begged to be admitted as a humble member of The Church. This was in the early part of November, 1848, before a High Council over which Elder Orson Hyde presided. On that occasion Oliver Cowdery said: "Brethren, for a number of years I have been separated from you. I now desire to come back. I wish to come humbly and be one in your midst. I seek no station, I only wish to be identified with you. I am out of The Church. I am not a member of The Church, but I wish to become a member of it. I wish to come in at the door. I know the door. I have not come here to ask precedence. I come humbly and throw myself upon the decisions of this body, knowing as I do, that its decisions are right and should be obeyed."

Soon after this he was re-baptized. He was on his way to join the main body of The Church when he stopped at Kanesville, Iowa, where the above occurred. Before continuing his journey west he resolved to visit his wife's friends, the Whitmers, then living at Richmond, Missouri; and while there he was taken with an illness from which he died, on the 3rd of March, 1850, in his forty-fifth year. According to the testimony of Phineas Young, who was present at his death, "his last moments were spent in bearing testimony of the truth of the gospel revealed through Joseph Smith, and the power of the holy Priesthood which he had received through his administration."

David Whitmer never denied his testimony to the truth of the Book of Mormon, through all the years of his separation from The Church, but repeatedly reaffirmed it, especially in the closing years of his life. Three days previous to his death, which occurred on the 25th of January, 1888, he called his family and a number of his friends to his bedside, and turning to his physician, said:

"Dr. Buchanan, I want you to say whether or not I am in my right mind, before I give my dying testimony."

The doctor answered: "Yes, you are in your right mind, for I have just had a conversation with you."

He then addressed himself to all around his bedside in these words: "Now, you must all be faithful in Christ. I want to say to you all, the Bible and the record of the Nephites (Book of Mormon) is true, so that you can say that you heard me bear my testimony on my death-bed. All be faithful in Christ, and your reward will be according to your works. God bless you all. My trust is in Christ forever, worlds without end. Amen." [C]

[Footnote C: Richmond Democrat, February 2, 1888.]

CHAPTER XXX
THE APOSTASY AT KIRTLAND

The spirit of apostasy referred to in the last chapter was by no means confined to Missouri. It extended more or less throughout The Church, but more especially at Kirtland. During the winter of 1836 and the early summer of 1837, a wild spirit of speculation swept over the United States, and the members of The Church had been carried away with it.

Money had been plentiful, easy to borrow, and a spirit of reckless extravagance and speculation had taken hold of the people. When the reaction from this only seeming state of prosperity set in, financial ruin stared the people in the face. As a result of these conditions and the spirit engendered by them, "evil surmisings, fault-finding, disunion, dissension and apostasy followed in quick succession" among the saints in Kirtland. "It seemed," says the Prophet Joseph, in speaking of the conditions existing in the early summer of 1837—"It seemed as though all the powers of earth and hell were combining their influence in an especial manner to overthrow The Church and make a final end."

Many of the leading brethren became especially bitter against the Prophet of God, as though he were the sole cause of the evils he was striving against, and which were brought about by the brethren not giving heed to his counsels. "No quorum in The Church," remarks Joseph, "was entirely exempt from the influence of those false spirits who were striving against me for the mastery; even some of the Twelve were so far lost to their high and responsible calling, as to begin taking sides, secretly, with the enemy." [A]

[Footnote A: History Joseph Smith, Millennial Star, Vol. 16, p. II]

Early in 1837 the Kirtland Safety Society Bank was organized. It was one of the many banks which sprung up all over the United States about that time, and which under the current banking laws issued bank currency; and with hundreds of other similar institutions throughout the land, went down in the financial maelstrom which swept over the country in the latter part of 1837.

Among those disaffected at Kirtland there were some who held the Prophet responsible for the failure of the Safety Society Bank. Some charged that they had been given to understand that the bank was instituted by the will of God, and that "it would never fail, let men do what they would." [B] The Prophet disclaimed having made any such statement, or having authorized any one else to make it. On the contrary, he declared in open conference, held at Kirtland on the 3rd of September, 1837, that he had always said "that unless the institution was conducted on righteous principles, it would not stand." [C]

[Footnote B: A statement of this character was made by Elder Boynton, one of the Twelve Apostles, at a conference held at Kirtland, September 3, 1837.]

[Footnote C: History Joseph Smith, Millennial Star, Vol. 16, p. 56.]

But notwithstanding his disclaimers, apostates in Kirtland held him responsible for its failure; and by early January, 1838, the spirit of these men became so bitter that the Prophet Joseph and Sidney Rigdon had to seek safety in flight in the direction of Far West. They fled by night from the city on horseback, but subsequently were joined by their families in wagons and thus made the tedious journey with teams.

The weather was cold, and sometimes they were obliged to secrete themselves in their wagons to escape their enemies, who followed them for about two hundred miles from Kirtland. The mobbers frequently crossed their track. Twice they were in the same house with the brethren; and once they stopped at the same house over night, with only a partition wall between them, through which the Prophet and his companion could hear their oaths, threats and imprecations. They even went into the room of the brethren, looked upon them, but concluded they were not the men they were pursuing.

Part of the time the Prophet and Sidney traveled together, but for greater security they sometimes traveled alone. At Terre Haute, Indiana, they separated and did not meet again until they arrived at Far West. Joseph reached the latter place on the 14th of March, and Sidney Rigdon on the 4th of April following.

The saints at Far West received the Prophet and Elder Rigdon with every demonstration of joy. Indeed, when they heard that Joseph was en route for Missouri, a delegation of brethren with teams and money went to meet him a hundred and twenty miles from Far West, and greatly assisted him in completing a journey with dispatch and safety which had been fraught with so many dangers.

CHAPTER XXXI
ADAM-ONDI-AHMAN

Joseph was forever active. His appearance in the midst of the saints was always the signal for increased activity in all phases of the work. A day or two after his arrival at Far West, while walking over the prairie, in company with several of the brethren, in one of those sudden out-bursts of inspiration so frequent and natural with and to him, he gave the following as the

POLITICAL MOTTO OF THE CHURCH OF JESUS CHRIST OF LATTER-DAY SAINTS.

The Constitution of our country formed by the Fathers of Liberty: peace and good order in society; love to God, and good will to man. All good and wholesome laws; virtue and truth above all things, and Aristarchy [A] live for ever; but woe to tyrants, mobs, aristocracy, anarchy and toryism, and all those who invent or seek out unrighteous and vexatious law suits, under the pretext and color of law or office, either religious or political. Exalt the standard of Democracy! Down with that of priestcraft, and let all the people say, Amen! That the blood of the fathers may not cry from the ground against us. Sacred is the memory of that blood which bought for us our Liberty.

[Footnote A: Aristarchy—a body of good men at the head of government.]

That is a motto that will challenge the admiration of all patriots, and is worthy of living in the archives of the great Republic.

Conferences, the convening of High Councils, preparing elders to go on missions, making arrangements for settling the ever-increasing numbers of the saints on the new lands of Far West, were the common labors of the day.

In May, 1838, Joseph and other leading brethren started on an exploring expedition to the north, for the purpose of finding new districts where more stakes of Zion might be laid off, and the gathering saints find homes. They traveled north until they reached Grand River, a stream sufficient for steamboat navigation in the rainy seasons, but so fluctuating that it is not practically a navigable stream. Time has cut the channel very deep, and left the wood-lined banks in places quite precipitous.

After reaching Grand River, Joseph and his party followed up the beautiful stream which lead them a north-westerly course. Having traveled some thirty miles from Far West, they camped on the north side of Grand River, at Tower Hill, a name which the Prophet Joseph gave it, because of finding an old ruined Nephite tower or altar on the hill. Half a mile north of Tower Hill, Joseph and party selected and laid claim to a site for a city in township sixty, ranges twenty-seven and eight, sections twenty-five, thirty-six, thirty-one, and thirty. Some of the saints had been located at the place for several months and called it Spring Hill; but by the mouth of the Lord it was named ADAM-ONDI-AHMAN;[B] because, said he, it is the place where Adam shall come to visit his people, or the Ancient of Days shall sit, as spoken of by Daniel [C] the prophet.

[Footnote B: Doc. & Cov. Sec. 116.]

[Footnote C: Daniel 8:9-14.]

Adam-ondi-Ahman, then, or Diahman, as it was familiarly known to the Missouri saints, is located on the north bank of Grand River. It is situated, in fact, in a great bend of the Grand. The river comes sweeping down from the north-west, and here makes a bold curve and runs in a meandering course to the north-east for some two or three miles, when it as suddenly makes another curve and flows again to the south-east. We have already spoken of Grand River as a stream that has worn a deep channel for itself, and left its banks precipitous; but here at Diahman that is only true of the south bank. The stream, as it rushed from the north-west, struck this height of prairie land containing beds of lime-stone, and not being able to cut its way through, it veered off to the north-east, and left that height of land standing like a palisade that rises very abruptly from the stream to a height of from fifty to seventy-five feet; but the summit of these bluffs is the common level of the high, rolling prairie, extending off in the direction of Far West. The bluffs on the north bank recede some distance from the stream, so that the river bottom at this point widens out to a small valley. The bluffs on the north bank of the river are by no means as steep as those on the south, and are covered with a heavier growth of timber. A ridge or spur runs out from the main line of the bluffs into the river bottom some two or three hundred yards, approaching the stream at the point where the curve is made. The termination of the bluff is quite abrupt, and overlooks a considerable portion of the river bottom. On the brow of the bluff stood the old stone altar which the brethren found there. When it was first discovered, according to those who visited it frequently, it was about sixteen feet long, by nine or ten feet wide, having its greatest extent north and south. The height of the altar as the brethren found it, was some two and a half feet at each end but gradually rising higher to the center, which was between four and five feet high—the whole surface being crowing.

Such was the altar at Diahman when the brethren found it. Now, however, it is thrown down and nothing but a mound of crumbling stones mixed with soil, and a few boulders, mark the spot which is doubtless rich in historic events. It was here that the patriarchs, associated with Adam and in his company, assembled at this altar to worship their God. Here their evening prayers ascended to heaven in the smoke of the burning sacrifice, and here angels instructed them in heavenly truths—but more of this anon.

North of the ridge on which the ruins of the altar are found, and running parallel with it, is another ridge, separated from the first by a depression or miniature valley, varying in width from fifty to a hundred yards. This small valley, with the larger one through which flows Grand River, is the valley of Adam-ondi-Ahman. Three years previous to the death of Adam, he gathered the patriarchs Seth, Enos, Cainan, Mahalaleel, Jared, Enoch and Methuselah, together with all their righteous posterity, into this valley we have described; and there gave them his last blessing. And even as he blessed them, the heavens were opened, and the Lord appeared, and in the presence of their God, the children of Adam arose and blessed him, and called him Michael, the Prince, the Archangel. The Lord also blessed Adam, saying: "I have set thee to be the head—a multitude of nations shall come of thee, and thou art a Prince over them for ever." So great was the influence of this double blessing upon Adam, that though he was bowed down with age, under the out-pouring of the Holy Ghost he predicted what should befall his posterity, to their latest generations. Thus we find the valley of Diahman a hallowed spot, made so because of these sacred associations.

But all the interest concerning Diahman is not associated with the past, it is connected with the future as well. For it is in this same valley that the "Ancient of Days," Adam, will come and meet with his posterity, when thousand thousands shall minister to him, and ten thousand times ten thousand shall stand before him; here is where the books will be opened and the judgment shall sit. Here, too, the Son of Man will appear to this vast multitude, in the clouds of heaven, and coming to the Ancient of Days, shall give to him dominion and glory, and issue a decree that all people, nations and languages shall serve and obey him; and his dominion shall be everlasting, and his kingdom one that shall never be destroyed.[D]

[Footnote D: Daniel 7th chapter; see also Doc. & Cov. Sec. 107.]

Such were the scenes of the past enacted in the "Valley of Diahman:" such are the splendid scenes to be enacted there in the future! No wonder if Satan has contended with the saints for the possession of this holy ground! Does not the fact of its being chosen as the place where the Kingdom of God shall be established in power no more to be destroyed, explain in part why there was such an effort on the part of the powers of darkness to drive the saints away from it? And, again, do not the very efforts made by Satan to drive away the saints, sustain the words of the prophets that declare this to be holy ground?

On the evening of May 21st, 1838, a few days after the arrival of Joseph's exploring party at Diahman, a council of the whole party was called, and it was decided not to go farther north, but counsel the people to settle at Diahman, and secure the land between there and Far West. So rapidly did the saints gather to this place, that about one month from the time it was selected, a stake of Zion was organized there. John Smith, uncle of the Prophet, was chosen president; Reynolds Cahoon and Lyman Wight were selected to be his counselors. A High Council was also organized, and Vinson Knight was chosen acting Bishop *pro tempore*.

CHAPTER XXXII
THE FOURTH OF JULY, 1838

The Fourth of July, 1838, is a memorable day in the history of Far West. The saints had long been vexed by their enemies. They had seen their homes destroyed, their helpless women and children driven into the wilderness by cruel mobs, when the exiles could be traced by the blood left in their tracks. They had been robbed of their possessions and maltreated in their persons until they were driven almost to desperation. They took advantage therefore of Independence Day to declare their intentions no more to quietly submit to the outrages perpetrated against them. Joseph Smith was president of the day; and his brother Hyrum, vice-president; Sidney Rigdon, orator; and Reynolds Cahoon, chief marshal. They marched in procession through the town and at last formed a circle around a large excavation—one hundred feet long by eighty wide—in the public square; and there, with appropriate ceremonies, they laid the corner stones of the House of the Lord at Far West. This was followed by speeches, music, prayers, reading the Declaration of Independence, etc. Sidney Rigdon, orator of the day, stirred with indignation in contemplating the sufferings the saints had endured, allowed his eloquence to carry him beyond the limits of calm wisdom, and many of the words spoken by him on that occasion, though corrected by the Prophet Joseph, were later made use of by the enemies of The Church, to the injury of the saints.

As an example of Elder Rigdon's unwise and intemperate language on the occasion referred to, I quote the following paragraph from his speech:

> Our cheeks have been given to the smiters—our heads to those who have plucked off the hair. We have not only when smitten on one cheek turned the other, but we have done it again and again, until we are wearied of being smitten, and tired of being trampled upon. We have proved the world with kindness, we have suffered their abuse, without cause, with patience and have endured without resentment until this day, and still their persecutions and violence do not cease. But from this day and this hour we will suffer it no more. We take God and all the holy angels to witness, this day, that we

warn all men, in the name of Jesus Christ to come on us no more for ever, for from this hour we will bear it no more, our rights shall not be trampled upon with impunity; the man, or the set of men who attempt it, do it at the expense of their lives. And that mob that comes on us to disturb us, it shall be between us and them a war of extermination; for we will follow them until the last drop of their blood is spilled, or else they will have to exterminate us, for we will carry the seat of war to their own houses and their own families, and one party or the other shall be utterly destroyed. Remember it then, all men. We will never be the aggressors, we will infringe on the rights of no people, but shall stand for our own until death. We claim our own rights and are willing that all others shall enjoy theirs. No man shall be at liberty to come into our streets, to threaten us with mobs, for if he does he shall atone for it before he leaves the place, neither shall he be at liberty to vilify and slander any of us, for suffer it we will not, in this place. We therefore take all men to record this day, that we proclaim our liberty this day, as did our fathers, and we pledge this day to one another our fortunes, our lives, and our sacred honors, to be delivered from the persecutions, which we have had to endure for the last nine years or nearly that time. Neither will we indulge any man, or set of men, in instituting vexatious law suits against us, to cheat us out of our rights; if they attempt it we say woe unto them. We this day, then, proclaim ourselves free with a purpose and determination that never can be broken, no, never! No, never!! No, never!!!—COLLECTION OF FACTS.— *Rigdon in Missouri, by J. M. Grant, p.* 11.

CHAPTER XXXIII
KIRTLAND CAMP

It may not be inappropriate here to break the direct line of my narrative, for the purpose of noticing events that are but indirectly connected with the Missouri persecutions; and yet are peculiarly characteristic of "Mormon" movements. The seventies that were in Kirtland in the spring of 1838, met in the House of the Lord there, and discussed the best method of removing the quorum to Missouri. It was manifest both by vision and by prophecy, that they should go up in a camp, pitching their tents by the way; and the liberty of going with the camp was to be extended to those that were not seventies, on the condition that they would comply with the rules of the camp. A commission of seven, all seventies, was appointed to lead the camp; and there were also appointed a chief engineer, a historian, and a general treasurer. The camp was divided in companies of ten, with a captain over each company. The rules governing "Kirtland Camp," as it is called in Church history, were few, and smack of a primitive simplicity:

1. The engineer shall receive advice from the counselors (the commission of seven) concerning his duties.

2. At four o'clock a. m., the horn shall blow for rising, and at twenty minutes past four for prayers, at which time each captain of ten shall see that the inmates of his tent are ready for worship.

3. The head of each division shall keep a roll of all his able-bodied men to stand guard, in turn, as called for by the engineer; one half in the former, the other half in the latter part of the night.

4. Each company of the camp is entitled to an equal portion of the milk whether it owns the cows or not.

5. Appointed a herdsman for the camp, who was to call for the assistance necessary to care of the stock.

6. Provided the camp should not travel more than fifteen miles a day, unless absolutely necessary.

A company of two hundred and forty-nine males, and two hundred and sixty-six females, a total of five hundred and fifteen souls, with twenty-seven tents, ninety-seven horses, twenty-two oxen, sixty-nine cows, camped about a quarter of a mile south of the Lord's House in Kirtland, on the fifth of July, 1838; and the next day started for Missouri. The journey was long and tedious; many difficulties were encountered and numerous obstacles overcome. A spirit of murmuring was frequently manifested, much sickness was in the camp, and because of their disobedience, evil spirits plagued them by getting possession of their bodies. At times they would camp by the way-side to rest their jaded teams, when the brethren would generally get a small contract of work to do; such as harvesting a field of grain, building fences or making road. In this way they spent the summer in journeying to Missouri, where they arrived late in autumn.

A company of saints organized in a similar manner, in Canada, under the leadership of John E. Page, in their journey to Missouri met with the camp from Kirtland, on Sunday the 12th of August, and John E. Page preached to the Kirtland Camp. As they passed through the country they received varied treatment at the hands of the people. At times they were allowed to pass on in peace, and then threatened with violence; and at times actually assaulted. Their toils and sufferings, their faithfulness and rebellions, their rejoicings and sorrows, their preaching the word in the wilderness, their hunger, fatigue, sickness, deaths, and the final arrival of the travel-worn remnants of the camp in Far West and Diahman would, if related in detail, make a long interesting chapter, but we have not space to say more here.

CHAPTER XXXIV
GALLATIN

The sparsely settled counties of upper Missouri, as well as the newly organized county of Caldwell, seemed to promise an asylum where the exiles from Jackson and Clay Counties, and the gathering saints from the East, could find peace and rest. But the illusion was soon to be dispelled, the hope blighted. They were to receive another testimony that the Church of Christ was still militant, and not triumphant; and that the true disciple of Christ must endure patiently the fortunes of that warfare.

Renewed hostilities with the Missourians began in this way: On the 6th of August, 1838, an election was held at Gallatin, in Daviess County; and the old settlers under the leadership of H. P. Peniston, made a determined effort to prevent the "Mormons" from voting. Some of the bullies among the Missourians persistently insulted the brethren, which was endured patiently for a time; but when at last a drunken rough—one Dick Welding—attempted to strike a brother by the name of Samuel Brown, Perry Durphy caught his arm, and this was made an excuse by the Missourians to begin a general assault.

The Missourians, although outnumbering the brethren, found themselves overmatched and beat a hasty retreat to get arms. Among those who fought hardest for his rights as an American citizen, and in the defense of his brethren, was John L. Butler; and as soon as they left, Butler called the brethren together and said: "We are American citizens; our fathers fought for their liberty, and we will maintain the same principles." Here he was interrupted by the county officials who told the brethren that the whole disturbance was a premeditated thing, to prevent them from voting, and requested them to withdraw, as they feared it might end in bloodshed.

By this time the Missourians began to collect, armed to the teeth and greatly reinforced; and as the brethren were unarmed, they retired to their homes, collected their families and concealed them in the hazel thickets. The rain fell in torrents through the night; the women and children were lying on the ground, while the men guarded them.

Judge Morin, of Daviess County, some two weeks before the time of election, had told Levi Stewart and others that there was a movement on foot then to prevent the "Mormons" from voting; and advised them if they went to the election at Gallatin to go armed, prepared to assert their rights. The brethren, however, had not heeded the friendly warning, and went to the polls unarmed, with the result above stated.

The report of the trouble at Gallatin which reached Far West was very much exaggerated. It stated that three of the brethren had been killed, and were refused burial, and that the people of Daviess County were arming to drive the saints from their homes in Diahman. Upon the reception of the report, the Prophet Joseph, his brother Hyrum, and other leading men started for the settlement of the saints, their company increasing on the route, by brethren living between Far West and Diahman joining them. The company arrived at the house of Lyman Wight, and there learned the truth in relation to the Gallatin trouble.

The whole country was in an uproar, in which ministers of the gospel and county officials joined; and by their connection with it made the disturbance formidable.

The whole company that had come with Joseph from Far West rode over to a spring on the prairie, a short distance from Wight's house, and a committee called upon Judge Adam Black, the justice of the peace for that district, and judge-elect for the county, to learn if he justified the course of the proceedings at Gallatin, on the part of the old settlers; to which he replied he did not. As he was a justice of the peace, they desired to know if he would administer the law justly and not join the mob. The question was put to him because rumor had it that he was connected with the mob element. He replied that he would administer the law fairly, and consented to give a statement in writing to that effect, and also denied having any connection with the mob. As this occurrence at Black's residence was made the excuse for commencing those hostilities which terminated so disastrously to the saints, I give Black's agreement in full—orthography and capitalization as in the original:

> I, Adam Black, a justice of the Peace of Davies county do here by Sertify to the people, coled Mormin, that he is bound to suport the Constitution of this State, and of the United States, and he is not attached to any mob, nor will he attach himselff to any such people, and so long as they will not molest me, I will not molest them. This the 8th day of August, 1838.

ADAM BLACK J. P.

While the judge-elect was making out this, to him, weighty document, Mrs. Black was chastising the brethren with the valor of her tongue, in a manner that, doubtless, would have made the ancient Xantippe green with envy. After securing this agreement of peace from Judge Black, the company returned to Wight's, where they met some citizens from Millport, and arranged to hold a conference the next day at noon with the principal men of Daviess County. Among those who attended that meeting, the day following, were Joseph Morin, State senator-elect; John Williams, State representative-elect; the clerk of the circuit court and others. Those men, and the principal elders of The Church, entered into a solemn agreement to preserve each other's rights, and stand in each other's defense. If men in the respective parties should do wrong, they were not to be upheld or screened from justice by their friends; but must be delivered up to be dealt with according to law and justice.

But like some hardened sinner, who "even in penance will plan sins anew," so with the Missourians; while some of their leading men were entering into covenants of peace, others of them were planning the destruction of the saints. The very day following the agreement of peace referred to, Wm. P. Peniston, who had incited the mob disturbance at the Gallatin election, went before the circuit judge, Austin A. King, and made out a complaint against Joseph Smith, Lyman Wight and others, accusing them of having surrounded the house of Adam Black, and under threats of immediate death, compelled him to sign a most disgraceful paper; also that the same men and their followers had threatened to take his life on sight, and the same threat extended to others. He claimed that the body of men following Joseph Smith numbered some five hundred, that they were armed, and that their actions were of a highly insurrectionary character, and that their object was to intimidate and drive from the county all the old citizens, and possess themselves of their lands, or to force such as would not leave to accept their measures and submit to their dictation. In the latter part of the month, Adam Black, himself, swore out a complaint to the same effect; adding that the "Mormons" would not submit to the law.

As soon as it was heard that Joseph Smith and a body of followers had gone armed into Daviess County to inquire about their friends, a committee of Ray County citizens came up to Far West to inquire into the reasons of such a movement. A meeting was called and a committee appointed to give the committee from Ray all the information required.

Joseph's movements were watched very closely. On the occasion of his returning from a visit to a company of saints camped on the forks of Grand River, between thirty and forty miles from Far West, he and the small company of brethren with him were chased some distance by a body of armed men, but they escaped.

It was reported that Joseph would not submit to civil process, that he defied the law. A charge had been trumped up in Daviess County against him, for going there in arms to inquire about the Gallatin election troubles, and on the morning of the 13th of August the sheriff of Daviess County and Judge Morin called upon Joseph and informed him that they had a writ for his arrest. Joseph expressed his willingness to be tried, but as the people of Daviess County were very much—though unjustly—exasperated at him, he wished to be tried in his own county, and the laws gave him that right. Upon this insistence the sheriff refused to serve the warrant, and he said he would see Judge King about it. Joseph agreed to remain at home until his return; which he did. On his return the sheriff informed the Prophet that he was out of his jurisdiction.

The excitement which had been aroused, however, could not be abated. On the contrary, it spread into surrounding counties and its intensity increased.

CHAPTER XXXV
BOGGS IN ACTION—DEFENSE
CONSTRUED INTO OFFENSE

This excitement in Daviess and surrounding counties, and the Indian difficulties which were threatening about the same time, induced Governor Boggs [A] to send an order to Gen. David R. Atchison, third division of Missouri militia, ordering him to raise within the limits of his district, four hundred mounted men, armed and equipped as infantry or riflemen, to be held in readiness to quell disturbances arising either from the excitement concerning the "Mormon" troubles, or Indian outbreaks. This order was dated August 30, 1838.

[Footnote A: This was Lilburn W. Boggs who, during the troubles in Jackson County, was lieutenant-governor of the State, and who not only quietly looked on and saw the saints driven from their homes by mob violence, but secretly aided and encouraged the mob in its atrocities.]

In order to show his willingness to honor the law, Joseph, under the counsel of General Atchison, under whom and General Doniphan, Joseph and Sidney Rigdon were studying law, volunteered to be tried for going armed into Daviess County before the circuit judge, Austin A. King. The judge was notified of Joseph's action, and the place selected for trial was the house of a Brother Littlefield, about fifteen miles north of Far West, where the little village of Winston is now located. But as the plaintiff, Wm. P. Peniston, failed to put in an appearance, the trial was postponed until the next day, to take place at the house of a Mr. Raglin, one of the chief mobocrats. The result of the trial was that Joseph and Lyman Wight were bound over in a five hundred dollar bond to appear at the next session of the district court; though Judge King afterwards said nothing worthy of bonds had been proven against them.

The leaders of the mob had sent out representatives into the surrounding counties, asking the people to join them in driving the "Mormons" from the State. They were usually successful in getting assistance, but when the people of Chariton County were appealed to they determined to proceed carefully, and very wisely sent two delegates to Caldwell and Daviess counties, to make inquiries as to the cause of the excitement. These men were at Joseph's trial before Judge King, and at its close accompanied him and his party to Far West, where the information they received convinced them that there was no occasion for the people of Chariton County to join with the surrounding counties in an effort to drive the saints from their homes. Chariton County is due east of Caldwell, with Carroll and Livingston intervening.

The whole country was in a state of intense excitement, and so many wild rumors were afloat, that it was difficult to determine just what the situation was. The brethren, however, were very active in moving from point to point, wherever there was a threatened attack upon their people. Hearing that a wagon load of arms and ammunition was *en route* from Richmond to the mob infesting the vicinity of Diahman, Captain Wm. Allred took a company of ten mounted men and started to intercept the transport. They found the wagon broken down, and the boxes of guns concealed near the roadside in the tall grass; but no one was in sight. Shortly after this party had discovered the arms, they saw moving over the prairie, from the direction of the mob's camp, two horsemen and behind them a third man driving a team. These parties came up to the broken down wagon and were arrested by Captain Allred, by virtue of a writ he held for them issued by the civil authorities of Caldwell County. The prisoners and the guns were taken to Far West, and after an examination before Albert Petty, justice of the peace, they were held to bail for their appearance at the next term of the circuit court. The names of these parties were, J. B. Comer, held as principal, and Wm. L. McHoney and Allen Miller as being in the employ of Comer, engaged in furnishing a mob with arms for an illegal purpose.

Judge King was informed of the arrest of these men, and his advice was asked as to what disposal should be made of the prisoners. He replied that the prisoners must be turned loose and treated kindly. He had no advice to give about the guns, and was at a loss to know how to account for them being in the possession of Comer, as they belonged to government, and had been in the custody of Captain Pollard, living in the vicinity of Richmond. I have already related how the prisoners were held to bail. The guns were distributed among the brethren to be used in self-defense. A few days afterwards the prisoners were delivered up to Gen. A. W. Doniphan; and forty-two stands of the firearms were also collected and delivered to him.

The mob took a number of the brethren prisoners, and sent word to Far West and other settlements that they were torturing them in the most inhuman manner, by this means, doubtless, seeking to provoke the saints to some act of cruelty upon their enemies that might fall into their power, and thus give the mob an excuse for assaulting and driving the "Mormon" community from the State.

All parts of the State were flooded with the falsehoods about "Mormon" atrocities and cruelties—cruelties which never occurred. A bitter prejudice, however, was manufactured against the saints, and people generally believed the "Mormons" were capable of all the crimes known to hardened, sinful wretches; and that they were unfit to live.

In the meantime, the militia Governor Boggs had ordered to be held in readiness, was mustered into service. Under the direction of Gen. Doniphan six companies of fifty men each were collected and armed from the militia of Clay County, and at once marched into the vicinity of Diahman. Here Doniphan found the citizens of Daviess and surrounding counties to the number of two or three hundred under arms, and commanded by Dr. Austin, from Carroll County. They claimed to have collected solely for the purpose of defending the people of Daviess County against the "Mormons." Doniphan read to them the order of his superior officer, General Atchison, to disperse, but this they refused to do.

"I had an interview," said Doniphan, "with Dr. Austin, and his professions were all pacific. But they (Austin's men) still continued under arms, marching and counter marching." The general also visited the encampment of the brethren under the command of Colonel Lyman Wight. Doniphan's report says: "We held a conference with him, and he professed entire willingness to disband, and surrender up to me every one of the 'Mormons' accused of crime; and required in return that the hostile forces collected by the other citizens of the county, should also disband." As they refused to obey the order to disband, the safety of the brethren and their families required that they should continue under arms; and General Doniphan took up a position between the two opposing forces, hoping that if the parties were kept apart, in a few days they would disband without coercion.

In the course of two or three days General Atchison arrived with a body of militia from Ray County. He at once ordered the citizens from the surrounding counties to repair to their respective homes, a movement they began to make with many signs of reluctance. Only about one hundred of them obeyed the order. Atchison reported to Governor Boggs, that he had received assurance from the "Mormons" that all those accused of a violation of the laws would be in for trial the very day on which his report was dated—the 17th of September, 1838. "And," says the report, "when that is done, the troops under my command will be no longer required in this county, if the citizens of other counties will retire to their respective homes."

A day or two after this report, Atchison succeeded in disbanding the mob forces; and the brethren against whom charges were trumped up appeared before a court of inquiry and entered into bonds to appear at the next session of the circuit court. This much having been accomplished, Atchison thought it no longer needful to keep his whole force of militia in the field, hence he dismissed all his forces except two companies, which were left in the vicinity, under the command of Brigadier-General H. G. Parks. In reporting these latter movements to the governor, Atchison says in conclusion:

> The "Mormons" of Daviess County, as I stated in a former report, were encamped in a town called Adam-ondi-Ahman, and they are headed by Lyman Wight, a bold, brave, skillful, and I may add, a desperate man; they appear to be acting on the defensive, and I must further add, gave up the offenders with a good deal of promptness. The arms taken by the "Mormons" and the prisoners were also given up upon demand with cheerfulness.

The forces, then, which had been called out by order of General Atchison were disbanded, except the two companies that were left under the command of General Parks. Parks and these men remained in the vicinity of Diahman, watching both "Mormons" and Gentiles, assisting in serving civil process, and reporting occasionally to his superior officers. As these reports come from a source that is other than a "Mormon" one, he is a witness to the uprightness of the acts of the "Mormon" people at that time of considerable importance; and this must be our excuse for inserting several extracts from his official reports. In a report which Parks made to Governor Boggs, on the 25th of September, occurs the following:

> Whatever may have been the disposition of the people called "Mormons" before our arrival here, since we have made our appearance, they have shown no disposition to resist the law or of hostile intentions. There has been so much prejudice and exaggeration concerned in this matter, that I found things entirely different from what I was prepared to expect. When we arrived here, we found a large body of men from the counties adjoining, armed and in the field, for the purpose, as I learned, of assisting the people of this county against the "Mormons," without being called out by the proper authorities.

In the meantime, a committee of old citizens had agreed to meet with a committee appointed by the saints in Daviess County, for the purpose of making arrangements for either buying the property of the saints, or of selling theirs to the brethren. Speaking of this committee in a postscript to the above report, Parks says: "I received information that if the committee do not agree, the determination of the Daviess County men is to drive the 'Mormons' with powder and lead."

Two days later than the date of Parks' report, General Atchison wrote to the governor, saying:

> The force under General Parks is deemed sufficient to execute the laws and keep the peace in Daviess County. Things are not so bad in that county as represented by rumor, and in fact from affidavits. I have no doubt your Excellency has been deceived by the exaggerated statements of designing or half crazy men. I have found there is no cause of alarm on account of the "Mormons;" they are not to be feared; they are very much alarmed.

These statements, accompanied by the former statements of Atchison and Doniphan, which said the "Mormons" were only acting on the defensive, and had surrendered the arms they had taken from the mob, together with the prisoners, with promptness and cheerfulness, prove that the saints in collecting and arming were merely acting in self-defense, and not with any desire to outrage the laws or injure the Missourians.

CHAPTER XXXVI
DE WITT

Dr. Austin, of Carroll County, who had commanded the mob forces about Diahman, being compelled to disband his forces, at least part of them, he esteemed his force insufficient to drive out the brethren from Diahman; so he conceived the idea of striking a blow in another quarter. In the south-east part of Carroll County, about fifty miles south-east of Far West, and near the point where Grand River empties into the Missouri, is the little settlement called De Witt. Here in the autumn of 1838, a number of the saints were located, quite a number of whom had come from Ohio during the summer of 1838, and were still camped in their wagons and tents. It was to this smaller and weaker settlement that the gallant(!) Dr. Austin lead the remainder of his mob forces, after about one hundred of his original number had returned to their homes in obedience to the orders of General Atchison.

At various times through the summer the mob had threatened the saints in and around De Witt, but it was not until the 20th of September that any serious demonstration of mob violence occurred. On that day about a hundred, perhaps a hundred and fifty men, rode into the settlement and threatened the people with death if they did not agree at once to leave the State, but after some deliberation, they gave them until the 1st of October in which to make their departure. The action of the mob was promptly reported to the governor, and he was asked by the saints to take such steps as would put a stop to all lawless proceedings. The petition making this prayer was signed by over fifty of the brethren living at De Witt, but the governor gave no heed to their prayers for the suppression of lawlessness.

The saints at De Witt of course paid no attention to the demand of the mob made on the 20th of September, that they leave the State by the first of October. So, on the 2nd of that month, early in the morning, about fifty men rode into De Witt and began firing upon the peaceful inhabitants of the place. Henry Root made out an affidavit to the foregoing effect, and at once went to General Parks with it, who was still in the vicinity of Diahman with his two companies of militia. Leaving Colonel Thompson in command at Diahman, General Parks at once ordered two companies of militia under the command of Captains Bogart and Houston to arm and equip, as the law directed, with six days' provisions and fifty rounds of powder and ball. With these companies he marched for De Witt. Just before leaving he sent a messenger to a Colonel Jones, of Carroll County, to call out three companies of the militia and join him at Carrollton, the county seat of Carroll County. This order, however, was ignored.

In his report to General Atchison, General Parks says that when he arrived at De Witt he found the place surrounded by Dr. Austin's men, to the number of some three hundred, provided with a piece of artillery ready to attack the "Mormons" gathered in De Witt. But he expressed the opinion that the "Mormons" could beat Austin even if he had five hundred troops. In the meantime his own forces were mutinous, and refused to act against the mob; hence he had sent word to General Doniphan to raise companies from Platte, Clay, and Clinton counties, as he had no faith that troops ordered from Livingston and other counties would come.

During the time that trouble was threatened at Diahman, which for the time was happily suppressed by General Atchison, Governor Boggs, in addition to the militia ordered out under Atchison, Doniphan and Parks, had directed General S. D. Lucas, of the fourth division of the Missouri militia, to march with four hundred men to join General Atchison at Diahman. Orders similar in their nature were issued to Major-Generals Lewis Bolton, John B. Clark and Thomas D. Grant. But the success of General Atchison in scattering the mob forces about Diahman led to the disbanding of the militia under the generals just named.

This apparently was not relished at all by S. D. Lucas, who, it will be remembered, took an active part in connection with Governor Boggs against the saints in the Jackson County troubles. Hearing of the difficulty arising at De Witt, he thought it another opportunity to strike a blow at the defenseless people he before had assisted in murdering and driving from their homes. He passed down the Missouri River, near where De Witt was located, about the time the actual hostilities began there, and reported the situation to Governor Boggs, and in concluding his letter he says:

> If a fight has actually taken place, of which I have no doubt, it will create excitement in the whole of upper Missouri, and those base and degraded beings (the "Mormons") will be exterminated from the face of the earth. * * * It is an unpleasant state of affairs. The remedy I do not pretend to suggest to your Excellency. My troops were only dismissed subject to further orders, and can be called into the field at an hour's warning.

While Lucas pretended in the above not to suggest a remedy to the governor, he really does so, and plainly offers to carry out the plan. General Lucas says: "Those base and degraded beings (the saints) will be exterminated from the face of the earth," and then follows that statement up by saying that his troops, amounting to four hundred, had only been dismissed subject to further orders, and could be called out at an hour's warning! This act on the part of Lucas was in reality a suggestion to Governor Boggs to exterminate the saints, and an offer on his part to do the job, if he only had orders to call out the men he had but a few days before disbanded. The circumstance is the more significant since his covert suggestion was subsequently acted upon by Governor Boggs.

The people of Chariton County were again asked to assist against the "Mormons," this time to drive them from De Witt; and again the people of that county held a public meeting on the question, and sent a committee of two to inquire into the situation and report. As their report is a complete vindication of the action of the saints in this instance, I make an extract from it:

> We arrived at the place of difficulties on the fourth of October, and found a large portion of the citizens of Carroll and adjoining counties assembled near De Witt well armed. We inquired into the nature of the difficulties. They said there was a large portion of the people called "Mormons," embodied in De Witt, from different parts of the world. They are unwilling for them to remain there, which is the cause of their waging war against them. To use the gentleman's language, they are waging a war of extermination, or to remove them from the said county. We also went into De Witt, to see the situation of the "Mormons." We found them in the act of defense begging for peace, and wishing for the civil authorities to repair there and as early as possible settle the difficulties between the parties. Hostilities have commenced, and will continue until they are stopped by the civil authorities.

As soon as word was brought to Joseph that the saints were shut up by mob forces in De Witt, he at once started for the scene of the trouble to allay, if possible, the excitement among the people. He had some difficulty in getting there, as the mob had all the roads strongly guarded, and allowed neither ingress nor egress to the place they were actually besieging. But by going unfrequented roads and through the woods, he arrived at the besieged town, and found the saints surrounded by a host of their enemies, with their provisions nearly exhausted, and no prospects of obtaining more.

The first thing Joseph did on his arrival was to talk with several gentlemen of respectability and of good standing in the neighborhood, and who were not connected with The Church, but who had witnessed the proceedings of the mob against the saints, and now offered to make affidavits respecting the treatment the saints had received at the hands of the mob forces, and their present perilous situation; and further offered to send a messenger with these papers, and lay the case before the governor. Their proposition was gladly accepted. The affidavits were made out, and a Mr. Caldwell dispatched at once with them to the governor. Instead of sending the people of De Witt any hope of relief, however, the governor said to Mr. Caldwell:

> The quarrel is between the "Mormons" and the mob, and they can fight it out.

This was the death blow to all hopes that had been entertained of receiving relief from the governor when the case should be fairly presented to him. Following close upon this answer that was returned from the chief executive, General Parks sent word to the besieged saints, that his troops under Captain Bogart had mutinied, and in order to prevent them joining the mob he was under the necessity of drawing them away. This act of course turned the people of De Witt over to the tender mercy of the mob led by Dr. Austin, Major Ashley, a member of the State legislature, and Sashiel Woods, a Presbyterian minister.

The saints were hopelessly shut up in De Witt. If their stock wandered outside of the immediate settlement it was shot down by the mob; and if the people went to the outskirts in search of food, they too became the targets of their merciless enemies. Provisions were exhausted, and some of the brethren died of exhaustion and starvation, while all were worn out with constantly watching the movements of their enemies. In this extremity the saints were advised by some of the prominent non-"Mormon" citizens in the vicinity of De Witt to leave that county, and they would be paid for all their losses, Henry Root and David Thomas having secured a promise of the mob that if the "Mormons" would leave De Witt, they should not be molested while doing so. The saints were compelled to accept these terms, and a committee was appointed to appraise the property of the "Mormons." The names of two of this committee are all that have been preserved—Judge Erickson and Major Florey. The only property that was appraised, however, was the real estate; the personal property the saints had lost, and the stock that had been shot down by the mob and upon which they had fed, was not taken into account at all.

The saints gathered up what teams and wagons they had left, and placing the sick, the aged and infirm, together with what personal property they could take with them, they left their fields and their homes in the hands of their enemies, and wended their slow way over the prairie in the direction of Far West. Ever and anon as they looked back with mournful glance in the direction of De Witt, they could see the smoke ascending heavenward from some of their burning homes. That was a dreary march to Far West. They were continually harassed by gangs of the mob who followed them, and others that they met in going to the appointed rendezvous in the vicinity of De Witt. Several brethren died on the way, and had to be buried without coffins, under the most sorrowful circumstances. One sister, who had not recovered from child-birth, through the exposure consequent upon being compelled to leave a comfortable home, died and was buried in a grave bordering the banks of a beautiful stream. The company arrived among their awe-stricken brethren and sisters at Far West on the 12th of October.

CHAPTER XXXVII
MILLPORT

No sooner had the saints departed from De Witt than the Presbyterian preacher, Woods, called the mob that had infested that settlement together, and in a speech of frenzied hate he suggested that they proceed at once to Daviess County and assist their friends in driving the "Mormons" from their homes in that county, as they had already done in Carroll County. He assured them the civil authorities would not interfere to defend the "Mormons," and they could get possession of their property just as well as not. He reminded them that the land sales would soon come off, and if they could but get rid of the "Mormons" they could secure all the lands they would want. To appreciate the force of this part of the preacher's appeal to the mob, the reader must remember that the whole country was wild on land speculations, and that some of the saints were badly tinctured with it, as explained in a previous chapter. The speech had the desired effect, and forthwith the entire body with their cannon started for Daviess County.

While these events were transpiring in Carroll County, Cornelius Gilliam, who, it will be remembered, called upon Zion's Camp at Fishing River several years before, had been engaged in raising a mob in Platte and Clinton counties to accomplish the same object that Parson Woods and his mob had in view. General Doniphan learned of these movements, both on the part of Gilliam and Woods, and sent word to Joseph Smith that a body of eight hundred men were moving upon the settlement of his people in Daviess County. He gave orders for a company of militia to be raised at Far West and marched at once into Daviess County, to defend those who were threatened, until he could raise the militia in Clay and adjoining counties to put down the insurrection. Accordingly a company of one hundred militia-men were gotten in readiness to march into Daviess County. The command was given to Colonel Hinckle and he started for Diahman.

After General Parks had left the vicinity of De Witt with his mutinous militia, he returned to Diahman, where he had left Colonel Thompson in command, and resumed control of affairs in that section.

The mob about Diahman, hearing of the fate of De Witt, and learning of the approach of that mob and the efforts of Gilliam in the same direction, became bolder, and at once began to threaten the saints and burn some of their houses and stacks of hay and grain. These depredations were committed chiefly at a place called Millport, a short distance from Diahman. The house of Don Carlos Smith was burned down, after being plundered, and his wife with two helpless babes were driven out into the night. She made her way to Diahman, carrying her children and having to wade Grand River where the stream was waist deep.

The next day General Parks passed the ruins of this house, belonging to Don Carlos Smith, who was then on a mission in Tennessee, and it seemed to arouse within him a just indignation. He at once went to the house of Lyman Wight and gave him orders to call out his companies of militiamen—Wight holding a colonel's commission in the fifty-ninth regiment of the Missouri militia, commanded by General Parks—and gave him full authority to put down mobs wherever he should find them assembled. He said he wished it distinctly understood that Colonel Wight had full authority from him to suppress all mob violence. The militia that Colonel Wight called out was divided into two companies; one company, consisting of about sixty men, was placed under the command of Captain David Patten, and the other of about the same number was commanded by Wight in person.

Captain Patten was ordered to go to Gallatin and disperse the mobs that were reported to be in that vicinity, while Wight and his company started for Millport.

When Patten's company came in sight of Gallatin, he found a body of the mob, about one hundred strong, who were amusing themselves by mocking and in various ways tantalizing a number of the saints whom they had captured. Seeing the approach of Patten's men, and knowing the determination of the leader, the mob broke and ran in the greatest confusion, leaving their prisoners behind them.

On his march to Millport, Colonel Wight found the whole country deserted by the mob which had infested it, and their houses in flames or in smoldering ruins. The mob having learned that General Parks had ordered out Wight's companies of militia, was seized with sudden fear and swore vengeance, not only upon the "Mormons," but upon Generals Parks and Doniphan as well. To accomplish this purpose, they had loaded up their most valuable personal effects and setting fire to their log huts, they sent runners throughout the State with the lying report that the "Mormons" had "riz" and were burning the houses, destroying property, and murdering the old settlers.

CHAPTER XXXVIII
CROOKED RIVER

That was a cunning piece of diabolism which prompted the mob of Daviess County to set fire to their own huts, destroy their own property and then charge the crime to the saints. It was an act worthy of an incipient Herod. But it was not without a precedent in Missouri. Two years before that, something very similar occurred in Mercer County, just north-east of Daviess. In June of the year 1836, the Iowa Indians, then living in St. Joseph, made a friendly hunting excursion through the northern part of the state, and their line of travel led them through what was known as the Heatherly settlement, in Mercer County. The Heatherlys, who were ruffians of the lowest type, took advantage of the excitement produced by the incursion of the Indians, and circulated a report that they were robbing and killing the whites, and during the excitement these wretches murdered a man by the name of Dunbar, and another man against whom they had a grudge, and then fled to the settlements along the Missouri River, representing that they were fleeing for their lives. This produced great excitement in the settlements in the surrounding counties; the people not knowing at what hour the Indians might be upon them. The militia was called out for their protection; but it was soon ascertained that the alarm was a false one. The Heatherlys were arrested, tried for murder, and some of them sent to the penitentiary.

This circumstance occurring only two years before, and in a county adjacent to Daviess County, doubtless suggested the course pursued by the mob in burning their own houses—chiefly built of logs—and fleeing to all parts of the State with the report that the "Mormons" had done it, and were murdering and plundering the old settlers. These false rumors spread by the mob, were strengthened in the public ear by such men as Adam Black, Judge King of Richmond, and other prominent men who were continually writing inflammatory communications to the governor. The citizens of Ray County called a public meeting and appealed to the governor to protect the people of upper Missouri from the "Mormons," whom they termed a "fearful body of thieves and robbers." It seemed as if the very prince of lies and all his hosts had suddenly broken loose, and sought to overwhelm the saints with a flood of falsehood. It was at this particular crisis that Thomas B. Marsh, the president of the Twelve Apostles, and Orson Hyde, one of the members of the same quorum, fled to Richmond and there testified to the most wicked falsehoods, calculated to bring destruction upon their former brethren. Thomas B. Marsh made an affidavit before Henry Jacobs, a justice of the peace, at Richmond, of which the following is an extract:

> They have among them (the "Mormons") a company consisting of all that are considered true "Mormons," called Danites, who have taken an oath to support the heads of The Church in all things, whether right or wrong. I have heard the Prophet say that he would yet tread down his enemies, and walk over their dead bodies; that, if he was not let alone, he would be a second Mohammed to this generation, and that he would make it one gore of blood from the Rocky Mountains to the Atlantic Ocean.

To this Marsh swore, and Hyde corroborated by affidavit, saying that he knew part of it to be true, and he believed the other.[A]

[Footnote A: It may be as well to say here that some time after this, when the clouds of hatred that at this time threatened the saints with destruction had drifted aside, and these men had time to reflect upon the terrible wickedness of their action, Orson Hyde, in tears, came back to the people he sought to destroy, and humbly begged to be restored to his position. And having manifested a spirit of repentance, he was received back into his place, went on a mission to Jerusalem, and for many years labored faithfully for the advancement of The Church. Thomas B. Marsh, after leading a vagabond life for years, with the brand of Judas upon his brow, and the gnawing of the worm that never dies at his heart, when the saints had weathered the storms of persecution not only in Missouri but also in Illinois as well, and their lives had fallen in the pleasant valleys of the Rocky Mountains, he too, a mere wreck of his former self, weak and driveling and childish; broken down in health and spirits, came humbly bending to the people upon whom he had sought to bring ruin, and begged—humbly begged, the privilege of ending his days in their midst. He arose in a congregation where thousands were congregated, referred to his wrecked condition, and told them it was the effect of apostasy, and warned all against walking in the path which he had trod to his infinite sorrow. His life furnishes a sad page in the history of the Latter-day Saints. He fell as Judas fell, and as Judas failed to stay the work of God in his day, so Marsh failed to break down God's work in these last days: he succeeded only in bringing upon himself the ruin and shame he tried to bring upon The Church.]

Since in this statement made by Thomas B. Marsh and Orson Hyde the "Danites" are spoken of, and as much has been said of this organization, and many false statements made over and over again, accusing The Church of having such an association as described by Marsh and Hyde, I here give in brief an account of that organization so far as The Church knows anything in relation to it.

A Doctor Sampson Avard joined The Church a short time previous to the apostasy of Marsh and Hyde. He was one of those restless, ambitious men who desire to become great, and lord it over their fellow men. Possessing neither the intelligence nor the integrity to rise to positions of honor and trust in The Church by open, fair means, he resolved to become a leader by craft and villainy. He employed the art of flattery in his conversations with the brethren, appointed frequent meetings at his own house which was guarded by one or more of his trusted associates, who would give him a sign if any one approached whom he had not trusted. With an air of mystery he would intimate that he had been appointed by the heads of The Church to accomplish some important work of a secret character, and at last put those whom he had won by his flattery, under an oath of eternal secrecy, not to reveal anything that he should communicate to them.

By these means he continued to enlarge his band, which he named *The Danites,* claiming of course that it was a very ancient order or society. He gave to them certain secret signs by which members of the band could recognize each other either day or night. He gave them to understand that he had authority from the heads of The Church for what he was about to do. He then proceeded to organize his men into companies of tens and fifties, placing a captain over each. Up to this time Avard had never intimated that anything unlawful or contrary to the spirit of the gospel was to be carried out. But now that he had the companies organized and all under an oath of secrecy, he thought he could with safety let the mask fall. After instructing the men as to what their duties were under their several captains, he took the captains into a secluded place and there told them they would soon be permitted to go among the Gentiles and take their property as spoil, and by robbing and plundering the Gentiles, they were to waste them away and with the property thus confiscated build up the Kingdom of God. If any of the band were recognized by their enemies, "who could harm them?" he asked: "for," said he, "we will stand by each other, and defend one another in all things. If our enemies swear against us, we can swear also." At this point some of the brethren expressed surprise, in fact, astonishment. But Avard continued by saying:

> As the Lord liveth I would swear to a lie to clear any of you;
> and if this would not do, I would put them or him under

the sand as Moses did the Egyptian. * * * And if any of us transgress, we will deal with him amongst ourselves. And if any one of this Danite society reveals any of these things, I will put him where the dogs cannot bite him.

This lecture of the doctor's revealed for the first time the true intent of his designs, and the brethren he had duped suddenly had their eyes opened, and they at once revolted and manfully rejected his teachings. Avard saw that he had played and lost, so he said they had better let the matter drop where it was. As soon as Avard's villainy was brought to the knowledge of the president of The Church he was promptly excommunicated, and was afterwards found making an effort to become friends with the mob, and conspiring against The Church.

This is the history of the Danite band, "which," says the Prophet Joseph, "died almost before it had an existence."

And now I return to the main line of my narrative. Captain Bogart, who, it will be remembered, held a command in the militia under General Parks, both in the operations about Diahman and before De Witt, and who on one occasion manifested a determination to mutiny and join the mob, was one of the bitterest enemies the saints had, and the most active of the mob. On the twenty-fourth of October, 1838, he, with about forty of his followers, called at the house of a Brother Thoret Parsons who lived on the east branch of Log Creek southeast of Far West. He warned Parsons to leave by ten o'clock the next day and remarked that he expected to give Far West "hell" before noon the next day; provided he was successful in joining his forces with those of Niel Gilliam who would camp that night six miles west of Far West, and that he himself should camp that night on Crooked River. A messenger was dispatched at once with this information to Far West, and Parsons followed the mob to watch their movements.

The day on which this occurred Joseph Holbrook [B] and a Brother Judith were watching the movements of a small detachment of Bogart's men, and saw eight of them enter the house of a Brother Pinkham, where they took three prisoners and four horses, together with some arms and food; and warned the old gentleman Pinkham to leave the State at once or they "would have his d—d old scalp." This detachment then started to join Bogart's main company, and Holbrook and Judith started for Far West. They arrived there near midnight and reported what they had seen in the vicinity of the mob's encampment. The blast of the trumpet and the roll of the drum soon brought together a large crowd of men to the public square.

Men slept very lightly in those days, as they had to be constantly on hand to repel the attacks of their enemies. The men had been assembled by order of Judge Higbee, and he requested Lieutenant-Colonel Hinkle to raise a company to disperse the mob, and rescue the prisoners. Volunteers were called for, and in a few minutes seventy-five men had answered the call and were placed under the command of David W. Patten, who it will be remembered held a captain's commission in the state militia. He was also a member of the quorum of the Twelve.

[Footnote B: This was Judge Holbrook, late of Bountiful, Davis County, Utah.]

The company marched out some distance from Far West, where it halted, and the body was divided into three divisions, the commands of which were given to David W. Patten, James Durphy, and Charles C. Rich, the whole being under the direction of David W. Patten. The march to the scene of action is thus described by one of the company:

> The night was dark, the distant plains far and near were illuminated with blazing fires, immense columns of smoke were seen rising in awful majesty, as if the world was on fire. This scene of grandeur can only be comprehended by those acquainted with scenes of prairie burning, as the fire sweeps over millions of acres of dry grass in the fall season, and leaves a smooth, black surface divested of all vegetation. The thousand meteors blazing in the distance like the camp fires of some war hosts, threw a fitful gleam of light upon the distant sky, which many might have taken for the Aurora Borealis. This scene, added to the silence of midnight, the rumbling sounds of the trampling steeds over the hard surface of the plain, the clank of the swords in their scabbards, the occasional gleam of bright armor in the flickering firelight, the gloom of surrounding darkness, and the unknown destiny of the expedition, or even the people who sent it forth; all combined to impress the mind with deep and solemn thoughts, and to throw a romantic vision over the imagination, which is not often experienced except in the poet's dreams, or in the wild imagery of sleeping fancy.[C]

[Footnote C: Autobiography of Parley P. Pratt, ch. 21.]

The mob were encamped in a bend of Crooked River near the line of Caldwell and Ray counties, and I should judge all of fifteen miles directly south of Far West. The stream here lies imbedded in a deep ravine, in fact this may be said of all the streams in this part of Missouri. There has been but little disturbance of the earth's crust in this locality, and the streams, having run in their present course for ages, perhaps ever since our Father Adam and the patriarchs dwelt in the land, have worn their channels deep. At any rate, at the place where the mob was camped, and which old settlers pointed out to me as "Bogart's Battle Field," the stream lies in the bottom of a deep ravine, the sides of which are quite steep and covered with a heavy growth of underbrush and timber. A dugway road has been cut on the north side of the ravine leading down to a point where the stream is fordable. It is just above this ford where Bogart and his men were encamped in a little bottom immediately on the bank of the river.

When the brethren from Far West were within two or three miles of this encampment they dismounted, and, leaving their horses in the care of a part of their company, the rest proceeded on foot to the brow of the hill under which the mob was encamped. It must be remembered that Captain Patten did not know the exact locality of the mob, but supposed they had camped somewhere about the ford of the river. Near the brow of the hill the companies separated, Patten's division going to the right, Rich's to the left, and Durphy's between them. They were proceeding along silently when suddenly the stillness was broken by some one exclaiming, "Who comes there?" followed instantly by the sharp report of a rifle, and a young man of the name of Patrick O'Banion reeled from the ranks and fell, mortally wounded. Captain Patten ordered a charge down the hillside upon the mob below, which was promptly obeyed. The mob left their encampment and formed in a line under the bank of the river. Patten's men formed in a line facing them, and the mob opened fire, which was promptly answered by the brethren and then followed a moment's silence, which was broken by C. C. Rich calling the watchwords:

"God and Liberty."

Patten ordered a second charge upon the enemy and then the fight was hand to hand. The fight, however, was but of short duration; the mob soon began leaping into the stream and making for the other side.

The late Judge Holbrook of Davis County, Utah, was struck at by a fierce Missourian with a sword, but by throwing up his left arm he saved his head, and before the mobber could recover himself the judge had cut him down. Two of the hindmost men of the mob were pursued by Captains Patten and Rich. The one followed by Patten suddenly wheeled round and shot him in the bowels, and he fell mortally wounded. Gideon Carter's face was so literally shot to pieces that he was almost beyond recognition. Several others were wounded in this engagement, about nine, I think, but they recovered. The mob had the advantage of position in the engagement, as they formed under the bank of the river, which answered all the purposes of a breastwork. It will be remembered too that it was not yet daylight—the dawn was only just breaking in the east when the fight began. The mob in their flight left their horses and all their camp utensils. These the victors took charge of, and making litters on which to carry their wounded and dying, they started on the return to Far West. Several miles from Far West the mournful train was met by a number of the brethren, among whom was the Prophet Joseph and his brother Hyrum and the wife of Captain Patten. Tender hands had carried him on a litter from the battle field, but he suffered excruciating pains and asked to be laid down by the wayside that he might die. He was taken to the house of a Brother Winchester about three miles from Far West, where he died that night.

I need not dwell upon the heartrending sorrow of the wife at the loss of a noble husband, or the grief of the whole people who mourned the departure of a great and good man, and one of the leading spirits in these last days. He died full of faith, having done as he often said he would do, if need were— lay down his life for his friends. Just before he breathed his last he said to his grief-stricken wife, "Whatever you do else, O, do not deny the faith!"

Young O'Banion died shortly afterwards, and they were buried together with military honors. The body of Gideon Carter was afterwards brought up from the battle ground, and interred at Far West. The loss of the mob has never been correctly ascertained, but at the time they scattered before the impetuous charge of Patten's men, each one supposed he was the only survivor left to tell the tale of the mob's destruction.

This battle on Crooked River, though perfectly justifiable on the part of the saints, was made the excuse for raising armies against them for their destruction. The following inflammatory and untruthful message was sent to the governor as a report of what we have already related:

> SIR:—We were informed last night by an express from Ray County, that Captain Bogart and all his company, amounting to between fifty and sixty men, were massacred at Buncombe, twelve miles north of Richmond, except

three. This statement you may rely on as being true, and last night they expected Richmond to be laid in ashes this morning. We could distinctly hear cannon, and we knew the "Mormons" had one in their possession. Richmond is about twenty-five miles west of this place, on a straight line. We know not the hour or minute we shall be laid in ashes—our county is ruined—for God's sake give us assistance as soon as possible.

Yours, etc.,

SASHIEL WOODS,
JOSEPH DICKSON.

Woods will be remembered as the Presbyterian preacher who, after the saints were compelled to leave De Witt, called the mob which had infested that place and urged them to hasten to the assistance of their friends in Daviess County, to drive the "Mormons" away from their settlement at Diahman, that they might gain possession of their lands. These men say they distinctly heard cannon and they knew the "Mormons" had one. Yet these men were thirty-seven miles from where the engagement on Crooked River occurred, and no cannon was used—and the one in possession of the saints was only a six-pounder. "These mobbers," said Joseph, "must have had very acute ears; * * * so much for the lies of a priest of this world."

One of Bogart's men fled to Richmond and reported that ten of his comrades had been killed and the rest taken prisoners after many of them had been wounded; and he said it was the intention of the "Mormon banditti" that night to sack and burn Richmond. Upon the reception of this lying report C. R. Morehead was dispatched from Richmond to Lexington, a town located on the south bank of the Missouri on the high bluffs overlooking the river, and only about eight miles south of Richmond. He begged the people of that town to come to the assistance of Richmond, and they responded by sending one hundred well armed, and according to E. M. Ryland, "daring men, the most effective our county can boast of." An express was sent from Lexington to Messrs. Amos Rees and Wiley C. Williams of Jackson County, then en route for the city of Jefferson, ordering them to hurry on to the city of Jefferson, imparting correct (?) information to the public as they went along; and to send one of their party into Cooper, Howard and Boone counties in order that volunteers might be getting ready to flock to the scene of trouble as soon as possible. The letter said: "They [the volunteers before alluded to] must make haste and put a stop to the devastation which is menaced by these infuriated fanatics, and they *must go prepared, and with a full determination to exterminate or expel them from the State en masse."*

The italics are mine, and I use them because it was upon the strength of this message that Governor Boggs afterwards issued his celebrated exterminating order. And I pause here to call attention to the fact that these men, Wiley C. Williams and Amos Rees had started for Jefferson City as special messengers to the governor to secure the banishment of the saints from the State of Missouri. These untruthful reports of the trouble on Crooked River were favorable to their cause, and an express was sent after them to add this falsehood to those with which they were already laden, and to wish them "God speed" in their murderous affairs! We need not say the "Mormons" had not so much as thought of going to Richmond, or acting otherwise than on the defensive.

CHAPTER XXXIX
EXTERMINATING ORDER OF
GOVERNOR BOGGS

In the meantime the messengers from those parties who had burned their own homes and destroyed their own property at Millport had reached Jefferson City, and poured into the willing ears of the executive the villainous falsehoods that the "Mormons" with an armed force had expelled the old settlers from Daviess County, pillaged and burned their dwellings, driven off their stock, and destroyed their crops. They also said that Millport and Gallatin were in ashes, and that all the records of the county were destroyed. Upon the reception of this batch of falsehoods and an application from these people to be restored to their homes and protected in them, Governor Boggs set himself vigorously at work calling out militia forces to accomplish this object.

One can not help pausing a moment to notice the difference in the action of the State authorities in two cases that would have been just alike, provided the report of those parties who fled from Daviess County, by the light of their burning homes, had been true. In 1833 the saints were driven by brute force and under circumstances the most distressing, from their possessions in Jackson County. And not only was their property destroyed, but quite a number of them were killed, while the number that was exiled amounted to twelve hundred. The State authorities had the fullest evidence of these outrages—in fact the very man who at the time of the Daviess County troubles was governor of the State, was on the ground and knew of all the circumstances of cruelty and outrage. But when those things came before the State authorities, it took more than two whole years of correspondence to come to an understanding of what could and should be done, and then the decision was that the exiles would do well to move still further on, in fact, get entirely away from that section of the country where they had made their homes, as the prejudices of the people were set against them, and the popular sentiment in this country was *vox Dei!* But now, when a mere rumor comes that the "Mormons" have been guilty of inflicting upon the Missourians the outrages which aforetime had been perpetrated against them, there is no halting on the part of the authorities, but on the contrary the most vigorous efforts are put forth to punish the reputed offenders, and reinstate the supposed exiles!

Governor Boggs, then, began his efforts to restore these reputed exiles to their homes. He sent an order to General John B. Clark, of the first division of Missouri militia, directing him to raise two thousand men from the first, fourth, fifth, sixth and twelfth divisions of the militia to be mounted and armed as the law directs, provided with rations for fifteen days, and to rendezvous at Fayette in Howard County, about eighty miles southeast of Far West, by the third of November.

This order was dated the twenty-sixth of October, 1838. The next day, however, Amos Rees and Wiley C. Williams arrived in Jefferson City with their false report of the battle on Crooked River, and Governor Boggs changed his orders to General Clark the same day. This letter is Boggs' exterminating order. He said to General Clark:

> Since the order of the morning to you, * * * I have received by Amos Rees, Esq., and Wiley C. Williams, one of my aids, information of the most appalling character, which changes the whole face of things and places the "Mormons" in the attitude of open and avowed defiance of the laws, and of having made open war upon the people of this State. Your orders are, therefore, to hasten your operations and endeavor to reach Richmond, in Ray County, with all possible speed. The "Mormons" must be treated as enemies and *must be exterminated* or driven from the State, if necessary for the public good. Their outrages are beyond description. If you can increase your force, you are authorized to do so to any extent you may think necessary.

The governor also ordered Major General Wallock of Marion County, to raise five hundred men, and join General Doniphan of Clay County, who had been directed to raise a like number of men, and together they were to proceed to Daviess County to cut off the retreat of the "Mormons" to the north. General Parks had been ordered to raise four hundred men and join Clark at Richmond, and thus the campaign was planned. The troops were not to reinstate the supposed exiles of Daviess County in their homes and protect them, but they were to operate directly against the "Mormons"—in fact, make war upon them—exterminate them, or drive them from the State.

Up to this time Major General Atchison had apparently exercised his influence counseling moderation in dealing with the "Mormons." He was a resident of Clay County when the saints were driven into that county from Jackson. He, with General Doniphan and Amos Rees, had acted as counsel for the exiles, and had seen the doors of the temples of justice closed in their faces by mob violence, and all redress denied them. He was acquainted with the circumstances which led to their removal from Clay County, to the unsettled prairies of what afterwards became Caldwell County. He knew how deep and unreasonable the prejudices were against the saints. Can it be possible that he did not know how utterly unjustifiable the present movement against them was? Whether he was blinded by the false reports about Millport and Gallatin and Crooked River, or whether his courage faltered, and he became afraid longer to defend a people against whom every man's hand was raised, I cannot now determine, but one or the other must have been the case for I find him joining with S. D. Lucas in the following communication to Governor Boggs:

> SIR:—From late outrages committed by the "Mormons," civil war is inevitable. They have set the laws of the country at defiance and are in open rebellion. We have about two thousand men under arms to keep them in check. The presence of the commander in chief is deemed absolutely necessary, and we most respectfully urge that your excellency be at the seat of *war* as soon as possible.

> Your most obedient, etc.

> DAVID R. ATCHISON, M. G. 3rd Div.
> SAMUEL D. LUCAS, M. G. 4th Div.

General Atchison, however, was afterwards "dismounted," to use a word of General Doniphan's in relating the incident, and sent back to Liberty in Clay County by special order of Governor Boggs, on the ground that he was inclined to be too merciful to the "Mormons." So that he was not active in the operations about Far West. But how he could consent to join with Lucas in sending such an untruthful and infamous report to the governor about the situation in upper Missouri, is difficult to determine. The saints had not set the laws at defiance, nor were they in open rebellion. But when all the officers of the law refused to hear their complaints, and both civil and military authority delivered them into the hands of merciless mobs to be plundered and outraged at their brutal pleasure, and all petitions for protection at the hands of the governor had been answered with: *"It is a quarrel between the Mormons and the mob, and they must fight it out,"* what was left for them to do but to arm themselves and stand in defense of their homes and families? It is not admitted in the above that the saints had defied the laws of the country, for it was not so. The movement on Gallatin by Captain Patten and that on Millport by Colonel Wight was ordered by General Parks, who called upon Colonel Wight to take command of his company of men, when the militia under Parks' command mutinied, and disperse all mobs wherever he found them. Gallatin was not burned, nor were the records of the county court, if they were destroyed at all, destroyed by the saints. What houses were burned in Millport had been set on fire by the mob. The expedition to Crooked River was ordered by Judge Higbee, the first judge in Caldwell County and the highest civil authority in Far West, and was undertaken for the purpose of dispersing a mob which had entered the house of a peaceable citizen—one Pinkham—and carried off three people prisoners, four horses and other property, and who had threatened to "give Far West hell before noon the next day." So that in their operations the acts of the saints had been strictly within the law, and only in self defense.

CHAPTER XL
HAUN'S MILL

The mob forces were gathering from all quarters to destroy Far West. Niel Gilliam was in the west urging the citizens to drive the "Mormons" from the State. Generals Lucas and Wilson, who will be remembered as active leaders of the mob which expelled the saints from Jackson County, were collecting those same mob forces; while General Clark was in the south raising companies of men to carry out the exterminating order of Governor Boggs.

In addition to these preparations for the destruction of the saints, in the counties immediately surrounding Caldwell, there was a general uprising of the old settlers under no particular leadership, but roaming through the scattered settlements of the saints in small bands, murdering, stealing stock, house-burning, whipping the men and driving the terror-stricken women and children from their homes. In fact, the whole country surrounding Far West was infested with a merciless banditti, which daily were guilty of the most atrocious deeds of cruelty. The saints living in a scattered condition over the prairies who were fortunate enough to escape with their lives, came running into Far West at all times of the day and night, white with fear. Let is here be said that the Prophet Joseph and counseled his people to settle in villages, and have their farms on the outskirts thereof, after the pattern, as far as circumstances would permit, of the plan given by revelation for building up the city of Zion, described in a former chapter of this volume. He had urged, in addition to the improved opportunities this plan would give them for educating their children, etc., that they would be in a better condition to defend themselves against their enemies. But the saints, at least many of them, would not hearken to this advice; now, however, that the enemy was upon them, when it was too late for them to profit by it, they could see the wisdom of it.

It was one of these marauding bands, under the leadership of Nehemiah Comstock, which was guilty of a fiendish massacre at Haun's Mill, on the thirtieth of October. Haun's Mill was between ten and twelve miles nearly due east of Far West, on the south bank of Shoal Creek, which takes a meandering course, though in the main flowing east, and finally empties into Grand River. All told there were about thirty families of the saints located at Haun's Mill, several of which had just recently arrived from the eastern states, and were camped in their wagons and tents behind an old blacksmith's shop adjacent to the mill. The banks of the stream were lined with a growth of scattered trees and an undergrowth of hazel and other brush; while back from the banks is the rather sharp rolling prairie common to that part of Missouri.

This little body of saints had been threatened by mobs for some time and were therefore on their guard. On the twenty-eighth of October, however, Colonel Jennings, of Livingston County, whose band of mobbers had been most menacing to the peace and safety of the saints, sent one of his men to the settlement to make a treaty of peace. This proposition of peace was gladly accepted by the saints, in fact, it was what they most devoutly prayed for. There was to be mutual forbearance, and each party was to exert itself to the extent of its influence to prevent further hostilities. There were other mobs collecting in the vicinity, however, who were not affected by this agreement of peace entered into by the saints and Colonel Livingston— one particularly on Grand River, at William Mann's residence. Hence the brethren in the little settlement on Shoal Creek remained under arms.

The thirtieth of October, the day on which the fearful tragedy occurred, is said by some of the survivors to have been a most beautiful one: one of those days in mid-autumn, when smoky mists hang about the horizon—the sure sign of the Indian summer; when the sun shines with all the brightness, but without the scorching heat, of August; when the gentle breeze rustles through the ripened corn and softly stirs the leaves of the forests that have been kissed by the early frosts and autumn sun to purple and gold, and all the shades and tints known to the practiced eye of the artist; when the sinking sun paints the heavens with new glories; and when hill and plain, stream and sky, forest and field all reflect the fullness of nature's beauties. Oh, is it not passing strange that one of God's fairest days should be made to look upon so foul a deed as that committed at Haun's Mill! The merry laughter of the children as they played upon the banks of Shoal Creek, mingled with the snatches of songs the mothers sang as they went about their domestic employments, made sweet music to the fathers engaged in gathering the crops, or guarding the mill.

In their neighborhood all apparently was peace, and no premonitory shuddering warned the saints of their approaching fate. It burst upon them with all the suddenness of a clap of thunder from a cloudless sky. The sun had sunken more than halfway down the western sky, when some of those on guard saw a large body of armed and mounted men approaching the mill at full speed. They came through the scattering timber on the bank of the creek to the edge of the prairie, where they formed themselves in a three square position with a vanguard. David Evans ran out to meet them, swinging his hat and crying, "Peace! Peace!"

But there was no peace.

The saints by this time were in the wildest state of excitement, and running in every direction, many of the men taking refuge in an old blacksmith shop not far from the mill. The leader of the mob, numbering two hundred and forty, fired his gun, and after a pause of a few seconds about a hundred shots were fired into the old blacksmith shop, and at those fleeing for the protection of the woods. The mob then rode up to the shop and fired through the space between the logs until, as they thought, all had been killed or mortally wounded. They then entered, and among the dead and dying found Sardius Smith, a lad about twelve years old, who in his fear had crawled under the bellows for safety. He was dragged from his place of concealment by a Mr. Glaze, who placed the muzzle of his gun near the boy's head and literally shot off the top of it. The inhuman wretch afterwards shamelessly boasted of his damning deed. His brother, Alma, a boy of eight summers, was shot through the hip. He had seen his father and brother shot down, and fearing if he moved the heartless wretches would shoot him again, he remained quiet among the dead until he heard the voice of his mother gently calling his name in the darkness. She nursed him tenderly, prayerfully, and under the inspiration of heaven made such a collection of herbs and barks with which she dressed his wound that he recovered, grew to manhood, lived to a reasonably good old age, and lately died at Coalville, Summit County, Utah.

Thomas McBride, an old gray haired veteran of the American Revolution, was met by a number of the mob in front of Mr. Haun's house. The old man, trembling with age rather than from fear, surrendered his gun, saying: "Spare my life, I am a Revolutionary soldier." But the inhuman wretch to whom he made this simple, pathetic appeal, sufficient to have moved adamantine hearts, shot the veteran down with his own gun, and then a Mr. Rogers, of Daviess County, fell upon him and hacked him to pieces with an old corn cutter. And there lay the veteran soldier of the Revolution, covered with a score of unsightly wounds, either of which alone had been fatal—his brains oozing from his cracked skull, and his white hairs crimsoned with his gore! Oh, a hard fate to overtake one of that noble band, who gave the best years of his life to his country's service, that liberty might survive oppression!

As night drew her sable mantle over the ghastly scene about Haun's Mill, those who had escaped to the woods returned to learn the fate of their friends. I need not dwell upon the horrors of that awful night in which wives with bursting hearts sought for their husbands, and mothers searched for their sons among the mangled bodies of the dead. Nor need I pause to relate in detail the sights revealed by the morning light. According to the statement of the leaders of the mob, they had fired seven rounds each, making in all some sixteen hundred shots fired at a company in which there were not more than thirty men. Nineteen of the men and boys were killed outright in this inhuman butchery, and some twelve to fifteen were wounded more or less severely. The few men who escaped with their lives, the following day carried the bodies of the slain to an old vault which had been dug for a well, and there the butchered were interred in haste, as those performing these sad offices were under fear every moment that the mob would return to massacre the survivors of the tragedy of the day before.

This Haun's Mill butchery may very properly be regarded as the first fruits of Governor Boggs' exterminating order. On the twenty-eight of October, Colonel Jennings, of Livingston County, had entered into a treaty of peace with the saints at Haun's Mill, and each party agreed to use whatever of influence it possessed for peace; and while we cannot learn whether that same colonel was in the company which did the killing or not, still it is known that a few days after the massacre, he, in company with other leading men in upper Missouri, among whom was Mr. Ashby, member of the State legislature from Chariton, went about threatening the lives of the survivors, stealing their property, laying waste their crops and running off their stock. My own view of the circumstances is that after the treaty of peace entered into on the twenty-eighth, Colonel Jennings' men, with other mob forces, heard of the exterminating order of Governor Boggs, and gathered together under the leadership of Comstock and undertook to carry out the monstrous edict that was worthy only of a Nero, a Caligula, or a Domitian.

CHAPTER XLI
THE BETRAYAL OF FAR WEST

In the meantime the mob forces, called "the governor's troops," had gathered about Far West to the number of two thousand two hundred men, armed and equipped for war. The main body of these forces had marched from Richmond under the command of Major General Samuel D. Lucas, starting on the 29th of October. The following day he was joined by the forces of General Doniphan at the ford of Log Creek, not far from Far West. Here they received the exterminating order of Governor Boggs. This order made no provisions for the protection of the innocent, the "Mormons" were either to be exterminated or driven from the State, regardless of their guilt or innocence as individuals.

On the morning of the 30th, the citizens of Far West had been informed of the approach of large bodies of armed men from the south, and sent out a company of one hundred and fifty of their number to learn the character of these forces, whether they were friendly or otherwise. The scouting party was soon convinced that the intentions of the approaching forces were hostile, and found some difficulty themselves in returning to Far West without being captured by the mob militia. As they approached the city in the evening, they were discovered by General Doniphan, who received permission from General Lucas to try and capture them; but having a superior knowledge of the ground, they escaped.

Seeing these large bodies of men approach, what militia there was in Far West was drawn up in line just south of the city to oppose the advance of the formidable enemy. Both parties sent out a flag of truce, and they met between the two forces. In answer to the inquiry of the citizens of Far West as to who the mob forces were and what their intentions, the reply was, "We want three persons out of the city before we massacre the rest." [A] Hostilities, however, were postponed until the next day, and the mob began the work of encampment along the borders of a small stream called Goose Creek. During the night, the people in Far West constructed, as best they could, some rude fortifications south of the city, and were reinforced in the night by Lyman Wight and a small body of men from Diahman.

[Footnote A: P. P. Pratt's Autobiography, page 201. The man sent out with the flag of truce from Far West was the late C. C. Rich.]

The mob forces were also strengthened during the night by the arrival from the west of Niel Gilliam's bands, who were dressed and painted like Indians, and doubtless more savage than the savages whose dress, paint, and horrible yells they imitated. The mob forces under Comstock, with their hands dripping with the blood of their Haun's Mill victims, also joined Lucas during the night.

That was a terrible night of suspense for Far West. The people had learned of the massacre at Haun's Mill; they knew the murderous intentions of the mob forces encamped within two miles of their homes, and outnumbering the people of Far West by more than four to one, and clothed with a seeming authority by the highest officer in the State, to resist which, however outrageous or barbarous the conduct of the mob might be, would give further excuse for their extermination. How true the saying: "When the wicked rule, the people mourn!"

It was with heavy hearts and sinking hopes that the saints watched the first approach of the gray dawn that ushered in the 31st of October. About eight o'clock a flag of truce was sent out (Joseph and other Church writers say) by the mob forces; Lucas in his report to Governor Boggs says: "I received a message from Colonel Hinkle, the commander of the 'Mormon' forces, [Caldwell militia] requesting an interview with me on an eminence near Far West, which he would designate by hoisting a white flag. I sent him word I would meet him at two o'clock p. m., being so much engaged in receiving and encamping fresh troops, who were hourly coming in, that I could not attend before."

It may be, judging from the subsequent treachery of Colonel Hinkle, that he sent a secret messenger to Lucas requesting an interview, and that the white flag sent out by the mob forces, of which our Church annals speak, and which was met by Hinkle in person with a few others, was sent to give General Lucas' answer to Hinkle's earlier request for an interview. At any rate, the truce flag was sent out and was met by some of the brethren, among whom was Hinkle; and if anything special was learned, or accommodations arranged, or understanding arrived at by the conference held with the enemy's flag of truce, our writers have failed to mention it. The reasonable conclusion is, therefore, that the flag of truce merely brought to Colonel Hinkle the information that Lucas could not meet him until two o'clock; and that Hinkle did meet him at that time; and upon his own responsibility, without consulting with the citizens of Far West or their leaders, entered into, and bound the people to, the following terms of capitulation:

First. To give up all their [The Church] leaders to be tried and punished.

Second. To make an appropriation of their property, all who have taken up arms, to the payment of their debts, and indemnify for damage done by them.

Third. That the balance should leave the State, and be protected out by the militia, but to remain until further orders were received from the commander in chief.

Fourth. To give up their arms of every description, to be receipted for.

According to Lucas' statement, Hinkle, while he readily accepted these terms of capitulation, desired to postpone the matter until the following morning; to which Lucas replied that if that was done he would demand that Joseph Smith, Junior, Sidney Rigdon, Lyman Wight, Parley P. Pratt and George W. Robinson be surrendered to his custody as hostages for his faithful compliance with the foregoing terms; and if after reflection and consultation the people decided to reject the terms offered them, these hostages were to be returned at the point where they were delivered into his possession.[B]

[Footnote B: Report of Lucas to Governor Boggs, dated November 2, 1838. Headquarters near Far West.]

Let us pause here for a moment's reflection. If Lucas intended to deliver up those men again, what advantage was it for him to have them? According to his own statement he offered Hinkle terms of capitulation which he and the people affected were to consider and report their conclusions upon the following day; but Lucas demands the principal "Mormon" leaders as hostages for the faithful performance—of what? Merely to bind them to consider the terms of capitulation, according to Lucas' statement; and if those terms were rejected after due consideration and consultation, these hostages were to be restored to the people! Was there any need of hostages being given to insure the consideration of the terms of surrender offered? Not under the circumstances. The whole thing was a plan to get the leaders of The Church into the hands of the mob, that the governor's order of extermination or banishment might be carried out without the mob militia running the risk of some of them losing their lives; as their generals believed the saints would submit to any injustice or indignity, rather than endanger the lives of their prophet leaders by resisting it. These men were demanded as a pledge that the whole infamous agreement between Lucas and Hinkle should be faithfully performed on Hinkle's part; and not to insure the consideration of his terms of surrender as Lucas clumsily puts it. As I proceed with the narrative it will be seen that Lucas never intended to restore the prisoners to their friends.

Hinkle returned from the secret consultation with Lucas, and about four o'clock in the afternoon told Joseph Smith and the other men Lucas demanded as hostages, that the leaders of the governor's troops desired a consultation with them outside the city limits. Accordingly the brethren, in company with Hinkle, walked out of Far West in the direction of the enemy's encampment. When midway between that encampment and Far West, the little band of brethren were met by the mob forces. Lucas occupied a central place, followed by fifty artillerymen, with a four-pounder; while the remainder of the forces, amounting to over two thousand, came up on the right and left. As soon as Lucas came up, Lyman Wight shook hands with him and said: "We understand, General, you wish to confer with us a few moments; will not tomorrow morning do as well?"

Here Colonel Hinkle said:

"General Lucas, these are the prisoners I agreed to deliver to you."

Lucas brandished his sword and told these men from Far West that they were his prisoners, and that they would march into his camp without further delay!

"At this moment," says Lyman Wight, "I believe there were five hundred guns cocked and twenty caps bursted, and more hideous yells were never heard, even if the description of the yells of the damned in hell is true as given by the modern sects of the day." [C] Especially horrible and threatening were the yells and threats of Niel Gilliam's company, costumed and painted as Indians.

[Footnote C: Wight's affidavit, Times and Seasons, Vol. 4, page 267.]

The brethren had been basely betrayed by Hinkle, as he had never consulted with them or any of the leaders of the people in relation to the terms of surrender offered by Lucas; and by misrepresentation he had induced them to place themselves in the hands of their implacable enemies. So long as treason is detested, and traitors despised, so long will the memory of Colonel Hinkle be execrated for his vile treachery.

On reaching the enemy's camp, ninety men were called out to guard the prisoners. Thirty were on this duty at a time: two hours on and four hours off. The prisoners lay in the open air with nothing as a covering, and they were drenched with rain before morning. All night long they were mocked and taunted by the guard, who demanded signs, saying, "Come, Mr. Smith, show us an angel, give us one of your revelations, show us a miracle;" [D] mingling these requests with the vilest oaths. Sidney Rigdon had an attack of apoplectic fits, which afforded much merriment to the brutal guard.

[Footnote D: P. P. Pratt's Autobiography, page 204.]

All night long the prisoners were compelled to listen to the filthy obscenity of those who watched them, and hear them relate their deeds of rapine and murder, and boast of their conquest over virtuous wives and maidens by brute force. Thus the wretched night passed away.

The morning following, which was the 1st of November, Hyrum Smith and Amasa Lyman were brought into the mob's camp as prisoners.

According to Hinkle's agreement, the militia in Far West were marched out of the city and grounded their arms, which were taken possession of by Lucas, although they were not State arms, but were the private property of the men who carried them. The mob was now let loose upon the unarmed citizens of Far West, and under the pretext of searching for arms they ransacked every house, tore up the floors, upset haystacks, wantonly destroyed much property, and shot down a number of cattle just for the sport it afforded them. The people were robbed of their most valuable property, insulted and whipped; but this was not the worst. The chastity of a number of women was defiled by force; some of them were strapped to benches and repeatedly ravished by brutes in human form until they died from the effects of this treatment. The horrible threat made a few years before in Jackson County had been at last carried out—*We will ravish their women!*

At night a court-martial was held, consisting of some fourteen militia officers, among whom were Colonel Hinkle and about twenty priests of the different denominations. Sashiel Woods and Bogart, the Presbyterian ministers, were among them; and in addition to these spiritual dignitaries, there was the circuit judge, Austin A. King and the district attorney, Mr. Birch. The decision of the court was that the prisoners should be shot the following morning at eight o'clock, in the public square of Far West, in the presence of their families, as an example to the "Mormon" people.

Colonel Hinkle visited Hyrum Smith and told him that a court-martial had been held and that he had contended for his (Hyrum's) acquittal, but it availed nothing, and all were to be shot the next morning. General Wilson had made an effort during the day to corrupt Lyman Wight, and get him to testify to something against Joseph Smith, but in this he failed. About the time Hinkle went to Hyrum, General Wilson took Wight aside and told him the decision of the court-martial. "Shoot and be damned," said Wight. About this time General Doniphan came up to Wilson and Wight and, addressing the latter, he said: "Colonel, the decision is a damned hard one, but I wash my hands against such cold-blooded murder." And he further said that he intended to remove his troops the following day as soon as light, that they should not witness such heartless murder. General Graham and a few others, whose names unfortunately have not been preserved, had voted against the decision of the court-martial, but it availed nothing.

The bold stand taken by General Doniphan the next morning, in threatening to remove his troops and denouncing the execution of the prisoners as cold-blooded murder, alarmed Lucas, and he changed his mind about executing the decision of the courtmartial; in fact he revoked the decree, and placed the prisoners in charge of General Wilson with instructions to conduct them to Independence.

CHAPTER XLII
SAD SCENES AT FAR WEST

Before starting, the prisoners were conducted into Far West, permitted to get a change of linen, and take leave of their families, though in the presence of a brutal guard. This parting, which they had good reason to believe was their final one, was very distressing. Yet it was borne with manly fortitude. Parley P. Pratt's wife was sick with a fever, with an infant at her breast. The roof of the miserable hovel in which she lay afforded but little protection from the drizzling rain which at the time was falling. His large comfortable house had been pulled down by the mob, and he had been forced to find temporary shelter in this hovel, for his sick wife and her young family. Stretched out on the foot of the bed, on which his wife lay, was another woman who had been driven from her home the night before, who now was in the throes of child-birth. To leave a family sick and helpless and destitute and exposed to the insults of a lawless band of murderers, would appall the stoutest heart. In tears Elder Pratt went to General Wilson and told him the circumstances of his family with the view of getting time to provide for their comfort, but he was only answered with a mocking, exultant laugh.

The wife of Hyrum Smith was near her confinement, yet he was compelled to take his leave of her in the presence of his brutal guard, who peremptorily ordered her to get her husband a change of clothing within two minutes or he would be compelled to go without them; and after securing the clothing he was rudely hustled out of the house to join the rest of the prisoners.

The separation of Sidney Rigdon from his family was scarcely less distressing, and Joseph had been as roughly torn away from his family. The prisoners were placed in a wagon, around which crowded the friends and relatives, among whom were the aged parents of Joseph and Hyrum, their hearts wrung with anguish and their eyes blinded with tears, as they beheld their noble sons in the hands of their merciless enemies. No one was allowed to speak to them, the silent pressure of the hand was the only token of affection granted, and the wagon containing the prisoners moved on, surrounded by its military guard, and followed by the prayers of heart-sick wives and a grief-stricken people. Leaving the prisoners to pursue their journey to Independence, let us relate what happened about Far West and Diahman.

Joseph and his fellow-prisoners were started for Jackson County on the second of November, and General Clark arrived at Far West on the fourth. In the meantime, Lucas had sent Niel Gilliam's company and a part of General Parks' brigade, under command of General Parks, with orders to surround Diahman and disarm the people. And just before Clark arrived, Lucas, too, went to Diahman. The first thing done by Clark was to send orders to General Lucas to take all the men among the "Mormons" prisoners, and secure their property, with a view of paying with it the damages that had been sustained by the old settlers.

After this, the brethren remaining at Far West were drawn up in line, and the names of fifty-six called off, and as they stepped out from the line, they were put under arrest to await a trial, though they were not informed as to the nature of the charges against them. After these fifty-six had been secured, General Clark addressed himself to the remainder, and referred them to the terms of surrender that Colonel Hinkle had arranged for them without their consent, and even without consulting with them. Yet General Clark as rigidly enforced those terms as if the people had drafted them, or had given them their sanction after they were drafted. The first item in the terms of capitulation was that the leaders of the people should be given up to be dealt with according to law. "This," said Clark, "you have complied with."

The second item was that they should deliver up their arms. "This has been attended to," said the general.

The third stipulation was that they sign over their property to defray the expenses of the war. "This you have also done," complacently went on Clark. That was true. The saints had signed away their property at the point of the musket, while the mob which compelled them to go to such extremes, mocked them with their taunts and sneers, unchecked by the officers who commanded them.

After enumerating the things the saints had complied with, the self-important general concluded his speech in these words:

> Another article yet remains for you to comply with, and that is, that you leave the State forthwith; and whatever may be your feelings concerning this, or whatever your innocence, it is nothing to me. General Lucas, who is equal in authority with me, has made this treaty with you—I approve of it—I

should have done the same had I been here—I am therefore determined to see it fulfilled. The character of this State has suffered almost beyond redemption, from the character, conduct and influence that you have exerted. And we deem it an act of justice to restore her character to its former standing among the States by every proper means.

The orders of the governor to me were, that you should be exterminated, and not allowed to remain in the State; and had your leaders not been given up and the terms of the treaty complied with, before this you and your families would have been destroyed, and your homes in ashes. There is a discretionary power vested in my hands which I shall exercise in your favor for a season, for this lenity you are indebted to *my clemency*. I do not say that you shall go now, but you must not think of staying here another season, or of putting in crops; for the moment you do this the citizens will be upon you. If I am called here again in case of a non-compliance of a treaty made, do not think that I shall act any more as I have done, you need not expect any mercy, but extermination, for I am determined the governor's order shall be executed.

As for your leaders do not once think—do not imagine for a moment—do not let it enter your mind, that they will be delivered or that you will see their faces again, for *their fate is fixed—their die is cast. Their doom is sealed.* I am sorry, gentlemen, to see so great a number of apparently intelligent men found in the situation you are; and oh, that I could invoke that *Great Spirit*, the unknown God, to rest upon you and make you sufficiently intelligent to break that chain of superstition and liberate you from those fetters of fanaticism, with which you are bound, that you no longer worship a man.

I would advise you to scatter abroad and never again organize yourselves with bishops, presidents, etc., lest you excite the jealousies of the people and subject yourselves to the same calamities that have now come upon you.

You have always been the aggressors; you have brought upon yourselves these difficulties by being disaffected and not being subject to rule; and my advice is that you become as other citizens, lest by a recurrence of these events, you bring upon yourselves irretrievable ruin.

After listening to this harangue—this mixture of hypocrisy and conceit, affected pity and heartless cruelty, pretended patriotism and willful treason—the fifty-six brethren who had been arrested, for what, they knew not, neither did Clark appear able to inform them, were sent to Richmond where they were to be tried; and the remainder were dismissed to provide food and fuel for their families, and make preparations for leaving the State.

Governor Boggs appeared anxious about having his exterminating orders carried into effect, and occasionally stirred up General Clark to a lively remembrance of what he expected him to do, by sending him messages from time to time. Here is a specimen received directly after Clark had sent the fifty-six prisoners to Richmond:

> It will be a necessity that you hold a military court of inquiry in Daviess County, and arrest the "Mormons," who have been guilty of the late outrages committed towards the inhabitants of said county. My instructions to you are to settle this whole matter completely if possible before you disband your forces; if the "Mormons" are disposed voluntarily to leave the State, of course it would be advisable in you to promote that object in any way deemed proper. *The ring-leaders ought by no means to be permitted to escape the punishment they merit.*

As if inspired to new zeal by the receipt of this message, Clark ordered General Wilson, who, in the meantime, had returned from Jackson County, to go to Diahman and take charge of all the prisoners at that place, and ascertain those who had committed "crimes," put them under close guard, and when he moved to take them to Keytesville, the county seat of Chariton County, and between seventy and eighty miles from Diahman. A number of the brethren were taken prisoners at Diahman and were examined before Judge Adam Black, one of the ringleaders of the mob in bringing about the whole trouble. But even he was obliged to acquit the brethren brought before him, as they were innocent of the charges made against them. At the close of their examination, General Wilson ordered all the saints to leave Diahman within ten days, with permission to move into Caldwell County, and remain until spring, when they were to leave the State.

A committee of twelve men were granted the privilege of moving about freely between Far West and Diahman, with permission to move the corn and household goods from the latter to the former place. The stock, or the most of it, was taken possession of by the mob-militia. The committee of twelve were to wear white badges on their hats in order that they might be easily recognized by the forces that would be detailed to watch the movements of the "Mormon" people.

By this arrangement the saints at Diahman were driven from their comfortable homes to camp out through a long, dreary and severe winter in their wagons and tents, by reason of which exposure many perished, among whom were a number of delicate women and children.

CHAPTER XLIII
A PROPHET'S REBUKE

It is time now that we turn our attention to what befell Joseph Smith and his fellow-prisoners. The first day from Far West they made twelve miles, camping at night on Crooked River. A strong guard was placed around the prisoners, who watched them closely.

The next morning the Prophet Joseph had a word of comfort for his brethren. He spoke to each one quietly saying: "Be of good cheer, brethren, the word of the Lord came to me last night that our lives should be given us; and that whatever we might suffer during this captivity, not one of our lives should be taken." [A]

[Footnote A: Autobiography of Parley P. Pratt, page 210.]

The reader will pardon me if I anticipate sufficiently to say that this remarkable prophecy was verily fulfilled: not one of their lives was sacrificed.

The same day this prophecy was made, the prisoners reached the Missouri River, and were hurried across into Jackson County, for General Clark had sent word to Lucas to bring the prisoners to him at Richmond; but Wilson was determined to exhibit the prisoners at Independence. On the journey Wilson became more friendly towards his prisoners and conversed freely with them in relation to the disturbances which had taken place in Jackson County, in 1833. General Wilson, it must be remembered, was the man who kept a store about one mile west of Big Blue, and seven or eight miles west of Independence; and who was active in driving the saints from Jackson County and burning their homes. Of the part he took in these proceedings he boasted as if it was some laudable work he had accomplished, though he admitted that he and his associates then, and now, were the aggressors, and that the manner of life followed by the saints was blameless.

On the fourth the prisoners and their guards arrived at Independence, and though it was raining, the prisoners were driven about the streets for the purpose of exhibiting them to the crowds which had come together to see them. They were placed in an old, vacant house where many came to see them during that and the following day. Among those who came on the first day was a lady, who innocently inquired which one of the men it was the "Mormons" worshiped. Joseph was pointed out to her as the one, and she inquired of him if he professed to be the Lord and Savior. To which he replied that he "professed to be nothing but a man, and a minister of salvation, sent by Jesus Christ to preach the Gospel." This astonished the lady and her eager questions brought from the prophet, ever willing to preach the gospel either in freedom or in bondage, a discourse on the principles he was sent to teach. The lady broke down in tears, and left their dingy prison with a prayer for their safety and deliverance. Joseph's native eloquence and the truth he advocated had gained another triumph, for not only was the lady overcome with what she heard, but it had its effect upon all who listened.

In a day or two the prisoners were removed from their miserable quarters where the floor had been their bed and blocks of wood their pillows, to the best hotel in the city, where they were treated kindly and allowed to move about pretty freely, with a small guard to watch their movements. Subsequently, however, they had to pay their own expense at this hotel, and exorbitant charges were made for every comfort afforded them.

During the few days that Joseph and his fellow-prisoners remained at Independence, several messages were sent from General Clark's headquarters at Richmond to have the "Mormon" leaders sent there immediately. General Wilson, however, found it difficult to secure a guard to accompany them, as no one would volunteer, and when men were drafted they refused to obey orders. At last three men were obtained as a guard, and on the morning of the eighth of November they set out for Richmond. They traveled down the south bank of the Missouri River to a ferry kept by a Frenchman by the name of Roy. Here they crossed the river, and after going about a half a mile lodged for the night at a private house. The guard who accompanied the prisoners came more as a protection to them than to hinder them from escaping, and the people in and about Independence appeared willing for the prisoners to escape. The guards had been drinking during the day, and not infrequently the prisoners were sixty or eighty rods in the rear or ahead of them. When night found them at the private house before mentioned, sleep so overpowered the guards that they gave their arms into the hands of the prisoners that they might protect themselves if occasion to do so should occur; and that was quite likely since they were in a neighborhood filled with their most bitter enemies.

The night passed, however, without any disturbance, and the next morning the journey to Richmond was continued. Before starting a number of armed and rough-looking men, gathered about the prisoners with curses and threats, and the guards alarmed for their safety, sent a messenger to Richmond to obtain a stronger guard. Without waiting for its arrival, the little company proceeded on its journey, but had not gone far when they met Colonel Sterling Price and a guard of seventy soldiers.

Arriving at Richmond, Joseph and his brethren were thrust into an old, vacant house under guard. Soon afterwards they were visited by General Clark who was introduced to them. The prisoners made an effort to find out the charges against them, but Clark evaded their questions and shortly withdrew. Clark had left the room but a few minutes when Colonel Price came in accompanied by a blacksmith of the name of John Fulkerson, carrying a log chain and a number of pad-locks. The windows to the house were nailed down, and the seven prisoners from Independence were chained together by the ankles; Price's guard of ten men standing with guns poised, and their thumbs on the hammers for instant use.

In the meantime General Clark was searching for authority to try the prisoners before a court-martial, and it would appear from the testimony of a brother, by the name of Grant, that he had concluded to so proceed, and had even given the sentence of the court before an investigation had occurred; for this young man by the name of Grant, (given name not known), but a brother-in-law to William Smith, brother to the Prophet Joseph, lodged at the hotel where Clark made his headquarters. He saw that general select the men who were to shoot the "Mormon" leaders on the morning of the twelfth of November. He saw these men choose their rifles and load them with two balls in each; after which Clark said to them: "Gentlemen, you shall have the honor of shooting the "Mormon" leaders on Monday morning at eight o'clock." [B]

[Footnote B: Testimony of Hyrum Smith, Times and Seasons, volume 4, page 252.]

Some of the friends of the captive brethren intimated to the general that he had no authority to try the prisoners by court-martial; whereupon he sent to Fort Leavenworth to obtain the military code of laws, which he searched for several days for authority to try the prisoners as he had proposed, by court-martial. At last he had to give it up, but he did it with great reluctance. He visited the prison where Joseph and his brethren were confined, and told them he had decided to deliver them to the civil authorities; and informed them they were accused of "treason, murder, arson, larceny, theft, and stealing." The prisoners then were delivered into the hands of the civil authorities, and an investigation was begun before Austin A. King, the circuit judge, and Thomas C. Birch, the prosecuting attorney for the State.

The examination of the witnesses for the State continued from the eleventh of November to the twenty-sixth. Each night after the day's examination the prisoners who had been brought down from Independence were taken to their gloomy prison and chained together, while about fifty of their brethren and fellow-prisoners, who had been brought from Far West, were kept under guard in an open unfinished, court-house, exposed to the excessive coldness of that inclement season.

The constitution of Elder Rigdon was so delicate, that in consequence of the exposure and hardships he was forced to endure under this cruel persecution, his health broke down and at last he lost his reason; yet he was chained to his companions and compelled to remain in the presence of a noisy and unruly and unfeeling guard. His daughter, who was the wife of George W. Robinson, one of the prisoners fastened to the same chain with her father, was at last permitted to come to the prison and care for her afflicted father. Lovingly, tenderly this delicate young woman with her first born babe at her breast, nursed her afflicted father through those gloomy days, and through her tenderness and anxious care nursed him back to health and reason.

The guard, under Colonel Price, was perhaps the most foulmouthed and villainous that could possibly be brought together. They related to each other their deeds of murder and rapine, and boasted of raping virtuous wives and maidens, until the prisoners were heart-sick with the disgusting details of their crimes. Parley P. Pratt relates an incident that occurred in the prison one night when the guards were unusually obscene, which we give entire in that writer's own language:

> I had listened [to the guard's boasts of defiling wives and maidens by force] till I became so disgusted, shocked, horrified and so filled with the spirit of indignant justice that I could scarcely refrain from rising upon my feet and rebuking the guards; but had said nothing to Joseph, or any one else, although I lay next to him and knew he was awake. On a sudden he arose to his feet, and spoke in a voice of thunder, or as the roaring lion, uttering as near as I can recollect, the following:

> "*Silence!* ye fiends of the the infernal pit. In the name of Jesus Christ I rebuke you, and command you to be still; I will not live another minute and hear such language. Cease such talk, or you or I die *this instant.*"

He ceased to speak. He stood erect in terrible majesty. Chained and without a weapon; calm, unruffled, dignified as an angel, he looked upon the quailing guards, whose weapons were lowered or dropped to the ground; whose knees smote together, and who shrinking into a corner, or crouching at his feet, begged his pardon, and remained quiet till a change of guards.

I have seen the ministers of justice, clothed in magisterial robes, and criminals arraigned before them, while life was suspended on a breath, in the courts of England. I have witnessed a congress in solemn session to give laws to nations; I have tried to conceive of kings, or royal courts, of thrones and crowns, and of emperors assembled to decide the fate of kingdoms; but dignity and majesty have I seen but once, as it stood in chains, at midnight in a dungeon, in an obscure village in Missouri.

CHAPTER XLIV
"A STRONG POINT FOR TREASON"

Fifteen days were consumed in taking testimony for the State. At the expiration of that time the judge ordered the defendants to bring forth their rebutting testimony or he would thrust them into prison. "I could hardly understand what the judge meant," says Hyrum Smith, "as I considered we were in prison already." The names of forty persons, residents of Far West, were given to the court to be called as witnesses for the defense, and the subpoenas for them were placed in the hands of "Captain" or "Parson," which ever title the reader may be best pleased to know him by, for he was both captain of a gang of mobbers and a supposed minister of Christ, and now an arm of the civil power—any way it was Bogard of Crooked River battle fame. He took with him a force of fifty men and started for Far West; and in the course of a few days returned with the forty men. They were at once put under arrest and by this cunning were prevented from appearing as witnesses.

After executing this *coup de main* the judge petulantly exclaimed: "Gentlemen, you must get your witnesses or you shall be committed to jail immediately." Most of the brethren felt very much discouraged at the turn affairs had taken, but Hyrum Smith, under the advice of General Doniphan and Lawyer Reese, gave the names of some twenty other persons at Far West, who were desirable as witnesses. The same man was ordered to bring the witnesses to Richmond, but in the meantime the people at Far West had learned of the intrigue being practiced upon them, and the persons whose names Bogard took with him, who had not left the State, kept out of the way and he returned to Richmond with but one man who was wanted, and he was thrust into jail and not allowed to testify. The judge again urged the prisoners to bring on their witnesses, telling them it was the last day he would hold the court open for them.

While the brethren were in consultation with their lawyers a Mr. Allen passed the window and Hyrum Smith beckoned to him to come inside, and the prisoners then informed the court that they had one witness who was ready to be sworn. But at this juncture the prosecuting attorney, Birch, objected to having the witness testify, as this court was merely investigating the case, and not trying it, notwithstanding the frequent calls from the court asking the accused to procure witnesses. General Doniphan here lost his patience, and rising to his feet he said: "I'll be G—-d——d if the witness is not sworn. It is a d—-d shame to treat these defendants in this manner. They are not allowed to put one witness on the stand; while the witnesses they have sent for have been captured by force of arms and thrust into the 'bull pen,' to prevent their testifying."

No sooner, however, had Allen begun his testimony than he was taken by the nape of the neck by a brother-in-law of the priest Bogard, kicked out of the room and made to run for his life.

During this preliminary examination Judge King appeared extremely anxious to fasten the crime of treason upon Joseph Smith and his associates; and to that end he bent every energy, knowing that if a charge of that character were sustained against them he could refuse them bail. The judge asked one of the witnesses if the "Mormons" sent missionaries to foreign countries. He was answered in the affirmative. "Do the 'Mormons' profess a belief in the seventh chapter of Daniel, and the twenty-seventh verse?" [A] asked the judge.

[Foonote A: "And the kingdom and dominion, and the greatness of the kingdom under the whole heavens shall be given to the people of the saints of the Most High, whose kingdom is an everlasting kingdom, and all dominions shall serve and obey him" [meaning Christ.]—Daniel 7:27.]

"Certainly they do," replied the witness. "Then," said Judge King, turning to the clerk of the court, and speaking with that dignity all judges are supposed to possess, "put that down; that is a strong point for treason!"

The examination resulted in the Prophet Joseph, his brother Hyrum, Sidney Rigdon, Lyman Wight, Caleb Baldwin and Alexander McRae being committed on a charge of treason, and sent to Liberty jail, in Clay County.

Parley P. Pratt, Morris Phelps, Lyman Gibbs, Darwin Chase and Norman Shearer were committed on a charge of murder for the part they took in the battle of Crooked River; and were to remain in prison at Richmond.

The fifty-six other brethren that had been sent to Richmond as prisoners by General Clark, and the forty brought down by Bogard under the pretense that they were to be witnesses on behalf of their brethren, were either released or admitted to bail. Those admitted to bail, together with those who went on their bonds, were subsequently driven from the State so that the bail was forfeited. Having followed the brethren in bonds thus far, we must turn our attention to what befell the main body of the Saints.

CHAPTER XLV
EXODUS FROM MISSOURI

It will perhaps be remembered that the saints at Diahman were given a very limited time by General Wilson in which to leave for Far West—only ten days. Therefore in their flight to Far West they left much of their stock and property behind them.

On the first of December the "Mormon" committee that had been granted the privilege of moving freely between Diahman and Far West for a limited time proposed to a committee of Daviess County citizens, viz., W. P. Peniston, Dr. K. Kerr, and Adam Black, that the "Mormon" committee be allowed, first, to employ twenty teams and their drivers to move the property of the saints from Diahman to Far West; and, second, that they be allowed to collect all stock the "Mormon" people owned in Daviess County, and that on a given day a committee from said county examine the stock and accompany the "Mormon" committee and the stock out of the county, the brethren binding themselves on their part not to take any stock from the county after this general drive. These propositions were accepted by the Daviess County committee, and duly executed, though much of the stock belonging to the saints had been driven away, or shot down to supply the mob forces with beef.

It was during these trying times that Brigham Young, afterwards the President of The Church, began to exhibit those executive qualities which so eminently fitted him as a great leader. By the apostasy of Thomas B. Marsh, the presidency of the quorum of the Twelve Apostles devolved upon him, hence also the leadership of The Church during the absence of the First Presidency. Was God training him for leadership in that greater exodus to take place a few years later?

He called together those members of the High Council of the Far West stake of Zion that still remained in Far West, and enquired of them as to their faith in the Latter-day work, first telling them that his own faith was unshaken. All the members present expressed their undying faith in the gospel, and their confidence in Joseph Smith as a prophet of God. The council was then reorganized; the vacancies caused by absence or apostasy were filled up, and the council was prepared to do business.

Elders John Taylor and John E. Page, both of whom had previously been chosen by revelation for the office, were ordained members of the quorum of the Twelve Apostles, on the nineteenth day of September, under the hands of Brigham Young and Heber C. Kimball. This work of setting in order the High Council and filling the vacancies in the quorum of the Apostles being accomplished, Elder Young waited upon Bishop Partridge and proposed to him that they adopt some plan to remove the poor from the State, that they might not fall victims to the governor's exterminating order. The bishop's reply was rather ungracious, for he said: "The poor may take care of themselves, and I will take care of myself!" "Well," said Elder Young, "if you will not help them out, I will." Here, however, I would suggest to the reader not to judge the bishop too harshly for the petulant expression he allowed to escape him at that moment. Let it be remembered that when the bishop first became connected with The Church he was a man of considerable means: and now, in consequence of frequent drivings, and caring for his brethren, he found himself stripped of nearly all his earthly possessions, and sorely perplexed as to the future. No wonder then, if, in a moment of forgetfulness, he made the remark quoted above. Those were days that tried men's souls, be not surprised if good men and true had their periods of despondency.

Elder Young's activity and zeal in the matter of caring for the poor were unbounded. A public meeting was called, not only of the saints but also of the citizens of Caldwell County and the poverty and distress of many of the saints presented to them. Several gentlemen, not members of The Church, expressed themselves as being of opinion that an appeal should be made to the citizens of upper Missouri, inviting their assistance towards furnishing means to remove the poor from Caldwell County. Whether such an appeal was made or not, I cannot say, but rather think not, as a resolution was adopted at this meeting as follows: "*Resolved*, That it is the opinion of this meeting that an exertion should be made to ascertain how much [means] can be obtained from individuals of the society [church]; and that it is the duty of those who have, to assist those who have not, that thereby we may, as far as possible, within and of ourselves, comply with the demands of the Executive." So that the generosity of the people of upper Missouri I think was not appealed to by the saints that were driven from among them.

At a subsequent meeting, similar in character to the one alluded to, Elder Young offered this resolution: "*Resolved*, That we this day enter into a covenant to stand by and assist each other, to the utmost of our abilities, in removing from this State, and that we will never desert the poor who are worthy, till they shall be out of the reach of the general exterminating order of General Clark, acting for and in the name of the State." This resolution was adopted, and a committee of seven appointed to superintend the removal of the saints. A committee was also appointed to draft a covenant that should bind the saints in an agreement to assist each other to the extent of their available property to remove from the State of Missouri, in accordance with the orders of the governor; this covenant was drawn up in due form and signed by the faithful brethren. Elder Young secured eighty names to this covenant the first day he took hold of it, and three hundred the next. The Prophet Joseph, not willing to be behind the other brethren in the good work, hearing what was going on through those who visited him while in prison, from his gloomy dungeon at Liberty, sent the brethren a hundred dollars to assist in removing the Saints.

Charles Bird was appointed to go down towards the Mississippi and make deposits of corn for the use of the saints as they should make their way out of the State. He was also to make contracts for ferriage and arrange whatever else might be necessary for their comfort and security. Thus all things were prepared for the exodus of The Church from the unfriendly State of Missouri.

No sooner had these arrangements been perfected than Elder Young, whose wisdom and activity had doubtless given offense to the enemies of The Church, had to flee from Far West to escape the vengeance of the mob. He went to Illinois. In his labors, Elder Young had been materially assisted by the support and counsels of Heber C. Kimball, John Taylor and the members of the various committees that had been appointed, to whom was now left the execution of the plans that had been laid for the removal of The Church.

I can not dwell upon all the details of that exodus. All I need say here is that it was managed with consummate wisdom; and, in view of all the difficulties in the way, with less suffering than could have been expected.

By the twentieth of April nearly all the saints, variously estimated from twelve to fifteen thousand, had left the State where they had experienced so much sorrow; and found a temporary resting place in the State of Illinois, chiefly in the city of Quincy and vicinity, but a few settled in the then Territory of Iowa.

CHAPTER XLVI
AGAIN THE PASSIVELY GOOD—PETITIONS

It must not be supposed that all the people of Missouri sanctioned the outrages committed against The Church. On the contrary there was here and there an honorable man who protested against the conduct of the mob and the authorities; and occasionally some newspaper would deplore the action of the State against the saints.

Among the men who were moved with sympathy by their sufferings was Michael Arthur. He wrote to the representatives in the State legislature from Clay County, relating the vile atrocities that were heaped upon the heads of the defenseless saints after they had surrendered their arms to General Clark. He represented that the "Mormons" were willing to leave the State, in fact that they were making every effort that their limited means would permit them to make to get away, and suggested that a company of reliable men under the command of Geo. M. Pryer be authorized to patrol on the line between Daviess and Caldwell counties with authority to arrest any one they found disturbing the peace, that the "Mormons" might be protected while they were making preparations to leave the State. And if it was impracticable to organize this company of men, then he suggested that the arms taken from the "Mormons" be returned to them, that they might defend themselves from the barbarous attacks of their enemies.

Nor were the saints wanting in attention to the instructions of the Lord in the matter of petitioning for a redress of their grievances. For as soon as the legislature was convened they sent a statement of all the wrongs heaped upon them during their sojourn in the State of Missouri, from the time they first settled in Jackson County to the treaty forced upon them at Far West by Generals Lucas and Clark, and the outrages that had been committed against them since the surrender of their arms.

After detailing the story of their wrongs, they asked: first, that the legislature pass a law rescinding the exterminating order of Governor Boggs; second, they asked an expression of the legislature, disapproving the conduct of those who compelled them to sign a deed of trust at the muzzle of the musket, and of any man in consequence of that deed of trust taking their property and appropriating it to the payment of damages sustained, in consequence of trespasses committed by others; third, that they receive payment for the six hundred and thirty-five arms that were taken from them, which were worth twelve or fifteen thousand dollars; fourth, that an appropriation be made to reimburse them for their loss of lands from which they had been driven in Jackson County. The petition closed in these words:

> In laying our case before your honorable body, we say that we are willing, and always have been, to conform to the Constitution and laws of the United States, and of this State. We ask in common with others the protection of the laws. We ask for the privileges guaranteed all free citizens of the United States and of this State to be extended to us, and that we may be permitted to settle and live where we please, and worship God according to the dictates of our own conscience without molestation. And while we ask for ourselves this privilege, we are willing all others should enjoy the same.

Elder David H. Redfield was appointed to present this petition to the legislature; and on that mission he arrived at Jefferson City on the seventeenth day of December. The same day of his arrival he had an interview with Governor Boggs, in which the governor manifested much interest, and on being informed that the Missourians were committing depredations against the saints, promised to write Judge King and Colonel Price ordering them to put down every hostile appearance.

In the course of this conversation Boggs admitted that the "stipulations entered into by the Mormons to leave the State, and signing the deeds of trust, were unconstitutional and not valid." "We want the legislature to pass a law to that effect, showing that the stipulations and deeds of trust are not valid and are unconstitutional," said Redfield, and went on to say if they did not, the character of the State was forever lost.

Previous to the arrival of Redfield, the governor's exterminating order, General Clark's reports, the report of the *ex parte* investigation at Richmond, and a lot of other papers, had been forwarded to the legislature and referred to a special joint committee. That committee reported the day following Redfield's arrival at Jefferson City, the eighteenth of December. And to show in what bad repute these documents were held by this committee, I need only say that it refused to allow them to be published with the sanction of the legislature, because the evidence adduced at Richmond in a great degree was *ex parte* and not of a character to be desired for the basis of a fair and candid investigation. The report concluded with three resolutions: one to the effect that it was inexpedient at that time to prosecute further the inquiry into the cause of the late disturbances; another to the effect that it was inexpedient to publish any of the documents accompanying the governor's message in relation to those disturbances; the last favored the appointment of a joint committee from the house and senate to investigate the troubles and the conduct of the military operations to suppress them. These resolutions were subsequently referred to a joint select committee with instructions to report a bill in conformity thereto, and to which I shall again allude.

The day after, the committee reported in relation to that part of the governor's message relating to the "Mormon troubles," and on the documents accompanying it. The petition from the saints was read, amid profound stillness of the house, and at its conclusion an angry debate followed, in which quite a number of the members testified to the correctness of the statements made in the petition and to the cruelties practiced upon the saints, but they were in the minority.

On the sixteenth of January, Mr. Turner, the chairman of the select joint committee before alluded to, in conformity with the resolution passed, reported "A bill to provide for the investigation of the late disturbances in the State of Missouri." The bill consisted of twenty-three sections. It provided for a joint committee composed of two members of the senate and three members from the house, which was to meet at Richmond on the first Monday in May and thereafter at such time and places as it saw proper. The committee was to select its own officers; issue subpoenas and other processes, administer oaths, keep a record, etc.

This bill was introduced on the sixteenth of January, and on the fourth of February called up for its first reading, but on motion of Mr. Wright was laid on the table till the fourth of July. He knew that by that time, since the governor's exterminating order was still in force, that the "Mormons," in obedience to that cruel edict, would all have left the State, and then there would be no need of an investigation. That was the fate of the bill. It was never afterwards brought up.

The legislature in its magnanimity appropriated two thousand dollars to relieve the sufferings of the people in Daviess and Caldwell Counties, the "Mormons" were to be included. And now came an opportunity for the Missourians of Daviess County to display their generosity. Having filled their homes with the household effects of the saints; their yards with the stock they had stolen; their smoke houses with "Mormon" beef and pork; they concluded they could get along without their portion of the appropriation and allowed the two thousand dollars to be distributed among the "Mormons" of Caldwell County!

Judge Cameron and a Mr. McHenry superintended the distribution of this appropriation. The hogs owned by the brethren who had lived in Daviess County were driven down into Caldwell, shot down and without further bleeding were roughly dressed and divided out among the saints at a high price. This and the sweepings of some old stores soon exhausted the legislative appropriation, and amounted to little or nothing in the way of relief to the saints.

Subsequently this same legislature, while the petition of the saints for a redress of their wrongs was lying before it, appropriated two hundred thousand dollars to defray the expenses incurred in driving the "Mormons" from the State, and dispossessing them of their property! By that act the legislature became a party to the deeds of the mob forces, urged on in their cruelties by the executive of the State; for that legislature had sealed with its approval all that had been done, by paying the mob that had executed the plan devised for the expulsion of the "Mormon" people.

CHAPTER XLVII
THE ESCAPE OF THE PROPHET
FROM MISSOURI

The winter of 1838-9 must have been a trying one to Joseph the Prophet and his associates immured in Liberty prison. The gloom of their prison life must have caused them less sorrow than the anxiety they felt for the safety of their families and friends, who were being abused and insulted by a heartless mob, even while making arrangements to leave the State. Still there were occasional glimpses of sunshine breaking through the clouds. Some of the faithful brethren called occasionally, bringing them the news from their families and their people, and the progress being made in the preparations to leave the State. Letters also from their families were brought to them, so that they were not altogether cut off from that sweet communion which affection breeds. Nor was the Lord unmindful of them, but he communed with them, and through the Prophet Joseph some of the noblest revelations ever given to The Church were received in that gloomy stone prison known as Liberty jail.[A]

[Footnote A: See Doc. & Cov. Sec. 121, 122 and 123.]

Nor were Joseph and his companions neglectful in making every proper effort to obtain justice from the State authorities. On the contrary they exhausted every means their minds could conceive of to regain their liberty. They petitioned the legislature, but without availing anything. Failing here, they petitioned the supreme court of the State twice for a writ of habeas corpus, but each time the petition was denied by Judge Reynolds, who subsequently became governor of the State..

They then petitioned the county court, and in about three weeks afterwards Judge Turnham came into their prison and said he had permitted Sidney Rigdon to get bail, but he had to do it in the night; and that he would have to make his escape in the night as his enemies had sworn they would kill him if they could find him. The judge said that he dared not admit the others to bail, lest it should cost him his own life, as well as theirs. The judge informed the prisoners that the whole scheme for the expulsion from the State of the "Mormon" people was arranged early in the spring, and that every officer in the State from the governor down was connected with the plot. He said the governor was now heartily sick of the whole transaction and would grant them a release if he dared; but the matter had gone beyond his control. However, the judge bid the prisoners to be of good cheer, as the governor had arranged a plan for their escape.

In April the prisoners were taken to Daviess County, where they expected to be tried. Here they found Judge Thomas C. Birch on the bench—formerly the prosecuting attorney for the State in the *ex parte* examination of the Prophet and his companions before Judge King at Richmond, and the man who was connected with the court-martial that condemned them to be shot in the public square at Far West. They were arraigned by a grand jury, composed of men connected with the massacre at Haun's Mill, some of whom, while under the influence of liquor, boasted of their deeds of cruelty at that horrible butchery. This grand jury did double service. During the day it acted as a court of inquiry, at night members of it were chosen by turns to act as a guard over the prisoners!

After ten days passed in this manner, the jury reported indictments against the prisoners, for "treason, murder, arson, theft and stealing."

The prisoners asked for a change of venue to Marion County. That was denied, but one was given them to Boone County, and Judge Birch made out the mittimus without date, name, or place; and the prisoners in charge of the sheriff and four other men and a two horse team and wagon started for Boone County.

Passing through Diahman the prisoners were allowed to purchase two horses of the guard, giving some clothing for one, and their note for the other. The third day out from Gallatin three of the guards and the sheriff got drunk and went to bed. The sheriff, previously having shown the prisoners the mittimus made out by Judge Birch, now also informed them that Birch had told him not to take the prisoners to Boone County. After exposing the plan that had been laid for their escape by the authorities, the sheriff assured the prisoners that he should take a good drink of whiskey and go to bed, and they could do as they pleased. Accordingly when all the guards but one were asleep, that one, who, by the way, was sober as well as awake, assisted them to mount their horses and escape. Ten days later they arrived among their friends in Illinois. The Prophet in a signed summary of the persecutions endured by himself and his people in Missouri says:—

> Before leaving Missouri I had paid the lawyers at Richmond
> thirty-four thousand dollars in cash, lands, &c.; one lot
> which I let them have, in Jackson County, for seven thousand
> dollars, they were soon offered ten thousand dollars for it,

but would not accept it. For other vexatious suits which I had to contend against, the few months I was in the State, I paid lawyers' fees to the amount of about sixteen thousand dollars, making in all about fifty thousand dollars, for which I received very little in return; for sometimes they were afraid to act on account of the mob, and sometimes they were so drunk as to incapacitate them for business. But there were a few honorable exceptions.

Among those who have been the chief instruments and leading characters in the unparalleled persecutions against The Church of Latter-day Saints, the following stand conspicuous, viz.: Generals Clark, Wilson and Lucas; Colonel Price, and Cornelius Gilliam; Captain Bogart also, whose zeal in the cause of oppression and injustice was unequalled, and whose delight has been to rob, murder and spread devastation among the saints. He stole a valuable horse, saddle and bridle from me, which cost two hundred dollars, and then sold the same to General Wilson. On understanding this, I applied to General Wilson for the horse, who assured me, upon the honor of a gentleman and an officer, that I should have the horse returned to me; but this promise has not been fulfilled.

All the threats, murders and robberies, which these officers have been guilty of, are entirely overlooked by the executive of the State; who, to hide his own iniquity, must of course shield and protect those whom he employed to carry into effect his murderous purposes.

I was in their hands, as a prisoner, about six months; but notwithstanding their determination to destroy me, with the rest of my brethren who were with me, and although at three different times (as I was informed) we were sentenced to be shot, without the least shadow of law (as we were not military men), and had the time and place appointed for that purpose, yet through the mercy of God, in answer to the prayers of the saints, I have been preserved and delivered out of their hands, and can again enjoy the society of my friends and brethren, whom I love, and to whom I feel united in bonds that are stronger than death; and in a State where I believe the laws are respected, and whose citizens are humane and charitable.

During the time I was in the hands of my enemies, I must say, that although I felt great anxiety respecting my family and friends, who were so inhumanly treated and abused, and who had to mourn the loss of their husbands and children who had been slain, and, after having been robbed of nearly all that they possessed, were driven from their homes, and forced to wander as strangers in a strange country, in order that they might save themselves and their little ones from the destruction they were threatened with in Missouri, yet so far as I was concerned, I felt perfectly calm, and resigned to the will of my Heavenly Father. I knew my innocency, as well as that of the saints, and that we had done nothing to deserve such treatment from the hands of our oppressors. Consequently, I could look to that God who has the hearts of all men in his hands, and who had saved me frequently from the gates of death, for deliverance; and notwithstanding that every avenue of escape seemed to be entirely closed, and death stared me in the face, and that my destruction was determined upon, as far as man was concerned, yet, from my first entrance into the camp, I felt an assurance that I, with my brethren and our families, would be delivered. Yes, that still small voice, which has so often whispered consolation to my soul, in the depth of sorrow and distress, bade me be of good cheer, and promised deliverance, which gave me great comfort. And although the heathen raged, and the people imagined vain things, yet the Lord of Hosts, the God of Jacob, was my refuge; and when I cried unto him in the day of trouble, he delivered me; for which I call upon my soul, and all that is within me, to bless and praise his holy name. For although I was "troubled on every side, yet not distressed; perplexed, but not in despair; persecuted, but not forsaken; cast down, but not destroyed."

The conduct of the Saints, under their accumulated wrongs and sufferings, has been praiseworthy; their courage in defending their brethren from the ravages of the mobs; their attachment to the cause of truth under circumstances the most trying and distressing which humanity can possibly endure; their love to each other; their readiness to afford assistance to me and my brethren who were confined in a dungeon; their sacrifices in leaving Missouri, and assisting the poor widows and orphans, and securing them houses in a more hospitable land; all conspire to raise them in the estimation of all good and virtuous men, and has secured them the favor and approbation of Jehovah, and a name as imperishable as eternity. And their virtuous deeds and heroic actions, while in defense of truth and their brethren, will be fresh and blooming when the names of their oppressors shall be either entirely forgotten, or only remembered for their barbarity and cruelty.

Their attention and affection to me, while in prison, will ever be remembered by me; and when I have seen them thrust away and abused by the jailer and guard, when they came to do any kind offices, and to cheer our minds while we were in the gloomy prisonhouse, gave me feelings which I cannot describe; while those who wished to insult and abuse us by their threats and blasphemous language, were applauded, and had every encouragement given them.

However, thank God, we have been delivered. And although some of our beloved brethren have had to seal their testimony with their blood, and have died martyrs to the cause of truth; yet

Short though bitter was their pain,
Everlasting is their joy.

Let us not sorrow as "those without hope;" the time is fast approaching when we shall see them again and rejoice together, without being afraid of wicked men. Yes, those who have slept in Christ shall he bring with him, when he shall come to be glorified in him, and admired by all those who believe; but to take vengeance upon his enemies and all those who obey not the gospel.

At that time the hearts of the widows and fatherless shall be comforted, and every tear shall be wiped from off their faces. The trials they have had to pass through shall work together for their good, and prepare them for the society of those who have come up out of great tribulation, and have washed their robes and made them white in the blood of the Lamb.

Marvel not, then, if you are persecuted; but remember the words of the Savior: "The servant is not above his Lord; if they have persecuted me, they will persecute you also;" and that all the afflictions through which the saints have to pass, are in fulfillment of the words of all the prophets which have spoken since the world began.

We shall therefore do well to discern the signs of the times as we pass along, that the day of the Lord may not "overtake us as a thief in the night." Afflictions, persecutions, imprisonments and deaths, we must expect, according to the Scriptures, which tell us, that the blood of those whose souls were under the altar could not be avenged on them that dwell on the earth, until their brethren should be slain as they were.

If these transactions had taken place among barbarians, under the authority of a despot, or in a nation where a certain religion is established according to law, and all others proscribed, then there might have been some shadow of defense offered. But can we realize that in a land which is the cradle of liberty and equal rights, and where the voice of the conquerors who had vanquished our foes had scarcely died away upon our ears, where we frequently mingled with those who had stood amidst "the battle and the breeze," and whose arms have been nerved in the defense of their country and liberty, whose institutions are the theme of philosophers and poets, and held up to the admiration of the whole civilized world—in the midst of all these scenes, with which we were surrounded, a persecution the most unwarrantable was commenced, and a tragedy the most dreadful was enacted, by a large portion of the inhabitants of one of those free and independent States which comprise this vast Republic; and a deadly blow was struck at the institutions for which our fathers had fought many a hard battle, and for which many a patriot had shed his blood, and suddenly was heard, amidst the voice of joy and gratitude for our national liberty, the voice of mourning, lamentation and woe? Yes! in this land, a mob, regardless of those laws for which so much blood had been spilled, dead to every feeling of virtue and patriotism which animated the bosom of free men, fell upon a people whose religious faith was different from their own, and not only destroyed their homes, drove them away, and carried off their property, but murdered many a free-born son of America—a tragedy which has no parallel in modern, and hardly in ancient, times; even the face of the red man would be ready to turn pale at the recital of it. It would have been some consolation, if the authorities of the State had been innocent in this affair; but they are involved in the guilt thereof, and the blood of innocence, even of *children*, cries for vengeance upon them.

I ask the citizens of this vast Republic, whether such a state of things is to be suffered to pass unnoticed, and the hearts of widows, orphans and patriots to be broken, and their wrongs left without redress? No! I invoke the genius of our Constitution. I appeal to the patriotism of Americans, to stop this unlawful and unholy procedure; and pray that God may defend this nation from the dreadful effects of such outrages.

Is there not virtue in the body politic? Will not the people rise in their majesty, and with that promptitude and zeal which is so characteristic of them, discountenance such proceedings, by bringing the offenders to that punishment which they so richly deserve, and save the nation from that disgrace and ultimate ruin, which otherwise must inevitably fall upon it?

JOSEPH SMITH, Junior.

The other prisoners who had been left in Richmond during this dreary winter, in the spring were taken to Columbia, in Boone County, and during the summer also escaped and joined their fellow exiles in Illinois.

CHAPTER XLVIII
A PROPHECY THAT DID NOT FAIL

Before concluding this writing I wish to refer to a matter before briefly alluded to. On July 8, 1838, the Lord had given a revelation to the Twelve Apostles through Joseph, the Prophet, in which John Taylor, John E. Page, Wilford Woodruff and Willard Richards were chosen to fill the vacancies in the quorum of the Twelve, and the Apostles were to take leave of the saints in Far West on the twenty-sixth day of April, 1839, on the building spot of the Lord's House, and from thence depart over the great waters to preach the gospel in foreign lands.

It had been the constant boast of the mob throughout the persecutions we have been relating, that this was one of "Joe Smith's" revelations, at least, that should not be fulfilled.

Yet at the time appointed, the twenty-sixth day of April, five of the Twelve Apostles arrived there, having come from Quincy by various routes to elude the vigilance of their enemies, together with a number of Elders, High Priests and Priests. The five Apostles ordained Wilford Woodruff and George A. Smith members of their quorum, thus making the number of Apostles present seven, a majority of the Twelve, and hence competent to transact business as a quorum. They also ordained a number to the office of Seventy. They excommunicated a number of persons from The Church; prayer was offered up by the Apostles in the order of their standing in the quorum. A hymn known to the saints as Adam-Ondi-Ahman was sung. After this hymn was sung, Elder Alpheus Cutler, the master-workman of the Lord's House, laid the south-east corner stone in its position, and then said, in consequence of the peculiar situation of the saints, it was deemed prudent to discontinue further labor on the House until the Lord should open the way for its completion. The Apostles then took leave of some seventeen saints, who were present, and started on their way to fill their missions beyond the great Atlantic Ocean. Thus was fulfilled that revelation in every particular, notwithstanding the boasts of the mob which said it should fail of fulfillment. So important do I deem the fulfillment of this prophecy, however, that I give here the official report of the proceedings of that meeting, signed by the president of it:—

At a conference held at Far West by the Twelve, High Priests, Elders and Priests, on the twenty-sixth of April, 1839, the following resolution was adopted—

Resolved: That the following persons be no more fellowshipped in The Church of Jesus Christ of Latter-day Saints, but excommunicated from the same, viz.:—Isaac Russell, Mary Russell, John Goodson and wife, Jacob Scott, Senior, and wife, Isaac Scott, Jacob Scott, Junior, Ann Scott, Sister Walton, Robert Walton, Sister Cavanaugh, Ann Wanlass, William Dawson, Junior, and wife, William Dawson, Senior, and wife, George Nelson, Joseph Nelson and wife and mother, William Warnoch and wife, Jonathan Maynard, Nelson Maynard, George Miller, John Grigg and wife, Luman Gibbs, Simeon Gardner and Freeborn Gardner.

The council then proceeded to the building spot of the Lord's House; when the following business was transacted—Part of a hymn was sung, on the mission of the Twelve.

Elder Cutler, the master-workman of the House, then re-commenced laying the foundation of the Lord's House, agreeably to revelation, by rolling up a large stone near the southeast corner.

The following of the Twelve were present—Brigham Young, Heber C. Kimball, Orson Pratt, John E. Page and John Taylor, who proceeded to ordain Wilford Woodruff and George A. Smith (who had been previously nominated by the First Presidency, accepted by the Twelve, and acknowledged by The Church)—to the office of the Twelve, to fill the places of those who are fallen. Darwin Chase and Norman Shearer (who had just been liberated from Richmond prison, where they had been confined for the cause of Jesus Christ,) were ordained to the office of the Seventies.

The Twelve then offered up vocal prayer in the following order—Brigham Young, Heber C. Kimball, Orson Pratt, John E. Page, John Taylor, Wilford Woodruff and George A. Smith. After which we sung Adam-Ondi-Ahman, and then the Twelve took their leave of the following saints, agreeably to the revelation, viz.: Alpheus Cutler, Elias Smith, Norman Shearer, William Burton, Stephen Markham, Shadrach Roundy, William O. Clark, John W. Clark, Hezekiah Peck,

Darwin Chase, Richard Howard, Mary Ann Peck, Artimesia Grainger, Martha Peck, Sarah Grainger, Theodore Thurley, Hyrum Clark and Daniel Shearer.

Elder Alpheus Cutler then placed the stone before alluded to in its regular position, after which, in consequence of the peculiar situation of the saints, he thought it wisdom to adjourn until some future time, when the Lord shall open the way; expressing his determination then to proceed with the building; whereupon the conference adjourned.

BRIGHAM YOUNG, President.
JOHN TAYLOR, Clerk.

CHAPTER XLIX
A STATE'S SHAME

This brings me to the close of the story of the Missouri Persecutions. We have seen a people start out under the direction of the Lord to build up the City of Zion to his holy name; but because of their disobedience and failure to observe strictly those conditions upon which the Lord had promised them success in accomplishing so great a work, they were driven entirely from that county and state where that city is to be founded.

We have seen a proud, sovereign state of the great American Union, with a constitution that guaranteed the largest possible religious and civil liberty to its citizens, ignore both the spirit and letter of that constitution. We have seen its officers shamefully violate the laws passed in pursuance of it; and from the chief executive down enter into plots to destroy the saints of God, or drive them from the State; in accomplishing which, they were guilty of the most cruel barbarity. It is no palliation of their offense to say that the saints had not strictly kept the commandments of God. Their offenses were against the laws of God rather than the laws of man; delinquencies that fell not under the power of the State to correct. So far as the State of Missouri was concerned, she was not justified in trampling on her own constitution and laws, and permitting not only her people but the officers of the State to commit outrages against an innocent people that would put savages to the blush of shame.

I impeach the State of Missouri before the Bar of Nineteenth Century Civilization; and affirm that in the five years between 1833 and 1838, she permitted and became a party to acts of robbery, violence and blood which are a disgrace to the age and its boasted spirit of progress and toleration. I charge that Missouri was guilty of crimes the perpetration of which forbids the claim that in the United States of America, and in this enlightened century, there has been an abandonment of the barbarities of past ages.

Before the great Bar of History, I impeach the State of Missouri. In the years from 1833 to 1838 there were committed within her borders and against an unoffending, and law-abiding people, acts of shameful robbery, arson, mob-violence; willful, wanton slaughter of men, women and children; worst of all, rape upon virtuous wives and maidens; and, at the last, illegal banishment of some twelve thousand people from the State. For these crimes, repeatedly committed and numerous, no offender was ever brought to punishment by the State. On the contrary the machinery of its government was employed and its officers exerted themselves to further oppress the innocent sufferers; so that instead of being a means for their protection, the government was made an engine for their oppression; and its legislature turning a deaf ear to the story of their wrongs, made liberal appropriations from the State treasury to defray the expenses of those who committed the outrages against them and drove them from the State.

I impeach the State of Missouri before the Bar of American Constitutions and Institutions; and charge that in the crimes permitted and by her officers perpetrated against the Latter-day Saints in the five years between 1833 and 1838, she both deserted and violated the principles of government upon which the State is founded. By failing—nay, worse, by refusing at first to protect by the majesty and righteous execution of her laws, and next by becoming an assailant and robber of the unoffending Latter-day Saints, she denied to them and deprived them of the right to property, the right to pursue happiness, the right to be free the right to worship God after the dictates of their own consciences. And by denying to them and depriving them of these rights, Missouri violated the fundamental principles of American government, and outraged American institutions.

Lastly, I charge Missouri's historians, both those who have written the history of the counties in which the outrages I have detailed occurred, as well as the historians of the State at large, with having glazed over these deeds of infamy. They have either withheld or misrepresented the facts, and have descended so low as to become apologists for the State and the officers that could perpetrate and become a party to such acts of injustice, rapine and murder.

The statements of fact in these pages are irrefutable and easy of verification. They can neither be successfully denied, gainsaid, nor explained away; nor can the impeachment of the State of Missouri before the Bar of History, Civilization or of American Institutions. The otherwise grand State of Missouri is stained with dishonor; because of her treatment of the Latter-day Saints on her escutcheon is to be seen the blotch of innocent blood unavenged.

In undertaking the task of writing this history, the one thought above all others in my mind has been the desire to present to the youth of the Latter-day Saints, many of whose fathers passed through these trying scenes, with a circumstantial account of them that they might know how much was endured by their fathers for the truth's sake; that they might learn to prize it, not only for what it is in itself, but also to prize it to some degree for what it cost the fathers. But at the close of my task I find myself convinced that it is equally important that the people of Missouri and of the United States should have the plain facts presented to them, that they may not unwittingly, as the general tendency now is, become in a manner parties to the crime by approving what was done in that period, and thus fall under the displeasure of God, whose words are equally strong against those who shed the blood of the saints and the prophets, and those who applaud such crimes.

APPENDICES

APPENDIX I.

"MORMONS" IN JACKSON COUNTY.

(Taken from the "History of Jackson County, Missouri," published by Union Historical Co., Kansas City, Missouri, 1881, pp. 250 to 269, inclusive.)

A very prominent feature of the early history of Jackson County was the trouble between the "Mormons" and other citizens during 1831 and 1832, which led to the expulsion of the former from the county during the latter part of the year 1832. This sect was brought into existence on the sixth day of April, 1830, near Manchester, New York. The first society consisted of six persons—Joseph Smith, Sr., Joseph Smith, Jr., Hyrum Smith, Samuel Smith, Oliver Cowdery and Joseph Knight. The three Smiths last mentioned were brothers, and sons of Joseph Smith, Sr., and Joseph Smith, Jr., was the reputed author of the new faith, and is the prophet of "Mormon" history. This Smith family came from Vermont, where Joseph, Jr., was born at Sharon, in Windsor County, December 23rd, 1805. They are represented by their neighbors, both in Vermont and New York, to have been a shiftless, worthless family. The parents are represented as having been dishonest, unreliable, ignorant and superstitious, and the sons seemed to have inherited all these peculiarities. A part of the business of the father was that of "water witch," in which capacity he went about the country with a hazel rod divining where water could be found by digging wells, by the writhings of the rod when held in the hands in a peculiar manner.

Young Joseph is reported to have been a wild, reckless boy, dishonest, untruthful and intemperate. As he grew toward adult age he adopted his father's profession of "water-witching," and afterwards added to it the more practical business of digging the wells he thus located. While in this capacity he discovered a smooth, round stone of peculiar shape while digging a well for a Mr. Chase near Manchester. This he adopted as a "peep stone," and pretended that by placing it in his hat in a peculiar way it had the miraculous power of revealing to him where lost and stolen articles could be found, and he then added this to his previous miraculous business of "water-witchery."

During the decade from 1820 to 1830 a great religious revival swept over the country, and gave rise to the phenomena known as "jerks!" This excitement raged greatly in western New York and in the neighborhood of the Smiths. Joseph, Jr., and some of his sisters and brothers became converted at one of the revivals, but Joseph was greatly vexed in spirit by the uncertainty as to which of the sects was the right one. He became a constant reader of the Bible for a time, but subsequently fell again into his old ways, and later events indicate that he fell also into some new ones, which have extended the peculiarities of his nature much beyond the sphere of his personal influence and beyond the period of his time. He put forth the claim that in September, 1823, God sent messengers to him to say that he was forgiven for his sins. Again in 1826, he claimed an angel visited him with the information that in the Hill Cumorah, not far from Manchester, were hidden certain golden plates which he was to unearth and translate. These plates were exhumed in September, 1826, as Joseph represents it, "with a mighty display of celestial machinery," and were delivered by the angels to him. These plates were afterwards translated by Joseph Smith, Oliver Cowdery, a school-master, and one Martin Harris, and published in the early part of the year 1830 as the "Book of Mormon."

Another account of the origin of the Book of Mormon is that it was written as a historical romance, to account for the Indians in America, in 1812, by a Mr. Solomon Spaulding, a retired preacher, and presented to Mr. Patterson, a bookseller in Pittsburg for publication, together with a preface representing it to have been taken from plates dug up in Ohio. Mr. Patterson did not think the enterprise would pay, and hence did not publish it; but Sidney Rigdon, afterwards quite noted in early "Mormon" history, was then at work in the office of Mr. Patterson, and it is suggested that he stole the manuscripts, and had his full share in bringing "Mormonism" into existence, though he did not appear in connection with it for some months after the organization of the first society.

But, however the book may have come, Joseph Smith appears from the first as prophet, and directed the movements of the new sect by what he claimed to be divine revelations, and put forth the most extravagant claims for himself and his prophetic powers. This was a time particularly favorable for the cultivation of such a superstition. The religious ideas prevailing at the time of the religious excitement referred to, embraced the belief in the direct dealings of God with man, very much after the manner represented in ancient Jewish history, which made such pretenses as these peculiarly liable to be accepted. Immediately after the organization of the first society, as above stated, there was an administration of the sacrament, and the laying on of hands for the "Gift of the Holy Ghost." Five days afterward, on the

11th of May, Oliver Cowdery preached the first sermon on the new faith, and before the close of the month, at Colesville, Browne [A] County, New York, there was what was claimed by the new sect to be miracles performed. From this the new sect took strong root with the ignorant and superstitious, and it gained members rapidly, notwithstanding the prophet was several times arrested for misdemeanors. In August, Paxley P. Platte [B] and Sidney Rigdon appeared as "Mormons," and soon after Orson Platte [C] was converted and baptized into the new sect.

[Footnote A: This should be Broome County.]

[Footnote B: Should be Parley P Pratt.]

[Footnote C: Should be Orson Pratt.]

The work of propagandation now became very active and effective. Smith put forth a revelation that mundane things were about to be brought to an end, a claim that was likely to strike terror into the hearts of the ignorant and superstitious, after the strong religious excitement that had been prevailing, and with the ideas of hell and the future state at that time current in theology. This was industriously proclaimed by the preachers, and accompanied with the narration of Smith's miracle, and the injunction to seek safety in the new Church. Its effect upon the ignorant and superstitious was very great, and by October, 1830, the society numbered fifty, and by June, 1831, about two thousand. Rigdon having taken up his residence near Kirtland, Ohio, had gathered around him about fifty very fanatical people. In January, 1831, he visited Smith in New York, and Smith returned with him to Kirtland, and soon afterward there was a gathering of all the adherents at Kirtland. This is known in "Mormon" history as the "First Hegira."

The sect, at this time, as at all others, was composed of ignorant, superstitious and fanatical people prepared by these qualities to accept anything marvelous that might be told them, or to do anything to which they might be directed by one imposed upon them as a prophet or something demanded of them by the Lord.

Such were the character of the people whom Smith attempted to settle in Jackson County. In June, 1831, Smith put forth a revelation to the effect that the final gathering place of the saints, which name they had now assumed, was to be in Missouri. Accordingly he set out with a few elders for the new land of promise, arriving at Independence in July. Here he put forth another revelation stating that this was the land, or as he put it, "the Zion that should never be moved," and that the whole land was "solemnly dedicated to the Lord and his saints." They began at once to build and at first erected a log house in Kaw township about twelve miles from Independence. On the 2nd of August, he gave out another revelation that the site of the great temple was three hundred yards west of the court house in Independence, and accordingly on the 3rd of August the spot was taken possession of by Joseph Smith, Sidney Rigdon, Edward Partridge, W. W. Phelps, Oliver Cowdery, Martin Harris and Joseph Coe, and dedicated with great ceremony, and followed by an "accession of gifts" from God. The next day, August 4th, another and larger party arrived from Kirtland, and the first "general conference" in the Land of Zion was immediately held. During this conference Smith gave utterance to another revelation, stating that the whole land should be theirs and should not be obtained "but by purchase or by blood." The situation, surroundings and leadership of these people seemed to impress their ignorant and superstitious minds with the idea that they were a chosen people designed in the purposes of God, to effect some great reformation in the world, and they seemed to have imagined that they occupied a similar position to that assigned by the Bible to the ancient Jews at the time of their escape from Egyptian bondage and replanting in Canaan. From this extravagance the way to others was open, easy and natural. In their poverty, the purchase of the "whole land" by them was manifestly not intended, and hence they seemed to expect that in some way the Lord would establish them in the possession of Missouri without that. Assuming this that they were the holy people of the Lord, that the Lord was the real owner of all things, and that all his possessions were free to them, they were not calculated to be respectful of the rights and interest of their non-"Mormon" neighbors *But though no overt acts of transgression upon such rights were being committed,* [D] the rapidly gathering members of the "Mormons," their ignorance, poverty and fanaticism, and the boastfulness and assurance with which they reiterated their belief in their destined possession of the country, backed by Smith's significant revelations and the dishonesty of the methods of the leaders, made the new sect an object of profound solicitude to the people.

[Footnote D: Italics are mine.—R.]

In August following the "general conference," Smith and Rigdon returned to Kirtland, where they established a mill and a bank, the latter being an irresponsible "wild cat" concern that failed soon after its notes were well afloat, which failure was attended by another revelation to Smith, directing him and Rigdon to depart at night for Missouri.

Soon after their arrival at Kirtland in August, W. W. Phelps was appointed to purchase a press and establish a Church paper in Independence, to be called the *Evening and Morning Star*. The prospectus for this paper appeared in February, 1832, and the paper itself in June following. On the 25th of March, 1832, Smith and Rigdon, while away from home, were seized by a mob and tarred, feathered and beaten for attempting to establish communism, and for forgery and dishonest dealings. In April, 1832, Smith being at Independence, a council was held and the printing press set up with religious ceremonies. In June the paper made its appearance and further excited the apprehensions of the citizens by an article on "Free People of Color," which was understood by the slave-holding population of Missouri to mean that the new sect were what was then appropriately called "abolitionists," and which in the excitement of that time about slavery, were as obnoxious to slave-holders as though they possessed the "cloven foot." This was a further cause of apprehension and led to a reply in a pamphlet entitled, "Beware of False Prophets!" In the spring of 1833, the "Mormons" numbered fifteen hundred in Jackson County. They had nearly taken possession of Independence, and were rapidly extending their settlements. They grew bolder as they grew stronger, and daily proclaimed to the older settlers that the Lord had given them the whole land of Missouri; that bloody wars would extirpate all other sects from the country; that it would be "one gore of blood from the Mississippi to the border," and that the few who were left unslain would be the servants of the saints, who would own all the property in the country.

At the same time they fell into equal extravagance regarding spiritual things, and declared themselves "kings and priests of the Most High God," and all other religious sects as reprobates, the creation of the devil designed to speedy destruction, and that all but themselves were doomed, cast away Gentiles, worse than the heathen and unfit to live. They notified all "Gentiles" who were building new houses and opening new farms that it was needless, that the Lord would never allow them to enjoy the fruits of their labor and that in a few months the "Gentiles" would have neither name nor place in Missouri.

At the same time that these extravagances were thus indulged, there does not appear to have been any more lawlessness among them or by them than would result from any equal number of low, ignorant people, so that while their presence was rapidly becoming insufferable, *they were doing nothing that would warrant their legal expulsion.* [E] Still their numbers constantly increased by accessions from the east and from time to time large and enthusiastic meetings were held. In addition to their paper they had established a Church store in Independence, which was kept by Bishop Partridge. During the spring and summer it began to be manifest that they would be strong enough at the fall election to control the election of officers, and the other settlers could not regard, except with grave apprehension, the filling of the county offices by members of such a sect. These apprehensions were intensified by scandalous stories, which about this time began to reach Missouri about the leaders of the sect in Ohio, and as the feeling of apprehension increased, there arose a state of restlessness and friction closely bordering upon open hostility. However, beyond some mutual petty annoyances, such as throwing stones at houses, breaking down fences, etc., there was no open action taken until the 20th of July, when a number of citizens, about four hundred, assembled to take action on the situation.

[Footnote E: Italics are mine.—R.]

The following account of this meeting is taken from a report published in the *Western Monitor*, at that time published by Weston F. Birch, at Fayette, Mo.:

"The meeting was organized by calling Colonel Richard Sampson to the chair, and appointing James H. Flournoy and Colonel Samuel D. Lucas as secretaries.

"Messrs. Russell Hicks, Esq., Robert Johnson, Henry Childs, Esq., Colonel James Hambriglet, Thomas Hudspeth, Joel F. Chiles, and James M. Hunter, were appointed to draft an address; the meeting then adjourned and convened again, when the following was presented:

"This meeting, professing to act not from the excitement of the moment, but under a deep and abiding conviction, that the occasion is one that calls for cool deliberation, as well as energetic action, deem it proper to lay before the public an *expose* of our peculiar situation, in regard to this singular sect of pretended Christians, and a solemn declaration of our unalterable determination to amend it.

"The evil is one that no one could have foreseen, and it is therefore unprovided for by the laws, and the delays of legislation would put the mischief beyond remedy.

"But little more than two years ago some two or three of these people made their appearance in the upper Missouri, and they now number some twelve hundred souls in this county, and each successive autumn and spring pours forth its swarms among us, with a gradual falling of the character of those who compose them, until it seems that those communities from which they come were flooding us with the very dregs of their composition. Elevated, as they mostly are, but little above the condition of our blacks, either in regard to property or education, they have become a subject of much anxiety on that point, serious and well-grounded complaints having already been made of their corrupting influence on our slaves.

* * * * * * *

"When we reflect on the extensive field in which the sect is operating, and that there exists in every country a leaven of superstition that embraces with avidity notions the most extravagant and unheard-of, and whatever can be gleaned by them from the purlieus of vice and the abodes of ignorance, it is to be cast like a waif into our social circles. It requires no gift of prophecy to tell that the day is not far distant when the civil government of the county will be in their hands; when the sheriff, the justices and the county judges will be 'Mormons,' or persons wishing to court their favor from motives of interest or ambition.

"What would be the fate of our lives and property in the hands of jurors and witnesses who do not blush to declare, and would not upon occasion hesitate to swear that they have wrought miracles, and have been the subjects of miraculous and supernatural cures; have conversed with God and his angels, and possess and exercise the gifts of divination and of unknown tongues, and fired with the prospect of obtaining inheritances without money and without price, may be better imagined than described.

* * * * * * *

"And we do hereby most solemnly declare,

"That no 'Mormon' shall in future move into and settle in this county.

"That those now here shall give a definite pledge of their intention, within a reasonable time, to move out of the county, shall be allowed to remain unmolested until they have sufficient time to sell their property and close their business without any material sacrifice.

"That the editor of the *Star* be required forthwith to close his office, etc.
* * * * * *

"That those who fail to comply with these requisitions be referred to those of their brethren who have the gift of divination and of unknown tongues to inform them of the lot that awaits them."

Compliance with these demands being refused, the people assembled, tore down the printing office, scattering the materials and paper on the ground, and took Bishop Partridge, and a man named Charles Allen, to the public square, where they stripped and tarred and feathered them. Mr. Gilbert, who was now connected with the store, agreed to close it, and the mob then dispersed until the twenty-third.

On the 23rd of July, this convention of citizens again convened and a committee was appointed to confer with the "Mormon" leaders. This committee was met by Messrs. Phelps, Partridge, Gilbert, and Messrs. Covil, Whitmer and Morley, elders of the sect. Between them an agreement was made to the effect that Oliver Cowdery, W. W. Phelps, William McLellin, Edward Partridge, Lyman Wight, Simeon Carter, Peter and John Whitmer, and Harvey Whitlock, were to remove from the county on or before January 1, 1834, and were to use their influence to secure the removal of all the saints—one-half by January 1st, the other half by April 1, 1834; John Corril and Algernon Gilbert were to be allowed to remain as agents to settle up the business of those removing; the *Star* was not again to be published nor any other press set up in the county; Mr. Phelps and Mr. Partridge, if their families removed by January 1st, were to be allowed to come and go in settling up their business. The committee of citizens pledged themselves to use their influence to see that no violence was to be used against the saints while compliance to the agreement was being observed.

This agreement as reported to the meeting, was unanimously adopted by the citizens, and the minutes signed by the chairman, Richard Sampson, and the secretaries, S. D. Lucas, J. H. Flournoy.

In September Orson Hyde and W. W. Phelps were appointed by the "Mormons" as a delegation to Governor Dunklin, then Governor of Missouri, and to represent the affairs already recited, and to ask for protection. They prepared and presented to the Governor, October 8th, a long memorial setting forth a long list of grievances, wrongs and intimidations which they had suffered at the hands of the people of Jackson County. The Attorney-General being absent, Governor Dunklin declined to take any action until his return, so that it was not until the 19th of October that they received his decision. The case presented to him was an *ex parte* one, and it received a decision which led the "Mormon" leaders to rely upon his protection. He denied the right of any citizens to take into their own hands the redress of the grievances, and recommended the "Mormons" to appeal to the civil courts by affidavit and legal process for redress of the wrongs complained of, and promised them a faithful enforcement of the laws.

In pursuance of this action of the Governor, the leaders resolved not to abide by the agreement made with the people in July. Preparations for removal from the county were stopped and their leaders engaged Messrs. Woods, Reese, Doniphan and Atchison to defend them and prosecute for them in the courts. This aroused the citizens again, and although the "Mormons" had not so violated the law as to enable the people to proceed against them by legal process, the prospect, from the facts already stated, were regarded by the people as so extraordinary as to warrant extraordinary measures. Their safety, it appeared to them, depended upon the expulsion of the "Mormons" from the county by force, and they at once began preparations to that end.

On the 31st day of October, a party of forty or fifty armed men, without other warrant than their own judgment of the requirements of the situation, visited a settlement of the "Mormons" on the Big Blue, destroyed ten houses and whipped a number of men. On the night of the 1st of November another party visited a settlement about twelve miles southwest of Independence, where Parley P. Pratt had assembled a force of about sixty men; here they encamped for the night and put out guards, two of which, Robert Johnson and a man named Harris, had an encounter with Pratt, whom one of them knocked down with a musket. They were then captured by Pratt's party and detained over night. The same night they were attacked in Independence and houses were stoned, doors broken down, etc. Part of A. S. Gilbert's house was pulled down and the doors of the store were broken in and the goods scattered on the street. A party of "Mormons," summoned from a neighboring settlement, saved part of the goods and attempted to have a man named Richard McCarty arrested for participation in the affair, but the Justice of the Peace applied to, Samuel Weston, refused to issue a warrant for the purpose. At the same time other "Mormon" settlements were visited by the people and great consternation was caused thereby among the women and children, the men having fled, but no injury was done them. The next day, November 2nd, all the Independence "Mormons," numbering about thirty families, left town and gathered together for protection. The same day people made another attack on the Big Blue settlement, when they unroofed another house. They attacked also another settlement about six miles from Independence. The next day, November 3rd, Joshua Lewis, Hiram Page and two other "Mormons" went to Lexington to ask protection from the circuit court, which was refused; while others applied to Justice of the Peace Silvers at Independence, with a like result. A number of persons at this time visited the "Mormons" and advised them to leave the country, as the people were so incensed at them that their lives were in danger. This was Sunday, and the "Mormons" had a rumor among them that a general massacre was impending for Monday.

When Monday came the citizens collected and took possession of a ferry belonging to the "Mormons" across the Blue, but they soon abandoned it and gathered in greater numbers at Wilson's store about one mile west of it. A party of "Mormons," numbering about thirty, started from an adjacent settlement to help those on the Blue, but hearing of the assembly of the citizens at the store, fled through the cornfields and were pursued by the citizens. Later in the day a party of about thirty arrived from the settlement on the prairie where Pratt had encountered the guards a few nights before, and between them and the citizens a fight occurred, in which Hugh L. Brozeal and Thos. Linville of the citizens were killed and a "Mormon" named Barber fatally wounded. This fight created the greatest excitement throughout the county.

The same day Richard McCarty caused Gilbert and Whitney to be arrested for assaulting him in Independence Saturday night, and for causing his arrest and attempting to prosecute him afterward. The situation of affairs now was that no "Mormon" could receive justice from the public courts any more than a citizen could have received justice in a trial by "Mormons." The conduct of the "Mormons" had so disrupted public peace and order that the county was virtually in the hands of a mob. In this situation Samuel C. Owens, clerk of the county court, advised Gilbert and Whitney to go to jail as a means of protection, and they, together with W. E. McLellin and a Mr. Coville and Morley, and one other "Mormon," took this advice. During the night, Gilbert, Coville and Morley were taken out for the purpose of an interview with their fellow "Mormons," but on being returned next morning were fired upon by a party of six or seven citizens. Coville and Morley ran and escaped, but Gilbert was retained by the sheriff. The balance of the party were released next day.

The next day, November 5th, brought still more exciting times, for rumors from both sides exaggerated the scenes that had transpired; the citizens gathered to the number of hundreds from all parts of the county; the "Mormons," too, were rallying, one hundred of them collecting about a mile west of Independence. There they halted, waiting to learn the condition of affairs. They were informed that the militia had been ordered out for their protection and that Colonel Pitcher was in command. Upon application to this officer the "Mormons" were told that there was no alternative, they must leave the county forthwith; and deliver into Col. Pitcher's hands certain ones of their number to be tried for murder; and to give up their arms. To these demands the "Mormons" yielded. The arms, about fifty guns of all sorts, were surrendered; the men present accused of being in the skirmish the evening before, were given up for trial; and after being kept in durance for a day and night Col. Pitcher took them into a cornfield near by and said to them, "Clear out!"

Following this event small parties went over the country warning the "Mormons" away wherever found, and not unfrequently using violence to the men when any of them were caught. This was continued by the infuriated citizens until the "Mormons" had all fled the county. They attempted to find refuge in adjoining counties, but Clay was the only one that would receive them.

This was the end of "Mormonism" in Jackson County, but not the end of the Mormon trouble, for through the influence of their attorneys, and in the absence of such open violations of law as would have warranted their legal expulsion from the county, they were able to impress Governor Dunklin with the idea that they were then the victims of a ruffianly mob and were being persecuted on account of their religion. Hence for several years afterward there was a sort of support given them by the governor, which, though insufficient to reinstate them in Jackson County, was sufficient to inspire them with the hope, and caused them to expect and to some extent propose to return. This kept up the trouble.

Whether the people were justified in so employing violence to rid themselves of an obnoxious sect, the members of which had not so violated the law as to warrant their legal expulsion, was shown by the events of the next few years. The "Mormons" settled finally in Clay, Carroll, Ray, Caldwell and Daviess counties, where they grew strong and prosperous, and, as in Jackson County, became correspondingly arrogant and unbearable. They took political possession of Daviess County, and there and in Caldwell County began to put in practice the things the people in Jackson County had apprehended and to prevent which they expelled them from the county. After making for themselves a record for treason, arson, burglary, theft, murder, and a long list of other crimes, they were finally, in 1838, expelled from the State by Governor Boggs, whom they attempted afterward, on the 6th day of May, 1842, to assassinate while sitting in his house at Independence.[F]

[Footnote F: For an investigation of this subject see "Rise and Fall of Nauvoo," by the author of "Missouri Persecutions."]

A quite detailed account of their efforts to get back to Jackson County, and of the action of Governor Dunklin, and the negotiations between them and the people of Jackson County, has been furnished in the following, which, it will be observed, is as favorable to the "Mormons" as possible:

November 21st, R. W. Wells, attorney-general of Missouri, wrote to the legal counsel employed by the saints, that he felt warranted in advising them that in case the "Mormons" expelled from Jackson County desired to be reinstated, he had no doubt the governor would send them military aid. He further advised that the "Mormons" might organize into militia and receive public arms for their own defense. Judge Ryland also wrote Attorney Amos Reese, stating that the governor had inquired of him respecting the "outrageous acts of unparalleled violence that have lately happened in Jackson County;" and wished to know whether the "Mormons" were willing to take "legal steps against the citizens of Jackson County."

He further wished to know whether a writ issued by him upon the oath of Joshua Lewis and Hiram Page had been handed to the sheriff for service; and if so what was the fate of the writ. This letter was dated November 24, 1833.

In answer to the governor's inquiries Mr. Gilbert wrote that officer on November 29th, giving the following reasons why an immediate court of inquiry could not be held. "Our Church is scattered in every direction: some in Van Buren, (a new county;) a part in this county, (Clay;) and a part in Lafayette, Ray, etc. Some of our principal witnesses would be women and children, and while the rage of the mob continues, it would be impossible to gather them in safety to Independence. And that your excellency may know of the unabating fury with which the last remnant of our people remaining in that county are pursued at this time, I here state that a few families, perhaps fifteen to twenty, who settled themselves more than two years ago on the prairie, about fifteen miles from the county seat of Jackson County, had hoped from the obscurity of their location that they might escape the vengeance of the enemy through the winter; consequently they remained on their plantations, receiving occasionally a few individual threats, till last Sunday, when a mob made their appearance among them; some with pistols cocked and presented to their breasts, commanding to leave the county in three days, or they would tear their houses down over their heads, etc." * * *

"An immediate court of inquiry called while our people are thus situated, would give our enemies a decided advantage in point of testimony, while they are in possession of their homes, and ours also; with no enemy in the county to molest or make them afraid."

This letter was read and concurred in by Mr. Reese.

Those people threatened on the 24th, as stated by Mr. Gilbert, fled into Clay County and encamped on the Missouri.

December 6th, an additional memorial of facts and petition for aid, was sent to Governor Dunklin, setting forth the facts of their dispersion, and signed by six of the elders of The Church. A letter accompanied the petition, informing his excellency of the wish and intention of the saints to return to their homes, if assured of safety and protection.

On Monday, December 24th, four families living near Independence, whose age and penury prevented their removal in haste, were driven from their homes; the chimneys of their houses were thrown down, and the doors and windows broken in. Two of these men were named Miller and Jones, Mr. Miller being sixty-five years old, and the youngest of the four.

A court of inquiry was held in Liberty, Clay County, during December, which resulted in the arrest of Colonel Pitcher for driving the saints, or "Mormons," from Jackson, for trial by court-martial.

Mr. Gilbert wrote Governor Dunklin from Liberty, Clay County, January 9, 1834, submitting for consideration the idea of the saints making the endeavor to purchase the property of a number of the most violent opposers, if such effort would be satisfactory, and help to solve the question peaceably.

Governor Dunklin replied to the memorials and petitions of the saints in a friendly manner, avowing his desire and design to enforce the civil law, and if practicable, to reinstate those unlawfully dispossessed of their homes. Two clauses in this letter disclose something in reference to the peculiar animus of the persecution waging against the "Mormon" population. He wrote: "Your case is certainly a very emergent one, and the consequences as important to your society as if the war had been waged against the whole State; yet the public has no other interest in it, than that the laws be faithfully executed. Thus far, I presume, the whole community feel a deep interest, for that which is the case of the 'Mormons' today, may be the case of the Catholics tomorrow; and after them any other sect that may become obnoxious to a majority of the people of any section of the State. So far as a faithful execution of the laws is concerned, the executive is disposed to do everything consistent with the means furnished him by the legislature, and I think I may safely say the same of the judiciary.

"As now advised, I am of the opinion that a military guard will be necessary to protect the State witnesses and officers of the court, and to assist in the execution of its orders, while sitting in Jackson County."

An order was sent by the same mail from the governor, directing the captain of the Liberty Blues, a military organization, to comply with the requisitions of the circuit attorney, in the progress of the trials that might ensue. This letter is dated February 4, 1834.

Suits were instituted by Messrs. Phelps and Partridge, in the proper courts of Jackson County, and a dozen or so of the brethren summoned by subpoena to attend the sitting of the court of inquiry to be held. These witnesses were met February 23rd, at Everett's Ferry by the Liberty Blues, fifty strong, commanded by Captain Atchison, to guard them into Jackson County. They crossed the river, and encamped about a mile from it. From reports brought into camp by scouts sent out, Captain Atchison sent an order to Captain Allen for two hundred drafted militia, and to Liberty for ammunition. The next day the party reached Independence, where the witnesses met the district attorney, Mr. Reese, and the attorney-general, Mr. Wells; and from them it was ascertained that all prospect for a criminal prosecution was at an end. Mr. Wells had been instructed by the governor, to investigate, "as far as possible," the outrages in Jackson; but the determined opposition presented to the enforcement of the law, by those who had driven the "Mormons" out, prevented the performance of executive duty.

The judge discharged Captain Atchison and his company of Blues, stating that their service was not needed and that officer marched out of town, with the witnesses under guard, to the tune of "Yankee Doodle."

While all this was transpiring time passed on and others were made to suffer. One old man Lindsay, nearly seventy, had his house thrown down, his goods, corn and other property piled together and fired, but was fortunate, after the parties who did it left, to save a part of his effects through the exertions of a son. Lyman Leonard, one of those who was compelled to return from Van Buren County was dragged from his house, beaten and left for dead, but revived and escaped. Joshua Sumner and Barnet Cole were beaten severely at the same time.

March 31st, 1834, Ira I. Willis went over from Clay County into Jackson to look for and reclaim a cow that had strayed. While at the house of Justice Manship, making proof to the ownership of the cow, he was set upon and cruelly whipped.

April 10th, 1804,[G] a petition was prepared memoralizing the President of the United States, and stating the facts of the expulsion of the people from Jackson County; and further setting forth that an impartial investigation into their several individual wrongs in the county where those wrongs were committed was impossible; they therefore asked that the executive power of the United States be exercised in their protection. This memorial and petition was signed by one hundred and fourteen of the expelled refugees.

[Footnote G: Doubtless should be 1834.]

In answer to this petition the President by order replied that the matter of the petition was referred to the War Department, and the department declined interference, as it did not appear that the emergency warranting such interference had occurred. This information was dated May 2nd, 1834, and signed by Lewis Cass. On the same day Governor Dunklin wrote to Messrs. Phelps and others, that the court of inquiry, before which Lieut. Col. Pitcher was to answer, had decided that the demand made by the officer for the surrender of the arms of the saints on Nov. 5th, 1833, was improper, and an order was sent to Col. Lucas to return them. This order directed Col. Lucas to deliver to W. W. Phelps, E. Partridge and others, fifty-two guns and one pistol, received by Col. Pitcher from the "Mormons," Nov. 5th, 1833.

The result of this order is seen from the following communication made to Gov. Dunklin, May 7th, 1834: "Since the 24th ult., the mob of Jackson County have burned our dwellings to the number of over one hundred and fifty. Our arms were also taken from the depository, (the jail,) about ten days since and distributed among the mob." * * * * * * *

The order for the restoration was forwarded to Col. Lucas, at Independence, May 17th, with a statement that he might return the arms to either of the three ferries on the Missouri, the line between Jackson and Clay counties. Of this delivery of the order the governor was informed by letter dated May 29th. To the letter and order to Col. Lucas, that officer stated that he would reply by May 22nd, but before that time he removed to Lexington and did not reply what he would do.

Some time in May the expelled "Mormons" and their friends in Clay County began the manufacture of weapons, in order to be prepared for defense if occasion again required it; and in this many of the influential men of the county encouraged them, in order, as they said, "to help the 'Mormons' to settle their own difficulties."

In the fall and before the agreement to leave Jackson County had been made, by the "Mormons" afterward expelled, a number of their brethren in Ohio, including Joseph Smith, Sylvester Smith, Frederick Williams and others, not far from one hundred and fifty men in all, had made arrangements to move into Missouri, with the intent to aid their followers there in defending themselves, or to share with them the fate that might await them. Of their intention thus to enter the State as immigrants, they notified their brethren in Missouri, who by letter dated April 24th, 1834, informed the governor, asking that their arms be restored to them and they be reinstated in their homes with the privilege of maintaining themselves in those homes, when so reinstated, by force; further asking the governor to give them a guard to escort them to Jackson County, when their friends from the East arrived. This letter was signed by A. S. Gilbert and four others.

This company above referred to, left Kirtland May 5th, 1834, and on June 5th, Mr. Gilbert notified the governor, in accordance with the opinion of Mr. Reese, district attorney, that the company was nearly to their journey's end; and again asked for an escort.

In answer to the communications of Mr. Gilbert and others, Governor Dunklin made answer, dated at Jefferson City, June 6th, 1834, from which letter, directed to Col. J. Thornton, the following extracts are taken:

"Dear Sir:—I was pleased at the reception of your letter, concurred in by Messrs. Reese, Atchison and Doniphan, on the subject of the Mormon difficulties. * * * A more clear and indisputable right does not exist, that the Mormon people, who were expelled from their homes in Jackson County, to return and live on their lands, and if they cannot be persuaded as a matter of policy to give up that right, or to qualify it, my course, as the chief executive officer of the State, is a plain one. The Constitution of the United States declares: 'That the citizens of each State shall be entitled to all privileges and immunities of citizens in the several States.' Then we cannot interdict any people who have a political franchise in the United States, from immigrating to this State, nor from choosing what part of the State they will settle in, provided they do not trespass on the property or rights of others. * * * And again, our Constitution says; That all men have a natural and indefeasible right to worship Almighty God according to the dictates of their own consciences.' I am fully persuaded that the eccentricity of the religious opinions and practices of the 'Mormons' is at the bottom of the outrages committed against them. They have the right constitutionally guaranteed to them, and it is indefeasible, to believe, and worship Joe Smith as a man, as an angel, or even as the true and living God, and to call their habitation Zion, the Holy Land, or even heaven itself. Indeed there is nothing so absurd or ridiculous, that they have not the right to adopt as their religion, so that in its exercise they do not interfere with the rights of others. * * * I consider it the duty of every good citizen of Jackson and adjoining counties, to exert themselves to effect a compromise of their difficulties, and were I assured I would not have to act in my official capacity in the affair, I would visit the parties in person and exert myself to the utmost to settle it. My first advice would be to the Mormons to sell out their lands in Jackson County, and to settle somewhere else, where they could live in peace, if they could get a fair price for them, and reasonable damages for injuries received. If this failed I would try the citizens and advise them to meet and rescind their illegal resolve of last summer; and agree to conform to the laws in every particular, in respect to the Mormons. If both these failed, I would then advise the plan you have suggested, for each party to take separate territory, and confine their numbers within their respective limits, with the exception of the public right of ingress and egress upon the public highway. If all these failed then the simple question of legal right would have to settle it. It is this last that I am afraid I shall have to conform my action to in the end, and hence the necessity of keeping myself in the best situation to do my duty impartially."

To facilitate any effort that might be made to effect a settlement of the troubles, the governor appointed Col. Thornton as an aid to the commander-in-chief, and requested him to keep himself and the governor closely informed of all that was transpiring.

The company emigrating from Ohio, under the charge of Joseph Smith, were joined at Salt River, Missouri, by a number from Michigan in charge of Hyrum Smith and Lyman Wright,[H] their united number being two hundred and five men. These were organized and drilled under Mr. Wright, who was appointed to the command of the whole force.

[Footnote H: Wight.]

June 9th, 1834, the governor issued a second order for the return of the arms, directed to Col. Pitcher, Col. Lucas having resigned his command and left the county. This order to Col. Pitcher required him to collect the arms, if not in his possession, and return them to Messrs. Phelps and Partridge and others from whom they were taken.

June 10th, Judge John F. Ryland wrote to Mr. Gilbert from Richmond, requesting that the "Mormons" be called together at Liberty the following Monday, the 16th, at which time he would meet them with a deputation of some of the most respectable citizens of Jackson County and explain to them his views, stating further that he dreaded the consequences likely to ensue if he failed in his efforts to secure an amicable adjustment between the parties. This request was acceded to. Mr. Gilbert and others notified their brethren of the time and place of meeting and its object; and on the 16th the meeting was held, the citizens of Clay County, including the "Mormons," numbering between eight hundred and a thousand, assembled at the court house, where they were met by the judge and a deputation from Jackson County. At this meeting the citizens of Jackson County, through a committee consisting of Mr. Samuel C. Owens and nine others, submitted propositions in substance as follows: That they would purchase the lands and improvements of the "Mormons" at a valuation to be fixed by arbitrators to be agreed upon by the parties; that when these arbitrators should have been chosen, twelve of the "Mormons" should be permitted to go with the arbitrators to point out the lands and improvements to be valued, the people of the county guaranteeing their safety while so doing; that when these arbitrators should have fixed said valuation, the people of Jackson County would pay the same with one hundred per cent added thereto within thirty days after said report. That upon said payment so made the "Mormons" should execute deeds for the lands, and make no effort ever after to settle as a community or as individuals within the county. Both parties were to enter into bonds to keep the terms of the agreement when made. A counter proposition was that the "Mormons" should buy all the lands of the people of Jackson County and their improvements on the public lands, the valuation to be made in the same way by arbitrators, and the same addition of one hundred per cent to such valuation when reported, payment to be made by the "Mormons" within thirty days after said report of valuation, as in the first proposition.

After the reading of this proposition, its adoption and enforcement were warmly urged by Mr. Owens, chairman of the deputation from Jackson County, and were as warmly met and opposed by Gen. Doniphan. Rev. M. Riley, of the Baptist church, urged the expulsion of the "Mormons," stating that they had "lived long enough in Clay County, and must either clear out or be cleared out." Mr. Turnham, the moderator of the meeting, answered this speech, counseling moderation, saying, among other things, "Let us be Republicans; let us honor our country and not disgrace it like Jackson County. For God's sake, don't disfranchise or drive away the 'Mormons.' They are better citizens than many of the old inhabitants." This expression was endorsed by Gen. Doniphan. Considerable excitement ensued, during which a quarrel occurred between some parties outside the door, in which one Calbert stabbed another man named Wales. Someone shouted into the door of the court room, "A man stabbed!" which broke up the meeting. Pending the restoration to order, Messrs. Phelps, McClellan and others consulted together and replied to the proposition, that they were not authorized to accede to either of the set of terms submited, but that they would give general notice and call a meeting of their brethren and make definite answer by the following Saturday or Monday, and that such answer should be placed in the hands of Judge Turnham, chairman of the meeting, earlier than the day named, if possible; assuring Mr. Owens and others that there was no design to open hostilities on the people of Jackson or other counties. They further pledged themselves to prevent any of their brethren coming from the east from entering into Jackson County.

Messrs. Phelps and Gilbert submitted to Mr. Owens and others of the Jackson committee a reply dated June 21st, 1834, stating that they had consulted with their brethren, as agreed, and were authorized to state that the propositions as made to them June 16th, could not be acceded to. In the same communication they gave the assurance that there was no intention on the part of themselves or their brethren to invade the county of Jackson in a hostile manner.

By this uniting, immediate conflict seemed to be averted, and the Jackson County committee returned home by way of the ferry, where is now the Wayne City landing. The boat was taken over to them and ten or twelve men and as many horses went aboard the boat. When about the middle of the Missouri the boat filled with water and sank; men, horses and all went down together. George Bradbury, David Lynch and James Campbell were drowned. S. V. Nolan could not swim, but catching hold of his horse's tail was hauled safely to the Jackson County shore. Samuel C. Owens and Thomas Harrington clung to the wreck of the boat and floated down a mile, and when the boat reached a sandbar Mr. Owens divested himself of all his clothes except his shirt, left the wreck and swam safely to the shore. He found a cow path which he followed to the main road. While traveling the path he found himself terribly annoyed by the sting of the nettle, but he walked to Independence, a distance of some four miles. Mr. Harrington hung to the boat and was drowned. William Everett swam to the Jackson shore and was washed against a drift and was found there ten days afterwards, one hand fast hold of a projecting snag. The other men swam back to the Clay County shore, where they all made it safe except Small-wood Nolan, who clung to a "sawyer" only a short distance from the shore. The men who made the shore built a fire and encouraged Nolan to "cling on" till they could rescue him. He did cling on with the grip of death. When daylight came and the men went in to take him off his scanty support, they found that the water was only waist deep and he could have waded to the shore with ease if he had known it.

It was rumored that the "Mormons" had secretly bored holes in the boat above the customary water mark, but when loaded would sink to the holes and then fill with water. But the most reasonable idea was that the boat did not generally carry such heavy loads, hence the timbers had become dry and the corking loose, and when the water pressed against it gave way and the boat filled.

Joseph Smith and his party passed through Richmond, Clay County, June 19th, and encamped between two branches of Fishing River, not far from their junction. Here they were met by five armed men, who informed them that sixty men from Ray and seventy from Clay counties were to meet others from different places and prevent their further progress. They also learned that two hundred from Jackson County were to cross the Missouri River at Williams' Ferry, there to meet the forces from Ray and Clay Counties, at Fishing River ford, and thence to attack and disperse or destroy them. Their designs, if entertained, were prevented, for on the night following a severe storm of wind and rain occurred, which raised the streams, flooded the country and prevented any hostile movements being made by either party.

Mr. Smith's band moved out on the prairie on the 20th and encamped, where, on the 21st, they were visited by Col. Sconce and two other leading men from Ray County, who were anxious to know what were their intentions. Mr. Smith replied, stating that they had come to assist their brethren, bringing with them clothing and other supplies to aid them in being reinstated in their rights; and disclaimed any design to interfere with, or molest any people. These men returned from their visit, satisfied of the intentions of Mr. Smith and those with him, and rode through the neighborhood, using their influence to allay the excitement.

Cornelius Gillium, sheriff of Clay County, went to the camp of Mr. Smith and party on June 22nd, and asked for Mr. Smith; and upon being presented to him, gave them some instructions concerning the peculiarities of the inhabitants of the county; and advised Mr. Smith and the rest as to the course that should be pursued by them to secure the protection of the people. Mr. Smith and those with him resumed their march to reach Liberty, Clay County, on the 23rd; but were met by Gen. Atchison and others when within six miles of the town, and were by them persuaded not to go to Liberty, as the people were too much incensed against them. The party, therefore turned away to the left and encamped upon the premises of a member of the fraternity named Burghardt, on the bank of Rush Creek.

From here a proposition for settlement was agreed to on the part of the "Mormons," and was by them sent to Mr. S. C. Owens and others, the committee from Jackson County. This proposition was in substance as follows:

That if the inhabitants of Jackson County would not permit them to return to their homes and remain in peace, then twelve disinterested men were to be chosen, six by each party to the strife, and these twelve men were to fix the value of the lands of those men resident in the county who were opposed to the "Mormons," and could not consent to live in the county with them; that when this valuation was made, the "Mormons" were to have one year in which to raise the money; that none of the "Mormons" should enter the county to reside until the money was paid; that the same twelve men were also to fix the amount of damages incurred by the "Mormons" in their expulsion, and the amount of damages so fixed should be taken from the aggregate sum to be paid by the said "Mormons" for the lands appraised by said arbitrators.

On June 25th, Mr. Smith caused his company to be broken into small bands, and scattered them among the resident members. He also apprised Generals Doniphan, Atchison and Thornton of what he had done, informing them that his company of emigrants would so remain dispersed until every effort for an adjustment of differences had been made on their part, "that would in anywise be required of them by disinterested men of Republican principles."

June 26th, by agreement among the elders of the "Mormons," a letter was prepared to Governor Dunklin, informing him of their arrival in Clay County, of their having been met by General Doniphan, of their present condition and the nature of the negotiations then pending, of the character of the proposals made by them, and notifying the governor that if the present effort for peace failed they should do all that could be required of them by human or divine law to secure peaceably their homes in Jackson County, their claim to which they would not abandon. They further notified the governor that within the week one of their brethren was taken by some citizens from Jackson County, and forcibly carried from Clay County across the Missouri, and after being detained in custody for a day and night was threatened and released. Also, that the houses of a number of their members in Clay County had been broken into and rifled of guns and arms during the absence of the men folks, the women being threatened and intimidated. On the same day they received a rejection of the proposals to Mr. Owens, by the way of their attorney, Mr. Reese.

While encamped on Rush Creek the cholera broke out among them, and out of sixty-eight attacked thirteen died, among them John S. Carter, Eber Wilcox and Algernon S. Gilbert, he who was expelled from Independence.

Mr. Gillium published the result of his visit to the "Mormon" camp, and the propositions made by them as stated above, in the *Enquirer*, July 1st, 1834, and the whole country then became acquainted with the purposes and wishes of these worshipers. We quote from this publication the following:

"We wish to become permanent citizens of the State, and bear our proportion in support of the government and to be protected by its laws. If the above propositions are complied with we are willing to give security on our part, and we shall want the same of the people of Jackson County, for the performance of this agreement. We do not wish to settle down in a body, except where we can purchase the land with money; for to take possession by conquest or the shedding of blood is entirely foreign to our feelings. The shedding of blood we shall not be guilty of, until all just and honorable means among men prove insufficient to restore peace."

This declaration was signed by Joseph Smith, Jr., F. G. Williams, then acting president of The Church, Lyman Wright, Roger Orton, Orson Hyde and John S. Carter, all leading men among the "Mormons." It was directed to John Lincoln, John Sconce, George R. Morehead, James H. Long and James Collins. The "Mormons" also appointed a committee of their number, who drafted an appeal to the people of the United States, in which they set forth the purposes expressed by them in their statement to Mr. Gillium. This appeal was published and scattered abroad, but it is not known what effect it had, other than possibly to exasperate the feeling in Missouri against them.

The message of the governor of Missouri to the general assembly of the State, then in session, communicated on November 20th, 1838, recommended a commission of both houses of the Legislature to inquire into the "Mormon" difficulties. The house, in committee of the whole on the state of the Republic, November 22nd, appointed a select committee of seven to co-operate with such number from the senate as that body might appoint, to inquire into the "causes of said disturbances, and the conduct of the military operations in suppressing them, with power to send for men and papers." The senate, on November 23rd, appointed Messrs. Turner, Noland and Scott, as their part of said committee, thus concurring in the action.

This committee reported in the senate, on December 18th, that they had taken the matters submitted to them into consideration, and decided that they "thought it unwise and injudicious under all the circumstances of the case to predicate a report from the papers, documents, etc., purporting to be copies of the evidence taken before an examining court, held in Richmond, Ray County, for the purpose of inquiring into the charges alleged against the people called 'Mormons,' growing out of the difficulties between that people and other citizens of the State."

The reasons given are: The evidence given in that examination was in a great degree *ex parte,* and not of a character to afford a "fair and impartial investigation." The papers had been so certified as to satisfy the committee of their authenticity. There were still charges pending against some of the "Mormons" for treason, murder and other felonies, which charges were to be tried before the courts in the several counties, where such crimes were charged to have been committed. Publication of the evidence and papers referred to might affect seriously the right of trial by a "jury of the vicinage," by prejudicing public sentiment against the accused. Were the committee to act and send for papers and persons, it might interfere with the action of the courts wherein the suits were pending. For this reason the committee recommended the appointment of a committee, who should, after the adjournment of the assembly, go into the vicinity of the scenes of the difficulties, there to make inquiry and make proper report to the legislature of their inquiry and examination when concluded. Among other reasons given for such recommendation occur these: that the "documents, although serviceable in giving direction to the course of inquiry, are none of them, except the official orders and correspondence, such as ought to be received as conclusive evidence of the facts stated." And that it "would not be proper to publish the official orders and correspondence between the officers in command, and the executive, without the evidence on which they were founded; and that evidence is not sufficiently full and satisfactory to authorize its publication."

The recommendations of the committee were concurred in by the senate, January 10th, and on the 16th Mr. Turner introduced a bill providing such inquiry; making it the duty of the commission when appointed to inquire into the causes of the disturbances. This bill passed after amendment, and being reported to the house was, on February 4th, 1839, laid on the table until July 4th, by 48 to 37.

Pending the expiration of the time for which this bill to inquire into the causes of the disturbance of the peace in the various counties of Clay, Ray and Daviess, the history of the "Mormons" of the State is about as follows:

After the removal from Jackson, and the acceptance of the final decision, nothing further appears of any settlement being attempted in Jackson County by the expelled party, or their brethren. Joseph Smith returned to Kirtland, Ohio, with many others, while some concluded to remain in the, to them, land of Zion; and these settled in and through the counties above named.

Things did not long remain in a peaceful condition, however, and it became apparent that there would again be trouble. To avoid this, if possible, it appears that some of the leading men among the "Mormons" were sent to Richmond, Ray County, and made inquiry as to whether the citizens would be willing that they should settle upon the territory north of and contiguous to the county of Ray, at that time unorganized. To this no answer was given, and, taking it for granted that no objections would be offered, many removed, and Mr. James M. Hunt, in his "Mormon War," written in 1844, declares that: "Here, for some time, the Prophet concentrated his followers; houses were erected, as if by magic—improvements were prosecuted with such rapidity as to promise a flourishing town and country in a very short time. The country round about was fast being settled, and undergoing improvements—every month bringing swarms of deluded fanatics, to forward the designs of their ambitious leaders."

Settlements were made at Far West; one on Grand River, in Daviess, called Adam-Ondi-Ahman, and one in Carrol County, called DeWitt. At these places says, Hunt, "members gathered, improving town and country rapidly." "It is due the 'Mormons,'" further says this writer, "here to state, that they were an industrious, agricultural people, or at least that portion of them who located in the country round about in the 'stakes,'" as these settlements were called by them.

Between the year 1834 and the beginning of 1838, these settlements, outside of Jackson, continued to thrive, disturbed, possibly, by now and then an outrage or reprisal, such as may occur in newly settled countries among any class of settlers, for which mutual wrongs, attempted redresses were sought before mutual courts, as some of the local minor courts were in the hands of the "Mormons," though the county and superior ones were held by other citizens; and each party claimed that injustice was done them by these courts by reason of partisan bias. The feeling was growing bitter against the "Mormons" on the part of the citizens, and the feelings of injury and resentment began to crystallize into provocation and resentment (especially so with some individuals) on the part of the "Mormons." Joseph Smith and Sidney Rigdon had settled with their families in the State, and under their direction the people had been organized and armed, more or less efficiently, to repel encroachments and protect themselves, as they stated, from unlawful aggressions. They had been told that the authority of the legislature and executive could not be brought to bear for their defense until remedies at the lesser courts failed them, and then only at the requisition of local civil officers, and had been advised whether judiciously or otherwise to defend themselves. There grew up some dissensions among themselves: a few, some of the prominent men among them, dissented from the rules of the society and the authority of Messrs. Smith and Rigdon; these were denounced as apostates, and attempts made to drive them out from the society and settlements, which resulted in mutual recrimination and the making public exaggerated accounts of the intentions of the "Mormon" leaders. Some of the brethren who were fanatical or more unwise than others, were guilty of a flagrant excess of language calculated to create suspicion and uneasiness in the minds of those already prejudiced against them as a people. There were some law-breakers among them who committed crimes and were not punished; all of which hastened the impending trouble. These things among themselves, and the constant manifestation of hostility from many of the citizens, lawless and irresponsible, and some of note and ability among the most respectable as well, with occasional depredation upon the "Mormons," resulted in making further peace very improbable.

In June, 1838, Sidney Rigdon preached a sermon, taking strong ground against the dissenters and the Missourians. This sermon was construed as a declaration of war against the apostates and of reprisal against the citizens. Mr. Hunt states that in this state of things, the citizens apprehended wrong-doers against them, but having to go before a "Mormon" justice and jury, they failed and were abused by the "Mormons" for bringing vexatious suits; and that the Gentiles were not idle in "setting afloat their grievances, and probably exaggerating them."

Mr. Rigdon is said to have delivered an oration July 4, 1838, at Far West, before a gathered multitude, which was called a treasonable speech. This oration we have carefully read and can now see that the passages construed as treasonable and dangerous, may have been but the indignant protest against violence that a possible enthusiast might unadvisedly use. They are as follows: "And that mob that comes on us to disturb us, it shall be between us and them a war of extermination; for we will follow them till the last drop of their blood is spilled, or they will have to exterminate us, for we will carry the seat of war to their own houses and their own families, and one party or the other shall be utterly destroyed. Remember it, then, all men! We will never be the aggressors—we will infringe on the rights of no people, but shall stand for our own till death. We claim our own rights, and are willing that others shall enjoy theirs. No man shall be at liberty to come into our streets, to threaten us with mobs, for if he does, he shall atone for it before he leaves the place; neither shall he vilify or slander any of us, for suffer it we will not in this place. * * * Neither will we indulge any man or set of men, in instituting vexatious law-suits against us to cheat us out of our rights; if they attempt it, we say woe be unto them."

August 1st, at an election in Daviess County, a quarrel ensued between some citizens and "Mormons." One of the latter was badly stabbed, and others on both sides wounded. From this occurrence, rumors flew in every direction. The "Mormons" at Far West were told that several of their number had been killed, and two hundred of them went into Daviess County to inquire into it. They found no one killed; but Mr. Adam Black, a justice of the peace of Daviess County, stated under oath, before John Wright and Elijah Foley, fellow justices, that Mr. Smith and others, to the number of one hundred and fifty-four, exacted from him about August 8, 1838, a written promise to support the Constitution of the State and the United States; and not to support a mob nor attach himself to any mob, nor to molest the "Mormons." To answer to this charge Mr. Smith, L. Wight and others were arrested, and recognized to appear for trial. Other disturbances followed, and upon representation of a deputation of citizens from Daviess County, Major-General Atchison, at the head of a thousand men of the Third Division of militia, went to the scene of trouble. The major-general found the citizens and the "Mormons" in hostile array. He dispersed both parties and reported to the governor, with the further statement that no further depredations were to be feared from the "Mormons." Almost simultaneously disturbances occurred in Carroll and Caldwell counties. The citizens determined to drive the "Mormons" from the State; the "Mormons" refused to be driven. A number of citizens made representations to General Atchison, on September 10th, that the citizens of Daviess had a "Mormon" in custody, as a prisoner, and that the "Mormons" had Messrs. John Comer, Wm. McHamy and Allen Miller prisoners, as hostages. Certain of the "Mormons," and other citizens of Carroll County, petitioned the governor from De Witt, stating the committal of lawless acts against them, among which was the ordering them to leave the county, giving them till October 1st, and asking interference and relief. This was dated September 22, 1838.

From reports filed with the governor, by Generals H. G. Parks, David R. Atchison and A. W. Doniphan, copies of which accompanied the messages of the governor to the assembly, it appears that when the proper authorities appeared on the scene of difficulty, the "Mormons" gave up, not only the prisoners they had taken in reprisal, but their arms, and also the men of their number against whom civil proceedings were pending. General Parks, in a report dated Mill Post, September 25, 1838, states: "Whatever may have been the disposition of the people called 'Mormons,' before our arrival here, since we have made our appearance, they have shown no disposition to resist the laws, or of hostile intention. * * * There has been so much prejudice and exaggeration concerning this matter, that I find things on my arrival here, totally different from what I was prepared to expect. When we arrived here, we found a large body of men from the counties adjoining, armed, and in the field, for the purpose, as I learned, of assisting the people of this county against the 'Mormons,' without being called out by the proper authorities." General Atchison wrote the governor from Liberty, Missouri, September 17, 1838: "I have no doubt your excellency has been deceived by the exaggerated statements of designing or half crazy men. I have found there is no cause of alarm on account of the 'Mormons;' they are not to be feared; they are much alarmed."

Hostile feeling culminated rapidly. The citizens, in absence of the militia, gathered their forces together, and, on the night of October 1st, attacked De Witt. A committee of citizens of Chariton County went into Carroll County, and found De Witt invested by a large force, the "Mormons" in defense and suing for peace, and wishing for the interposition of the civil authorities. They reported October 5, 1838. General Atchison reported October 16th, that the "Mormons" had sold out in Carroll County and left, and that a portion of their assailants were on the march to Daviess County with one piece of artillery, "where, it is thought the same lawless game is to be played over, and the 'Mormons' driven from that county, and probably from Caldwell." "Nothing, in my opinion," wrote this general in his report, "but the strongest measures within the power of the executive will put down this spirit of mobocracy."

The "Mormons" resisted, and in their turn plundered the store of Jacob Stollings at Gallatin, removing the goods, burned the store and other buildings in that place and Millport. The citizens of Ray, Daviess, Carroll, Jackson, Howard and some other counties gathered, and apprising the governor that the "Mormons," now growing desperate, had become the aggressors, the governor, L. W. Boggs, moved thereto by representations made to him, issued orders to General John B. Clark, placing him in command of all the force necessary, with instruction that he was in receipt of information of the most appalling nature, "which entirely changed the face of things, and places the 'Mormons' in the attitude of an open and armed defiance of the laws, and of having made war upon the people of this State * * * The 'Mormons' must be treated as enemies, and must be exterminated or driven from the State, if necessary for the public peace—their outrages are beyond all description."

In obedience to this order, General Clark, associated with General Lucas, proceeded to the seat of war, and, without much resistance, disbanded the armed forces of the "Mormons," demanded and received their arms, took Joseph Smith, Sidney Rigdon, Hyrum Smith and fifty other leading men prisoners for trial upon various charges—high treason against the State, murder, burglary, arson, robbery and larceny. These men were examined before Austin A. King, judge of the Fifth Judicial Circuit in the State of Missouri, at Richmond, beginning November 12, 1838. At this examination some were discharged for lack of evidence to hold them, but Joseph Smith, Lyman Wight, Hyrum Smith, Alexander McRae and Caleb Baldwin were held for trial and committed to jail in Clay County; some others were recognized for trial and gave bonds. A further demand was made to the effect that the "Mormons" make an appropriation to pay their debts and the indemnification for the damage to citizens done by them. The property said to have been taken by them was mostly restored upon demand of the officers.

The "Mormons" began leaving at once, and continued to leave until all were gone, except now and then a recalcitrant member, or one who had some personal friends among the citizens. Many sold out for what they could get, and many were compelled to go without selling at all. Their leaders were taken prisoners, their means of defense, as well as offense, were taken from them by law, and by the will of the citizens, enforced by the order of the governor, some twelve thousand people were driven from the State. The number of killed in this "Mormon" war is stated by the official report of the general in command in the following language: "The whole number of the 'Mormons' killed through the whole difficulty, as far as I can ascertain, are about forty, and several wounded." This is rather a damaging result against the State, after the terrible character given the "Mormons" by those opposed to them, and upon whose reports the governor ordered their suppression. Messrs. Smith, Rigdon and their comrades, in jail at Liberty, took change of venue to Boone County, but the officer charged with their delivery in Boone in his return of the order of removal to Daviess County states that the prisoners escaped. They afterwards reached Illinois in safety.

Such in brief is the history of that strange people called "Mormons," in Missouri; the events succeeding their departure from the county of Jackson and settlements in Ray, Clay, Caldwell, Daviess and other counties, has been hurried over as not properly belonging in our history of Jackson.

After this expulsion from Missouri, the "Mormons" settled in Illinois, where in six years, from 1838 to 1844, they increased rapidly and laid the foundation for a magnificent city. They began the erection of a stone temple upon a sightly location. Trouble followed them, the citizens were again aroused. Process was issued for the arrest of Joseph and Hyrum Smith, on charge of treason; awaiting trial upon which charge in the jail of Hancock County, Illinois, June 27th, 1844, they were attacked and killed by a mob. Two years after that, the "Mormons," under the leadership of Brigham Young, were expelled from Illinois, and Utah and polygamy are the outcome.

There is now in Jackson County a body of people calling themselves Latter-day Saints. They are in fact a branch of the Reorganized Church of Jesus Christ of Latter-day Saints, of which church, Joseph Smith, Jr., the eldest son of Joseph Smith, the putative father of "Mormonism," is the president. The present headquarters of the church is at Plano, Kendall County, Illinois; where they have a printing house, containing engine, press, type and other facilities for carrying on quite an extensive business. They number some fifteen thousand members now, dispersed through the United States in over four hundred congregations, including branches in Boston, Philadelphia, Chicago, St. Louis, Salt Lake City and many other prominent cities; and are most numerous in Illinois, Iowa and Missouri. In many places they have houses of worship, which they by the engagement and aid of the citizens have built; one of these buildings is in Independence.

This church, under Mr. Smith's presidency, has kept an active ministry at work in Utah, endeavoring to disabuse the "Mormons" of that Territory of the dogma of polygamy, which they assert to be no part of primitive "Mormonism;" and from the history of the sect during its stay in Missouri from 1835 to 1838, it would appear that these organizers are correct; for not a single charge of such dogma being held or taught appears in the many statements made against them, or in the published orders and reports of the officers engaged in expelling them from the State. They, at all events, oppose the tenet, and are directly antagonizing Utah "Mormonism."

APPENDIX II.

"MORMON" WAR.

*(Taken from the History of Clay County as published in
St. Louis by the National Historical Company, 1885.)*

In 1832 the "Mormons" under their Prophet Joe Smith came into Jackson County, where the previous year large tracts of land had been entered and purchased for their benefit and began to occupy and possess the land with the intention, as they said, of remaining for all time. "But their years in that land were few and full of trouble." They were in constant collision with their Gentile neighbors, who frequently tied them up and whipped them with cowhides and hickory switches, derided their religion, boycotted them where they did not openly persecute them, and at last engaged in a deadly encounter with them, tarred and feathered their bishops; threw their printing press into the river and finally drove them from their homes and out of the county.

Affrighted, terror-stricken, many of the "Mormons" took refuge in Clay County. Every vacant cabin in the south of the county was occupied by the fugitives. Many of them among the men obtained employment with the farmers, some of the women engaged as domestics, others taught school. A few heads of families were able to and did purchase land and homes, but the majority rented. The Clay County citizens treated them kindly and administered to their wants and rendered so many favors that to this day away out in Salt Lake the old "Mormons" hold in grateful remembrance the residents of the county of 1834-6.

An old citizen of Independence has recently published in the Kansas City *Journal* an interesting article on the "Mormon" troubles in Jackson County. One paragraph of this article reads as follows:

True history, however, must record the fact that the deluded followers of the so-called prophet Joseph Smith, in their first effort to organize and establish a religious, socialistic community in Jackson County, Missouri, were unjustly and outrageously treated by the original settlers. That is seen in the tragical and pitiful scene which occurred during the last part of their sojourn in this their promised inheritance, their Zion and New Jerusalem. With scarcely one exception the old settlers were the aggressors so far as overt acts of hostility were concerned. During the last year of their stay, the continued persecutions to which they were subjected excited the sympathy of many outside the county, especially of the people of Clay County, who gave them an asylum and assistance for a year or two after their expulsion. Indeed, material aid and arms were furnished them by citizens of Clay

County before their expulsion. A wagon with a quantity of guns was stopped near the south part of Kansas City and seized by parties on the watch.

The Jackson County people were indignant at the reception given the "Mormons" by the citizens of Clay County and stigmatized some of our citizens as Jack "Mormons," a term yet used. On one occasion a delegation of eleven Jackson County citizens, led by Major S. Owens and James Campbell came over to Liberty to hold a council with the Gentile citizens and "Mormons" of Clay County in regard to the lands from which the "Mormons" had been driven. The title to these lands was in the hands of the "Mormons," but the Gentiles wished to extinguish it by purchase, if it could be obtained at their—the Gentiles'—price. Accordingly, they offered the "Mormons" an insignificant sum for their lands and farms, many of which were already in possession of certain citizens of Jackson County, but this offer was refused. The Clay County people generally endorsed the refusal. Returning home that night in great ill humor with their neighbors on this side of the river, the delegation of Jackson County met with a sad misfortune. As they were crossing the river at Duckins Ferry, about the middle of the river the boat sank and five of them were drowned. Three of the unfortunate men were Ilu Job, James Campbell and——Everett. The casualty increased the indignation already felt against the people of Clay County.

By the year 1838, all or nearly all of the "Mormons" had left Clay County, and joined the "Mormon" settlement at or near Far West, or at other points in Caldwell and Daviess counties; and in October of that year the "'Mormon' War" broke out. Among the troops dispatched to Far West during that month were some companies of militia from Clay County, belonging to General Doniphan's brigade, of Major-General D. R. Atchison's division. Two of these companies were commanded by Corporals Prior and O. P. Moss.

Of Captain Prior's company Peter Holtzclaw was first lieutenant. He with twenty-five men from the north part of the county became separated from the main command and did not leave with it. The detachment marched across into Ray County and fell in with the Jackson county regiment, which had refused to march through Clay County owing to the animosity existing, and had crossed the river at Lexington.

All the Clay County men were in line confronting the breastworks when the "Mormon" camp at Far West was surrendered, and witnessed all the proceedings. They saw the white flag pass back and forth from the "Mormons," and saw the robber, Captain Bogard of the Missourians, fire on it; saw the cannoneers stand with lighted matches beside their pieces, having sent word to General Doniphan that they were ready to fire; saw suddenly a white flag go up; saw the "Mormon" battalion march out with "General" G. W. Hinkle, brave as a lion, at its head and form a hollow square and ground arms, and then saw Hinkle ride up to Doniphan, unbuckle his sword and detach his pistols from their holsters and pass them over to his captor, who quietly remarked, "Give them to my adjutant." Then they saw Hinkle dash the tears from his face, and ride back to his soldiers.

The "Mormons" agreed fully to Doniphan's conditions, that they should deliver up their arms, surrender their prominent leaders for trial, and the remainder of them, with their families, leave the State. As hostages, Joe Smith, Sidney Rigdon, Lyman Wight, G. W. Hinkle [A] and other prominent "Mormons" delivered themselves up to e held for the faithful performance of the hard conditions.[B]

[Footnote A: Hinkle was not among the hostages that were held for the faithful performance of his agreement with the mob, nor did those "hostages" deliver themselves up to the mob; they were betrayed into the hands of their enemies by Hinkle.—*B. H. R.*]

[Footnote B: Colonel Lewis Wood of this county, who was present, states to the compiler that at a council of the leading militia officers held the night following the surrender, it was voted by nearly three to one to put these leaders to death, and their lives were only saved by the intervention of General Doniphan, who not only urged his authority as brigadier, but declared he would defend the prisoners with his own life.—*N. H. C.*]

The "Mormon" leaders were taken before a court of inquiry at Richmond, Judge Austin A. King presiding. He remanded them to Daviess County, to await the action of the grand jury on a charge of treason against the State and murder. The Daviess County jail being poor and insecure, the prisoners were brought to Liberty and confined in the old stone jail (still standing) for some time. Many citizens of the county remember to have seen Joe Smith when he was a prisoner in the old Liberty jail.

In due time indictments for various offenses, treason, murder, resisting legal process, etc., were found against Joe Smith and his brother Hyrum, Sidney Rigdon, G. W. Hinkle, Caleb Baldwin, P. P. Pratt, Luman Gibbs, Maurice Phelps, King Follet, Wm. Osburn, Arthur Morrison, Elias Higbee and others. Sidney Rigdon was released on a writ of habeas corpus, the others requested a change of venue, and Judge King sent their cases to Boone County for trial. On the way from Liberty to Columbia, Joe Smith escaped. It is generally believed the guard was bribed. P. P. Pratt escaped from Columbia jail; the others were either tried and acquitted, or the cases against them were dismissed. The entire proceedings in the cases were disgraceful in the extreme. There never was a handful of evidence that the accused were guilty of the crimes with which they were charged. Those who were tried were defended by General Doniphan and James S. Rollins.—pp. 132-5.

APPENDIX III.

THE "MORMONS."

(*History of Daviess County, by D. L. Kort.*)

This sect of professed Christians, whose history is but a burlesque upon the pure morality of the meek and lowly, but glorious Nazarene, came to this country in 1836. Their chief settlement was in Far West, in Caldwell County, where their apostle, Joseph Smith, and all their chief dignitaries resided. Here in 1838 the corner stone of the temple was laid, with great ceremony and not a little deception; for Smith had foretold that the rock, which was of great size, would move at his command. This it apparently did do, but actually by means of ropes and pulleys worked through a concealed trench, by men at a distance.

The temple was to occupy a large square in the centre of the town, and was approached by four main streets, each one hundred feet wide, and was to exceed in magnificence any edifice in the United States. The temple was never built, but Far West attained a population of three thousand inhabitants, and was for some years the county seat of Caldwell County. Now, however, not one stone is left upon another, and the farmer's plow turns up their once busy streets and desecrates their holy ground.

In our own county their chief point was a place still known as "Diamond," but by the "Mormons" called Adam-ondi-Ahman, which we believe means "the grave of Adam." This place is the old Dr. Craven's farm now, owned and occupied by Major McDonald, and lies about three and a half miles northwest of Gallatin. It is a romantic spot, on the east bluff, overlooking the valley of Grand River; and to this day, owing perhaps to fissures in the underlying rock, the observer may behold the greasy cactus-lined walks of their "garden of Eden; laid off with almost mathematical precision. Adam's Grave is at the edge of the garden, and is a small mound of broken limestone, gravel and soil intermixed. From Diamond to Far West the "Mormons" had a very fair road, and all along it and interspersed throughout the county were many settlers of their faith.

A trace of wandering, a track of blood and temple building are the principal features in the history of this deluded people, deluded by a film so thin that even sense might see beyond. Taking their rise in the south of New York they soon migrated to Kirtland, Ohio, then to Jackson county, Missouri, then to Clay County, then to Daviess and Caldwell, then to Nauvoo, Illinois, and thence across the plains to Salt Lake, and even now there are rumors of another removal. In all these places they began to build a temple, and in all except the first they left the marks of blood, either their own or shed by them. The "Mormons" have always claimed that they were peaceable and law-abiding; yes, peaceable when not resisted in their outrages, law-abiding when obeying the laws of their prophet.

They have always claimed that they never shed blood only when attacked: but this is stark falsehood, as, witness the work of their Danite Destroying Angels, Mountain Meadow Massacre; and even the attacks they complain of were always induced by their infamous conduct.

The first cardinal principle in the tenets of their religion, as exemplified among our people, was: "The Lord has given the earth and the fullness thereof to his saints," the next was, "We are his saints." Thus armed and equipped and incited by their leaders, they roamed through the county, took whatever pleased their fancy, carried it to Diamond and placed it in the "Lord's storehouse." Nothing was safe, nothing was exempt from their rapacity, and our sturdy pioneers were justly indignant and panting for revenge. With them the "Mormon" war meant business, and we find the county court on the sixth of March, 1839, allowing an account of twenty-one dollars for powder and lead furnished the county during the "Mormon" war. So great was the numerical superiority of the "Mormons" that the citizens dared offer no resistance, but were simply at their mercy. On the 13th of October, 1838, the "Mormon" Legion formed their line of battle in front of the few houses in Gallatin, and ordered the citizens to leave at once. From there the legion proceeded to Millport and issued the same order. That night the citizens fled by the light of their burning homes, the principal part going to Livingston County. When they burned Gallatin the "Mormons" robbed the treasury: true, they did not find much money, but they took what they could lay their hands on. Shortly after this the State militia, under General Parks, entered the county, and the people arose en masse to assist him. Diamond, containing perhaps five hundred souls, surrendered without resistance. About the same time Smith himself surrendered Far West, and the war was over.

At the April term, 1839, of our circuit court, indictments for treason, arson, riot, burglary, and a host of other crimes were found against Joseph Smith, Hyrum Smith, Lyman Wight, Caleb Baldwin, Alexander McRae, W. S. Slade, H. H. B. Belt, Eli Bagley, Wm. Aldridge, Alanson Ripley, Amos Lubbs, Perry Durphery, John Lehomon and many others. Most of them were released on bail, which they forfeited, but Smith and the rest of the leaders, being refused bail, took a change of venue to Boone County, to which place the sheriff was ordered to convey them under military guard. On the way the prisoners effected their escape, it is claimed, by bribing their guard.

During the time between the surrender of the "Mormons" and the finding of the indictments against them, they had been in custody in Clay County, and a claim of four hundred and eighty dollars for guarding them in Liberty jail was presented to our county court, but disallowed. The claimants obtained a temporary writ of mandamus, which was venued to Caldwell County, and finally passed into oblivion. The general assembly on the eleventh day of December, 1838, appropriated two thousand dollars to relieve the suffering in Daviess and Caldwell caused by this "Mormon" war. This was for the relief of "Mormons" as well as others, and M. T. Green was appointed relief commissioner for this county.

APPENDIX IV.

CALDWELL COUNTY.

(By Crosby Johnson.)

Mormon emigration.—Shortly prior to the organization of the county, the "Mormons," driven from Jackson County, sent J. Whitmer and others to select a home in the wilderness. Far West was chosen, which was approved by The Church authority.

Far West.—The site chosen for Far West was a high, rolling prairie, visible for a long distance from all directions. The plat of the town as laid off embraced a square mile, to-wit: Northeast quarter, section fifteen; northwest quarter, section fourteen; southeast quarter, section ten; southwest quarter, section eleven. In the center of the town a large square was left as a site for a temple which it was their design to erect. The square was approached by four main streets, each a hundred feet wide. * * * As its population increased, additions to the town were laid out. At the time of the "Mormon" war the population of Far West was about two thousand five hundred, and it was the largest town in the State north of the Missouri.

"Mormon" War.—The "Mormons" as a people were honest, sober and industrious, but the object of the leaders was to make money and obtain power. Joe Smith and his brother Hyrum, with The Church funds, purchased of the government large tracts of land around Far West, which they did not scruple to sell to their followers at exorbitant prices. When the leaders set the example of speculating in the devotion of the people, it is scarcely to be wondered at if the subordinates went to greater extremes to fill their purses, and if they had but little respect for their obligations to each other, they had less for the laws of the State or the rights of their Gentile neighbors. Some of their daring leaders taught the doctrine that the Lord had given the earth and the fullness thereof as an inheritance to his people, and they were his people and had a right at pleasure to take what pleased their appetite or fancy. At the time of the difficulties in Jackson County, Joe Smith organized a band of men called the army of Zion, to protect his people against the attacks of their enemies. Among these were many who were too lazy to earn a living by the sweat of their brow. Desperado and vagabond joined his band for the purpose of plundering. Squads of them strolled about the county threatening the men, intimidating the women, and appropriating in the name of the prophet any property which pleased their taste. As the "Mormons" largely outnumbered the Gentiles, they elected to all offices of honor and trust persons of their own faith. Smith was careful that the persons selected should be subservient to the will of himself and his apostles. The Gentiles declared it was impossible for them to get a fair hearing before the "Mormon" magistrates and juries; that the trials were farces: that the leaders taught and the members acted on the principle that a Gentile had no rights that a "Mormon" was bound to respect, and that not the merits of the cause, but the creeds of the contestants determined which way the scales should turn.

Whether these complaints were true or false, they were believed by many and naturally excited deep indignation against the "Mormons." Tales of debauchery, theft and murder were told of them, and their expulsion from the county demanded. These bitter feelings engendered broils and riots. Crowds of excited fanatics pelted obnoxious Gentiles on the streets of Far West with clubs and stones. In retaliation armed Gentiles rode into public meetings where their lawless conduct was being denounced, seized the speakers and applied the lash until the blood trickled down their backs. Both sides ceased to resort to legal methods in the enforcement of their rights.

Amid so much excitement and insubordination the civil authorities were powerless to enforce the laws and punish offenses.

Finally, in 1838, the disorder became so great and outrages so frequent that the State authorities felt it their duty to interfere. Governor Boggs issued a proclamation calling out the militia to aid in restoring order and enforcing the laws. The generals in command were Generals John B. Clark, David R. Atchison, A. W. Doniphan. General Doniphan's brigade removed to Far West. The main body of the army of Zion under the command of G. M. Hinkle, whom Smith designated as commander in chief of the "Mormon" forces, was held in reserve to act as emergencies might require. Smaller forces were thrown forward to guard the approaches from the south and the east.

Haun's Mill.—On the thirtieth of October an engagement was fought at Haun's Mill on Shoal Creek, south of Beckenridge. At that point a "Mormon" outpost entrenched in the mill and a blacksmith shop was attacked by the Livingston County militia under Captain Comstock. After a brief struggle the "Mormons" threw down their arms in token of surrender, but one of the militia men, being savagely wounded, his comrades were so enraged that their officer was unable to check them until eighteen of the "Mormons" were killed and a number wounded. Haun, the proprietor of the mill, was killed and with the rest of the dead buried in a well that stood near by.

"Mormon" Exodus.—The surrender took place in November. The days were cold and bleak, but the clamor for the instant removal of the

"Mormons" was so great that the old and young, the sick and feeble, delicate women and suckling children, almost without food and without clothing were compelled to abandon their homes and firesides to seek new homes in a distant State. Valuable farms were sold for a yoke of oxen, an old wagon or anything that would furnish means of transportation. Many of the poorer classes were compelled to walk. Before half their journey was accomplished the chilly blasts of winter howled about them and added to their general discomfort. The suffering they endured on this forced march though great, was soon forgotten in the prosperity of Nauvoo, their new asylum. Their trials and sufferings instead of dampening the ardor of the Saints, increased it ten fold. "The blood of the martyrs became the seed of The Church."

The exodus of the "Mormons" reduced the population of the county from six thousand to less than one thousand; but the deserted farms and houses offered inducements to emigration that were not despised and new settlers rapidly filled the places of the departed ones.

Visions.—If that strange people who built Nauvoo and Salt Lake, who uncomplainingly toiled across the American Desert and made the wilderness of Utah bloom like a garden, had been permitted to remain and perfect the work which they had begun here, how different would have been the history of Far West. Instead of being a farm with scarcely sufficient ruins to mark the spot where it once stood, there would have been a rich populous city, along the streets of which would be pouring the wealth of the world, and instead of an old dilapidated farm house there would have been magnificent temples, to which devout Saints from the farthest corners of the world would have made their yearly pilgrimages. But the bigotry and intolerance of the Saints toward the Gentiles and especially toward dissenters from the new revelations of Joe Smith, rendered such a consummation impossible.

APPENDIX V.

"MORMON" DIFFICULTIES.

(History of Missouri, Union Historical Society, 1881.)

In 1832, Joseph smith, the leader of the "Mormons," and the chosen prophet and apostle, as he claimed, of the Most High, came with many followers to Jackson County, Missouri, where they located and entered several thousand acres of land.

The object of his coming so far west—upon the very outskirts of civilization at that time—was to more securely establish his Church, and the more effectively to instruct his followers in its peculiar tenets and practices.

Upon the present town site of Independence the "Mormons" located their "Zion," and gave it the name of "New Jerusalem." They published here *The Evening Star,* and made themselves generally obnoxious to the Gentiles who were then in a minority, by their denunciatory articles through their paper, their clannishness and their polygamous practices.[A]

[Footnote A: Although the work from which the above record is quoted is quite a pretentious history consisting of 1006 pages, yet it apparently has no regard for consistency of statement, for while it is said on page 47, that this Church (of Jesus Christ of Latter-day Saints—"Mormon") made themselves generally obnoxious by their polygamous practices, on page 269 the following occurs, speaking of the difference between the so-called Josephite Church, who now have a congregation and church building in Independence, Mo., and the Church of Jesus Christ of Latter-day Saints: "This church, * * * (i. e., Josephite Church,) has kept an active ministry at work in Utah, endeavoring to disabuse the 'Mormons' of that Territory of the dogma of polygamy, which they assert to be no part of primitive Mormonism; and from the history of the sect during its stay in Missouri from 1835 to 1838, it would appear that these organizers are correct; for not a single charge of such dogma being held or taught appears in the many statements made against them, or in the published orders and reports of the officers engaged in expelling them from the State."]

Dreading the demoralizing influence of a paper which seemed to be inspired only with hatred and malice toward them, the Gentiles threw the press and type into the Missouri River, tarred and feathered one of their Bishops, and otherwise gave the "Mormons" and their leaders to understand that they must conduct themselves in an entirely different manner if they wished to be left alone.

After the destruction of their paper and press, they became furiously incensed, and sought many opportunities for retaliation. Matters continued in an uncertain condition until the 31st of October, 1833, when a deadly conflict occurred near Westport, in which two Gentiles and one "Mormon" were killed.

On the second of November following the "Mormons" were over-powered and compelled to lay down their arms and agree to leave the county with their families by January 1st on the condition that the owner would be paid for his printing press.

Leaving Jackson County, they crossed the Missouri and located in Clay, Carroll, Caldwell and other counties, and selected in Caldwell County a town site, which they called "Far West," and where they entered more land for their future homes.

Through the influence of their missionaries, who were exerting themselves in the east and in different portions of Europe, converts had constantly flocked to their standard, and Far West, and other "Mormon" settlements, rapidly prospered.

In 1837 they commenced the erection of a magnificent temple but never finished it. As their settlements increased in numbers they became bolder in the practices and deeds of lawlessness.

During the summer of 1838, two of their leaders settled in the town of DeWitt, on the Missouri River, having purchased the land from an Illinois merchant. DeWitt was in Carroll County, and a good point from which to forward goods and emigrants to their town—Far West.

Upon its being ascertained that these parties were "Mormon" leaders the Gentiles called a public meeting, which was addressed by some of the prominent citizens of the county. Nothing, however, was done at this meeting, but at a subsequent meeting, which was held a few days afterward, a committee of citizens was appointed to notify Colonel Hinkle (one of the "Mormon" leaders at De Witt,) what they intended to do.

Colonel Hinkle upon being notified by this committee became indignant, and threatened extermination to all who should attempt to molest him or the Saints.

In anticipation of trouble, and believing that the Gentiles would attempt to force them from De Witt, "Mormon" recruits flocked to the town from every direction, and pitched their tents in and around the town in great numbers.

The Gentiles, nothing daunted, planned an attack upon this encampment, to take place on the 21st of September, 1838, and, accordingly, one hundred and fifty men bivouacked near the town on that day. A conflict ensued, but nothing serious occurred.

The "Mormons" evacuated their works and fled to some log houses, where they could the more successfully resist the Gentiles, who had in the meantime returned to their camp to await reinforcements. Troops from Howard, Ray and other counties came to their assistance, and increased their number to five hundred men.

Congreve Jackson was chosen brigadier-general; Ebenezer Price, colonel; Singleton Vaughn, lieutenant-colonel, and Sashel Woods, major. After some days of discipline, this brigade prepared for an assault, but before the attack was commenced Judge James Earickson and William F. Dunnica, influential citizens of Howard County, asked permission of General Jackson to let them try and adjust the difficulties without bloodshed.

It was finally agreed that Judge Earickson should propose to the "Mormons" that, if they would pay for all the cattle they had killed belonging to the citizens, and load their wagons during the night and be ready to move by ten o'clock next morning, and make no further attempt to settle in Howard County, the citizens would purchase at first cost their lots in DeWitt, and one or two adjoining tracts of land.

Colonel Hinkle, the leader of the "Mormons," at first refused all attempts to settle the difficulties in this way, but finally agreed to the proposition.

In accordance therewith, the "Mormons," without further delay, loaded, up their wagons for the town of Far West, in Caldwell County. Whether the terms of the agreement were ever carried out, on the part of the citizens, it is not known.

The "Mormons" had doubtless suffered much and in many ways—the result of their own acts—but their trials and sufferings were not at an end.

In 1838 the discord between the citizens and the "Mormons" became so great that Governor Boggs issued a proclamation ordering Major-General David R. Atchison to call the militia of his division to enforce the laws. He called out a part of the first brigade of the Missouri State Militia, under the command of General A. W. Doniphan, who proceeded to the seat of war.

General John B. Clark, of Howard County, was placed in command of the militia.

The "Mormon" forces numbered about 1,000 men, and were led by G. W. Hinkle. The first engagement occurred at Crooked River, where one "Mormon" was killed. The principle fight took place at Haun's Mill, where eighteen "Mormons" were killed and the balance captured, some of them being killed after they had surrendered. Only one militiaman was wounded.

In the month of October, 1838, Joe Smith surrendered the town of Far West to General Doniphan, agreeing to his conditions, viz: That they should deliver up their arms, surrender their prominent leaders for trial, and the remainder of the "Mormons" should, with their families, leave the State. Indictments were found against a number of these leaders including Joe Smith, who, while being taken to Boone County for trial, made his escape, and was afterward, in 1844, killed at Carthage, Illinois, with his brother Hyrum.